HAWTHORNE AS MYTH-MAKER

A STUDY IN IMAGINATION

HUGO MCPHERSON

UNIVERSITY OF TORONTO PRESS

UNIVERSITY OF TORONTO
DEPARTMENT OF ENGLISH STUDIES AND TEXTS
16

© University of Toronto Press 1969
reprinted in Canada 1971

ISBN 0-8020-5200-2

pour Louise

Preface

In the past quarter century, described by Mr. Randall Stewart as 'the golden age of Hawthorne criticism,' almost every facet of Hawthorne's life and art has been documented and analysed. Scholars have formulated – better than he himself could have done – his ideas on religion, politics, philosophy, and aesthetics, and have placed the man, his work, and his milieu in a flood of light. Randall Stewart has recruited the skills of science to decipher passages in Hawthorne's letters and journals that had been inked-out with loving prudery by his widow; New Critics have added greatly to our understanding by studying his art in terms of bipolar image schemes such as Head and Heart, Light and Dark, Marriage and Isolation; psychologists – seldom as skilled as Roger Chillingworth – have probed relentlessly into the remains of his psyche in an effort to diagnose repressed incest wishes and unresolved Oedipal problems.

But though much of this work fully deserves the praise which Mr. Stewart bestows upon it, a central mystery remains: if we recognize Hawthorne's moral and psychological depth and his highly conscious artistry, we understand less clearly the inward preoccupations which give coherence to his *œuvre*; and as a result we dismiss a number of perplexing details and incidents as 'Gothic trappings' or 'over-ingenious allegory' – labels which, like Swift's *lusus naturae*, betray something that the doctors do not understand. As Stanley T.

Preface

Williams has said of contemporary Hawthorne criticism and biography:

> Such revaluations bring us closer to him as a man but only reaffirm the cryptic nature of his preoccupation. What was it? Sophia could not define what lay behind the veil, and his friends alluded to another Hawthorne hidden within the stalwart, outward man. He himself spoke of depths in his mind which he could neither fathom nor explain. ... In any case, no outward event in Hawthorne's biography is so important as this secret place in his mind of solitude and meditation; within this refuge, he drew the breath of life itself. When this failed him, he died. (*Literary History of the United States*, p. 421)

The essays which follow will attempt to define, as fully as the evidence allows, the nature of Hawthorne's 'cryptic preoccupation,' that inward vision or drama of which his works are the particular if partial formulations. The essays, in short, are concerned with the myth-making nature of Hawthorne's imagination. Their prime concern is not to study his art in terms of an external frame of ideas but to allow the character types, image patterns, and narrative configurations of his art to speak for themselves.

Criticism has been demanding such an approach to Hawthorne's art for some time. Randall Stewart's Introduction to *The American Notebooks* (1932) brought a measure of order by classifying Hawthorne's recurring plots and character types. Q. D. Leavis, Harry Levin, Daniel Hoffman, Lionel Trilling, and others have affirmed the essentially myth-making and poetic core of Hawthorne's vision. Frederick C. Crews has also sensed this inward life in Hawthorne's work, but has unfortunately chosen to describe it in Freudian terms which fail to compass the richness, depth, and individuality of Hawthorne's mind. As we know, Hawthorne was deeply

Preface

influenced by Shakespeare, Spenser, Bunyan, Swift, and even Sir Walter Scott; moreover, the Puritan habit of studying 'types' and 'Providences' was second nature to him. His mythology, then, is likely to be moored to these antecedents, but because the centre of his reality is American, his creation will be primarily a myth for the New World.

In presenting my study I caution the reader on two points: the first essay is a broad, outline map of what I would call Hawthorne's 'personal mythology' – a map which should not be mistaken for the territory that will be explored in detail in parts II and III; and the concluding section on character types is something like the 'legend' of a map – a series of indicators rather than a rigid schema. After a decade of exploration in Hawthorne's land of romance I would be the first to deny that his vision can be compassed by even such an elaborate diagram as that which appears in my final essay. The second and third essays require no comment here beyond the information that part II is a detailed source study and analysis of the twelve mythological labours which Hawthorne performed between the composition of *Seven Gables* and his departure for Europe; and part III is a reading of the major romances which suggests that the so-called 'Gothic trappings' are meaningful and indeed essential parts of his statement.

Apart from my great debt to scholars and critics whose names appear prominently in every Hawthorne bibliography and in my own notes, I am particularly grateful to a number of persons who have been both champions of American studies and generous personal friends. Gordon Roper and Malcolm Ross of Trinity College, Toronto, inspired and guided my work in American studies; the late Professor A. S. P. Woodhouse of University College, Toronto, and Roy

Preface

Daniells of the University of British Columbia gave me welcome practical assistance. In the United States Norman Holmes Pearson of Yale University made his expert knowledge available to me, generously allowed me to read his unpublished collection of Hawthorne's letters, and his material on Hawthorne's early reading and college experience; and in a late phase of my work read the manuscript. In 1966 the Master and Fellows of Berkeley College at Yale admitted me to their fellowship for two valuable terms. In addition, the Humanities Research Council of Canada and the Canada Council made possible two summers of travel and study. During these periods I incurred further debts to the librarians and their staffs at the universities of Toronto, McGill, Harvard, Brown, Chicago, and Yale. The Library of Congress loaned me the book which enabled me to identify Hawthorne's major source for his mythological tales. This work has been published with the aid of grants from the Humanities Research Council, using funds provided by the Canada Council, and from the Publications Fund of the University of Toronto Press.

Finally, I acknowledge with gratitude subjective debts to Northrop Frye of Victoria College, Toronto, and Marshall McLuhan of St. Michael's College, Toronto; their approaches to the task of literary study have continuously illuminated my own thinking and practice. Louise McPherson's fresh criticism, patience, and Gallic point of view have extricated me from a variety of *impasses*.

H.M.

Montreal, Canada
February 1968

Contents

References

Quotations from Hawthorne's works cited only by volume and page will refer to the Riverside Edition, *The Complete Works of Nathaniel Hawthorne*, edited by George Parsons Lathrop (13 volumes, Boston and New York, 1882–83). References to volumes in the Hawthorne Centenary *Edition*, edited by William Charvat, *et al.* (Columbus: Ohio State University Press, 1962–   ) will be preceded by the letter C: for example, C, II, 84.

Acknowledgements

The author is grateful for permission to quote brief passages from the following works: Edward H. Davidson, *Hawthorne's Last Phase* (New Haven: Yale University Press, 1949); *Hawthorne's 'Dr. Grimshawe's Secret'* (Cambridge, Mass.: Harvard University Press, 1954), edited by Edward H. Davidson. Material from the following articles by the author has been used in the text: 'Hawthorne's Major Source for his Mythological Tales,' *American Literature*, XXX (1958), 364–65; 'Hawthorne's Mythology: A Mirror for Puritans,' *University of Toronto Quarterly*, XXVIII (1959), 267–78.

[An author's] external habits, his abode, his casual associates and other matters entirely on the surface. ... These things hide the man, instead of displaying him. You must make quite another kind of inquest, and look through the whole range of his fictitious characters, good and evil, in order to detect any of his essential traits.

Hawthorne, Preface to *The Snow Image*

A Man's life of any worth is a continual allegory – and very few eyes can see the mystery of his life – a life like the scriptures, figurative – which such people can no more make out than they can the hebrew Bible. Lord Byron cuts a figure – but he is not figurative – Shakespeare led a life of Allegory: his works are the comments on it –

Keats, *Letters*

Foremost in the roughest of professions, he [Lord Nelson] was as delicately organized as a woman, and as painfully sensitive as a poet. More than any other Englishman he won the love and admiration of his country, but won them through the efficacy of qualities that are not English, or, at all events, were intensified in his case and made poignant and powerful by something morbid in the man, which put him otherwise at cross-purposes with life. He was a man of genius. ... The wonderful contrast or relation between his personal qualities, the position which he held, and the life that he lived, makes him as interesting a personage as all history has to show. ... Nelson expressed his life in a kind of symbolic poetry.

Hawthorne, *Our Old Home*

PART I

The Shape of Hawthorne's Myth

THE TRADITIONAL VIEW OF NATHANIEL HAWTHORNE AS moralist and allegorist has broadened in recent years to include his achievement as myth-maker and symbolist. Unquestionably he was much concerned as moralist and thinker with problems of sin and salvation, the past, democracy, women's rights, the role of the artist, and the methods of art; but underlying these rational concerns is a deeper current of drama and narrative allied to the patterns of fairytale, romance, and myth. As Q. D. Leavis has expressed it, 'he turns ... history into myth and anecdote into parable.'[1] In his hands, character and situation become vehicles of meaning – a mode of knowing, or vision. But if criticism is friendly to this view it has not yet agreed what Hawthorne's myth or myths may be; nor has it investigated the possibility that a personal mythology gives coherence to the broader range of his work.[2] My purpose in this introductory essay, therefore,

1 'Hawthorne as Poet,' *Sewanee Review*, LIX (Spring 1951), 185. Though I differ with a number of points in Mrs. Leavis's two-part article, I regard it as one of the major contributions to Hawthorne criticism, and have quoted at length in my epigraphs two passages to which she alludes.

2 Listed alphabetically by author, the principal recent contributions to Hawthorne studies are as follows: Millicent Bell, *Hawthorne's View of the Artist* (New York, 1962); Malcolm Cowley, ed., *The Portable Hawthorne* (New York, 1948); Frederick C. Crews, *The Sins of the Fathers* (New York, 1966); Leslie A. Fiedler, *Love and Death in the American Novel* (New York, 1960); Richard Harter Fogle, *Hawthorne's Fiction: The Light and the Dark* (Norman Oklahoma, revised ed., 1964); Daniel G. Hoffman, *Form and Fable in American Fiction* (New York, 1961); A. N.

3

will be to define the term 'personal mythology' as I understand it, and to establish in broad outline – using Hawthorne's language as far as possible – the personae and conflicts of his inward drama.

The conception of an artist's work as rising out of a personal mythology is illuminated by two comments, one on Shakespeare, the other on Yeats. Keats once remarked in a letter that Shakespeare must have 'led a life of Allegory: his works are the comments on it.'[3] And F. O. Matthiessen, when he turned to explore Hawthorne's psychology, began with a similar comment on Yeats: 'That there are aspects of art which can hardly be reached by the scalpels of economic and social analysis was maintained by Yeats' belief that poetry is not "a criticism of life" but "a revelation of a hidden life." This belief would unquestionably have been accepted by Hawthorne.'[4] As these statements suggest, the imaginative

Kaul, *The American Vision* (New Haven, 1963); Harry Levin, *The Power of Blackness: Hawthorne, Poe, Melville* (New York, 1958); Roy R. Male, *Hawthorne's Tragic Vision* (Austin Texas, 1957); William Bysshe Stein, *Hawthorne's Faust: A Study of the Devil Archetype* (Gainesville Florida, 1953); Hyatt H. Waggoner, *Hawthorne: A Critical Study* (Cambridge Mass., revised ed., 1963).

The most valuable of these for insights into Hawthorne's mythology are Millicent Bell, Malcolm Cowley, Richard Fogle (see his essay on 'The Artist of the Beautiful'), Daniel Hoffman, and A. N. Kaul. Q. D. Leavis's article has been cited above. Randall Stewart, *Nathaniel Hawthorne: A Biography* (New Haven, 1948) remains the best objective account of Hawthorne's career. Walter Blair's 'Hawthorne,' in *Eight American Authors: A Review of Research and Criticism*, ed. Floyd Stovall (New York, 1963), is the standard work on earlier Hawthorne scholarship and criticism.

3 *The Letters of John Keats*, ed., Maurice Buxton Forman (London, 1935), p. 305.

4 *American Renaissance* (New York, 1941), p. 337.

I: The Shape of Hawthorne's Myth

foundation of a writer's work may well be an inner drama or 'hidden life' in which his deepest interests and conflicts are transformed into images or characters; and through the symbolic play of these creations, he comes to 'know' the meaning of his experience; the imaginative structure becomes a means of reaching truth. Thus, as Keats, Coleridge, and Yeats asserted, and as Hawthorne must have understood,[5] the total creation of the artist is not his written works but a living, interior drama; he lives 'a life of allegory,' and each of his works expresses one facet or another of the total structure.

Moreover, the coherence of an artist's work may depend as much on his personal mythology or 'life of allegory' as on any rational scheme of ideas, aesthetic theory, or external social or religious framework. With some writers this inner realm of the imagination is of negligible interest to either reader or critic, for the artist's statement is so directly and rationally accessible that one does not probe further. But if – as Northrop Frye has argued – a private, non-rational pattern, a personal myth 'is in fact ... the source of the coherence of his argument'[6] then the critic must recognize that myth, or fail, beyond certain limits, to understand both the artist's statement and method.

Such an investigation, in my view, is now overdue in Hawthorne studies, for though we have exhaustive information on his life, thought, and artistic techniques, we have not yet penetrated to the heart of that 'cryptic preoccupation' which has so perplexed his readers and critics. Unfortunately, Hawthorne himself was not of much help in clearing up the

5 Consider his remarks on Lord Nelson, quoted in my epigraph (VII, pp. 275–77).
6 *Anatomy of Criticism* (Princeton, 1957), p. 354.

mystery. He was far too reserved to risk a positive and deliberate statement of his vision as Poe and Yeats did; indeed it appears doubtful whether he was fully conscious of the shape of his personal myth, for in his notebooks he reflects:

A cloudy veil stretches over the abyss of my nature. I have, however, no love of secrecy and darkness. I am glad to think that God sees through my heart, and, if any angel has power to penetrate into it, he is welcome to know everything that is there. Yes, and so may any mortal who is capable of full sympathy, and therefore worthy to come into my depths. But he must find his own way there. I can neither guide nor enlighten him. It is this involuntary reserve, I suppose, that has given the objectivity to my writings; and when people think I am pouring myself out in a tale or an essay, I am merely telling what is common to human nature, not what is peculiar to myself (IX, 335–36).

The critic must attempt, therefore, to approach Hawthorne's secret 'depths' with the kind of tact and 'full sympathy' that he demands. In making the attempt, I shall begin by reconstructing briefly his personal legend as it is revealed in his works and in subsequent scholarship. From there I shall turn to his idealized reinterpretations of Greek myth (a source study which is new in Hawthorne scholarship), and thence to the sombre tales of experience, his New England myth.

The most striking features of Hawthorne's personal legend, if we step back far enough to observe its broad configurations, are these. First, he was fatherless, like the majority of his principal heroes – the last son of a long line of austere and even brutal men whose dark faith had led them to persecute Quakers for their spiritual intuitions, and witches for their dark knowledge; but he was haunted by his 'fathers,' and he lived in a house, if not of mourning, of decay – a home withdrawn from both the commercial power of the community

6

I: The Shape of Hawthorne's Myth

and the complacent society of Salem's Chestnut Street.
Second, he knew very early that he was an artist – no later,
certainly than his days at Bowdoin College where, at eighteen, he adopted the nickname 'Oberon'; much later he confessed that as a child his 'native propensities were towards
Fairy Land' (VII, 150). And though he recognized that his
vocation made him an observer, unhappily aware of his
separation from the practical community and the rewards of
love and the Heart, he persisted in his isolation 'like a man
under enchantment' for a twelve-year cycle. (The 'enchantment,' as Randall Stewart's biography reminds us, included
voyages to the Berkshires, to Canada, to a Shaker community, and long voyages into the countries of Spencer,
Swift, and Shakespeare – but the sense of detachment remained.) Third, as he tells us in 'The Custom House,' he
knew that his Puritan forebears would have sneered at the
spectacle of their nineteenth-century descendant trifling with
the gossamer of fiction, and probably consigned him to the
devil. He understood equally well that though his society
yearned for a national art which would give it status in the
eyes of Europe, its real values were a self-regarding philistin-
ism and materialism. In post-revolutionary New England the
artist was at best a Coverdale, a minor entertainer or dilettante for whom men of affairs had small respect.[7] Finally,
though far from matching the panache of one of his Greek
heroes, he was able to 'open an intercourse with the world,'
and to find a place in the human community through marriage to a virginal New England Venus, his 'dove,' Sophia.

7 Millicent Bell, in *Hawthorne's View of the Artist*, chapter VI, gives
the best account available of the dilemmas of Hawthorne's nineteenth-
century artist-writers.

Hawthorne as Myth-Maker

The legend thus far sounds a bit like a fairy tale (I make it sound deliberately so, since Hawthorne often talked about these years in the language of dream and fairytale): in synopsis, the young artist-hero 'Oberon,' menaced by his aged 'fathers,' goes on a twelve-year quest in an illusive world of spectres, and finally returns to claim his place and marry a 'princess.' The four points described above, however, help us to place in new perspective several prime features of Hawthorne's work: his obsession with the past, especially the Puritan past; his view of the rising democracy of the present; his suspicion of transcendental optimism; and his supreme conviction that artists are the 'unacknowledged legislators of the world.'

The celebrated ambivalence of Hawthorne's attitude toward the past has provoked almost equally ambivalent responses from critics: did his obsessive sense of personal and family guilt draw him to the past? Did the nature of his art require settings removed from the present? Or did his Romantic temper lead him to seek *any* refuge from the barrenness of his own age? All of these questions have been correctly answered in the affirmative. But what criticism has not sufficiently emphasized is the *presentness* of Hawthorne's fiction. As the legend I have been recounting suggests, the overwhelming question that faced the young Hawthorne was this: *In such a community, how could the child of such a history find his authority and place?* If the visionary Oberon was an exile in his community, the origin and meaning of his isolation might be discovered somewhere in the past. Hawthorne's leading response to his situation, therefore, was to return to the past in an effort to discover how and why and when the American career had gone wrong – to discover, by

8

I: The Shape of Hawthorne's Myth

studying the past, how a young man of his own energy and imagination could feel so alienated in the New England community of the 1830s. His New England fiction is thus an analysis of the historical process that produced the America of his own day. And this revelation of the relevance of the past in understanding the present is undoubtedly what led T. S. Eliot to praise Hawthorne's fiction as a true critique of America, and to dismiss Emerson's essays as 'an encumbrance.'[8] Certainly Hawthorne hated the past for its inexorable influence on the present; but at the same time he longed for a legacy of humane traditions without which the new society would remain inhospitable to such heroes as Oberon.

As these remarks on the relation of past and present suggest, Oberon-Hawthorne's concern to achieve his personal quest led him inevitably to consider the wider context of the American career. There could be no personal fulfilment unless the community strove unceasingly towards the ideals envisioned initially by the Puritans as the New Jerusalem, and revised by their descendants in the Declaration of Independence. Hawthorne dreamed this American dream as ardently as any patriot; and even in his last anguish he believed that his society would at length emerge as the culture hero of the western world, a youthful successor to John Bull. But was there genuine reason for optimism? Had 'the one true system' been discovered in the new republic? Were the ideals of the founding fathers being realized? As Hawthorne observed the reformers, bluestockings, transcendental prophets, merchants, and politicians of Salem and Boston, he feared that the American quest was far from achieving its goal; that its heroes were sham heroes; that the dazzle of its

8 Quoted in F. O. Matthiessen, *American Renaissance*, p. 193.

gilded materialism was as blinding as the darkness of the Puritan past. Young America had not used its best gifts or realized its ideal role.

The final episodes of Hawthorne's personal legend are anguished indeed; personally, he did achieve a measure of honour, and as the 'Flowers of Eden' bloomed at the conclusion of *The House of the Seven Gables*, he was able to hope that a new and better age was at hand; that America had exorcised its past; and that the Master Genius, a writer who had been welcomed to the fantasy of 'A Select Party,' might indeed appear and find welcome in America. But that hope slowly faded. Hawthorne discovered in England, 'Our Old Home,' that the hated fatherland was in many respects richer than the youthful republic with its imminent civil war. In the confusion of the last romances we find him alternately dreaming of a repentant American tycoon who is able to re-establish his connection with the English tradition, and a young writer who hopes that an elixir of life will permit him to live on until he witnesses 'the final triumph' of the republic.

In these fragmentary tales, as in Hawthorne's earliest works, what finally thwarts the quest and destroys the dream is the frailty of the Heart, that marble temple and foul cavern which was at once Hawthorne's central preoccupation and his leading symbol. Everything he has to say is related, finally, to 'that inward sphere.' For the Heart is the meeting place of all the forces – spiritual and physical, light and dark, that compete for dominance in man's nature.

Criticism has dealt at great length with the Heart and its complexities, but Hawthorne's 'personal legend' reveals its centrality in a new way. Those who read him as a Christian moralist recognize instantly an opposition between Head and

I: The Shape of Hawthorne's Myth

Heart, reason and passion which is related not only to Puritan theology but to the Neo-Classical view of man: 'Reason the card, but passion is the gale.' But to conclude that Hawthorne thinks of Reason as a presiding faculty which must restrain and direct the depraved Heart is to forget that he allied himself with the Romantics in regarding Imagination as the supreme instrument of vision. For Oberon-Hawthorne the realm of imagination is the realm of night, of moonlight and magic; it is in this realm that one truly 'sees.' Reason belongs in the daylight realm of empirical action, and is concerned with law, measurement, and mechanism; it is efficacious in getting the world's work done. Unquestionably the Head-Heart conflict was primary in the Puritan vision of man's experience, for Puritanism equated imagination not with Oberon's magic but with witchcraft and demonism. (Consider, for example, 'The Devil in Manuscript,' in which Oberon wonders whether his art is not the devil's work after all.) In Hawthorne's personal vision, however, we have not a bipolar Head-Heart conflict but a tableau in which the Heart is central, flanked by two suitors – the empirical, day-light faculty of Reason and the nocturnal, magical power of Imagination.

The heart, then, far from being a sink of evil as Calvinism would have it, is for Hawthorne the characteristically human realm – as complex as the Cretan labyrinth (IV, 238), sometimes as black as Hell itself; but though its 'gloom and terror may lie deep ... deeper still is the eternal beauty.'[9] And when the heart is touched by love, man discovers his true humanity. As Hawthorne wrote to Sophia: 'That touch creates us – then

9 Randall Stewart, *The American Notebooks by Nathaniel Hawthorne* (New Haven, 1932), p. 98.

we begin to be – thereby we are beings of reality, and inheritors of eternity.'[10]

This redefinition of the relation of the Heart to Reason and Imagination brings us to a final problem that is illuminated by Hawthorne's 'personal legend.' If the individual and the community are major subjects of his concern, the figure of the artist is of special concern, for merchants, law-makers, clergy, and philanthropists are not the only people who should lead. The supreme hero is the man of imagination; vision, or insight, is his magical power, and this gift must finally be recognized by society and given a place of practical authority. Indeed until this occurs there can be neither individual nor corporate fulfilment of the American dream.

But the artist's pursuit of vision is full of peril, for it cuts him off from human warmth and fellowship; he may perish of cold and loneliness, or end by feeling that he has lived a life of shadows. Moreover, if he loses sight of the humane purpose of his art he may, like the artist of 'The Prophetic Pictures,' commit the unpardonable sin of prying into human hearts without sympathy or love – may become a kind of wizard. (By contrast, his counterpart in the daylight realm, the scientist or man of reason, is equally in peril, for if he pursues gold or knowledge to the exclusion of humane values, he will perish in flame, or become a demon.) The power which the artist achieves must serve human needs – must win the Heart; and for Hawthorne the hero's return to the community is symbolized by 'marriage.' The artist must espouse the human realm and work creatively in it. Thus, as with another mythological figure, Joyce's Stephen Dedalus, sexual

10 *The Portable Hawthorne*, ed., M. Cowley, p. 613.

I: The Shape of Hawthorne's Myth

love becomes a metaphor for artistic fertility and for the creative use of the individual's powers.

In all of this I have said nothing of the celebrated Dark Lady, for though she haunts Hawthorne's fiction, she does not appear in his personal legend. Hawthorne's course of action, after the twelve-year quest in his chamber of shadows, was to 'open an intercourse with the world' and, like his hero Cadmus, to marry 'a daughter of the sky.' In the fiction to which I shall now turn, however, the Dark Lady will emerge as a force almost equal in importance to the heroes of Hawthorne's quest stories.

The foregoing account of Hawthorne's mythologizing habit of mind and his personal legend is, I believe, closer to the spirit of his art than interpretations which stress Freudian psychology, Christian theology, or New-Critical analysis of image patterns. But in what way does the personal myth inform his fiction? And what are the mythological situations that give his work coherence as an *œuvre*? Once more deferring detailed documentation until parts II and III, I shall describe these myths in outline.

The mythological substructure of Hawthorne's work has not been clearly identified before now because criticism has neglected two of his simplest and apparently most inconsequential works, *A Wonder-Book for Girls and Boys*, and *Tanglewood Tales* – twelve episodes from Greek mythology which he retold for children. The literary merit of these tales is not great, although several of them persist in the imagination with a tenacity that places them in a class far above the 'progressive reader' rituals of John and Betty. Their most

13

striking feature for the critic, however, is that Hawthorne allowed himself to treat these 'immortal fables' as ideal forms created in 'the pure childhood of the world,' and justified his radical re-working of them on the ground that they were 'indestructible' and that 'the inner life of the legends cannot be come at save by making them entirely one's own property' (IV, 210). The result is a body of stories which in their purified state may make 'very capital reading' for children; but at a deeper level they constitute an 'ideal' myth which reveals Hawthorne's highest aspirations for the individual, the community, and the artist. This happy narrative, so striking in contrast to the dark tales of New England experience, provides the most direct access to the 'inward sphere' of Hawthorne's imagination.

Three themes dominate in Hawthorne's recreation of the materials that he found in Charles Anthon's *Classical Dictionary*.[11] The first, as revealed in the legends of Perseus, Cadmus, Bellerophon, Jason, Theseus, and Hercules, is the narrative of the hero: a young man undertakes a dangerous quest; he undertakes it at the prompting, or command, of a jealous king, an uncle or father; its fulfilment involves the killing of a monster; and the hero's reward (with the exception of Hercules and Bellerophon, the rider of Pegasus) is kingship. A related narrative, the stories of Pandora, Circe,

11 See Charles Anthon, *A Classical Dictionary, Containing an Account of the Principal Proper Names Mentioned in Ancient Authors, and Intended to Elucidate All the Important Points Connected With the Geography, History, Biography, Mythology, and Fine Arts of the Greeks and Romans* ... (New York: Harper and Brothers, 4th ed., 1845, 1848). Hawthorne may have used an earlier edition of this work, but the attribution of the source is not in doubt. There is an 1845 copy of the *Dictionary* in the Stirling Memorial Library at Yale.

and Proserpina, deals with an attractive female who, like Eve, appears to be responsible in one way or another for mankind's fallen state. And the third situation, treated in the tales of Baucis and Philemon, Midas, and the Pygmies, underlines the ideas that man's happiness is inextricably involved with the happiness of his fellows; men must learn to be brothers. The pattern of a quest, however, is central, though it is not, finally, separable from the related themes of the Dark Lady and the brotherhood of man.

In Hawthorne's rendering of the hero's quest, the reader soon recognizes recurring images which characterize two sides of the hero's experience. The daylight world in which the quest begins is associated with sun, flame, money, iron, power, the senses, and the narrow rationalism of law; this is the empirical realm, the concrete dimension of man's temporal experience. The moonlit world which the hero enters is an insubstantial area where he will accomplish his mission 'as though in a dream'; it is associated with the air, invisibility, mirrors, fountains, and magic; this is the realm of imagination, the dusky area in which the hero discovers his power.[12]

12 DEFINITIONS: My choice of the term 'empirical' to describe the material, daylight side of the hero's experience presents a semantic problem: as one 'empirical' reader of my manuscript has pointed out, I load the word with a burden of meaning that no dictionary would justify. I ask, therefore, that the term be accepted as a convenient label to cover that area of experience which E. M. Forster describes as 'prose,' and other writers refer to as 'this-worldly.' This is the world of custom and custom houses, of rule-following, measuring, weighing, precedent-citing (what Emerson called 'a foolish consistency'). Custom, law, rigid logic, and hard commonsense all fit under this umbrella.

The semantic difficulty increases when the term is applied to the Puritan way of life, because Puritans thought obsessively of their ex-

15

Hawthorne as Myth-Maker

At the beginning of the quest, the materialistic 'forces' of the daylight realm – such sun-blinded tyrants as Polydectes and Minos – dominate. Guided only by law, lust, or prophecy, they are at once jealous of the young men who threaten their power and terrified of the dark mysteries of the night realm. Hence they send their young relatives on quests into the moonlit world in the full expectancy that they will be destroyed by a Gorgon or a Minotaur. But the heroes are aided in their tasks by spectral, mercurial 'forces' such as Quicksilver, a personification of the moon-mirror image; by Mercury's sister, Minerva, the goddess of wisdom; or by a pale, ethereal girl such as Ariadne. And the monsters which they overcome appear, finally, to be delusory monsters, most terrible to those who believe in their empirical reality. Thus Perseus sees the Gorgon Medusa only as a reflection in his shield, but she can turn the credulous Polydectes and his court to stone.

This central narrative of Hawthorne's, though given substance in dramatic personalities, is in one sense interior – a myth of the self. The hero's quest is an exploration of the

perience as spiritual. But their approach to such experience was dominated by ideas of law, rule, and covenant. For Hawthorne, their rigid insistence on divine decree and so-called 'logical' pattern was as repugnant and inhuman as the custom-house materialism of the nineteenth century; and the nineteenth-century rigidity was but a secularized version of the Puritan mechanism. Such terms as 'rationalistic,' 'this-worldly,' or 'materialistic' fail to cover this complex of ideas and attitudes; the term 'empirical' may be somewhat less offensive.

The term 'imaginative,' I trust, will present no difficulty. Malcolm Cowley's analysis of images associated with the imaginative realm in his 'Editor's Introduction' to *The Portable Hawthorne* is one of the most important contributions to Hawthorne criticism.

menacing darkness of his own identity; it involves a long, night journey, as with Perseus and Cadmus, or the entry of a labyrinth or forest, as with Theseus and Jason. The hero's victory is the recognition and control of these forces, and the application of his new power to the problems of his community. Hawthorne underlines this dimension of the quest as a private 'initiation' when he remarks of the Cretan labyrinth: 'There can be nothing else so intricate, unless it were the brain of a man like Daedalus, who planned it, or the heart of any ordinary man' (IV, 238). Until this ordeal is past – until the forces of the darkest reaches of the self are brought under control – the hero cannot act creatively in the empirical world. The ideal end of the quest is the achievement of a new balance between the opposed forces of matter and spirit, sun and moon, reason and imagination. Then the hero can rule, and perhaps marry.

In this sense, Hawthorne's 'ideal' myth is optimistic in tone: each new generation of heroes brings back to the world of things an imaginative power which enables him to become a king – a benefactor of his race. There are no counterparts here of the dying Hercules, Orpheus, or Adonis. Provided that young men of imagination continue to appear, the powers of vision will triumph. Moreover, there is a significant variation of the pattern: the young hero Bellerophon, by gazing long and patiently into the fountain (mirror) of Pirene, sees the reflection of Pegasus, and finally makes this magnificent creature of the air his servant and friend. Then, as master of this offspring of the dying Medusa, he combats earth-born Chimaeras by lifting them into the imaginative realm of air and destroying them there. The hero, in short,

17

may become a king, like Perseus, a city-builder, like Cadmus, or an artist, like Bellerophon. The myth expresses the ideals of the self, the community, and the artist.

But this central narrative is not as simple as it appears, for there are a dozen other forces or personalities, active or passive, imaginative or materialistic, who aid or hinder the quest, and who may even make it miscarry. The ideal hero's parents are characteristically gentle, kindly people, but as a rule the father has been deposed by the iron-hearted uncle or cousin who sends the hero on his quest. In the empirical realm, it appears, there are two kinds of parental forces – the aggressive, gold-blinded rulers and the benign, but essentially passive men of good will. The hero's aim is to restore his kindly relatives to honour, or, since they are often too old, to reinstate their values on his own behalf. In Hawthorne's version, Cadmus is the only mythological hero who marries: he espouses a 'daughter of the sky,' Harmonia, and begets a race in his own image.

The personalities of the night side of the hero's experience also fall into active and passive groups. On the one hand there are willing helpers like Quicksilver and Minerva and the frail Ariadne who, though they cannot accomplish the quest itself, give the hero every possible aid; on the other, there are the malign monsters whom the hero must destroy, just as he must depose the tyrants, perhaps equally monstrous, of the empirical world. The action of the myth thus involves not merely a reconciliation of the opposed realms of imagination and matter, sun and moon, but a realignment of the active and passive groups within the community. If the old tyrants are men who fear the moonlight monsters and live only for material things and sensory satisfactions, the new

18

heroes are imaginative or reflective types whose power stems from their achievements in the realm of vision. Perseus even feels that he might remain forever floating above the earth in his magic slippers, were it not for his affection for his mother. But earth is the locus of human action; and Perseus, like Shakespeare's Prospero, wins control of the realm of air, and then, motivated by love, returns to the realm of men.

Hawthorne's ideal myths, then, reveal how the hero's quest ought to end: he ought to supplant his aggressive, materialistic relatives and restore his benign, passively sunny parents to honour. By contrast, the hero's quest in the historical world of experience is painful and disillusioning.

Before we turn from the ideal myth to Hawthorne's narratives of New England experience, however, we must consider the two related mythological situations mentioned above. The first might be called 'the brotherhood of man' theme. Again and again Hawthorne talks of 'unhumanized' hearts that have turned to iron, gold, marble, or stone. But the Heart's true elements are warm if fallible flesh and blood, and its presiding values should be sympathy and love. The Heart is the emblem of 'our common nature,' and until mankind recognizes and affirms its warm values he will fail equally in his social and individual quests. Three of the mythological tales underline this key perception: Hercules' adventure with the Pygmies moralizes earnestly if awkwardly on the need to treat one's fellowman as a brother; 'The Miraculous Pitcher,' even though its milk is laced with saccharine, lends the authority of Jupiter to the law of love and brotherhood; and 'The Golden Touch' is a skilful parable which reveals that to seek wealth for its own sake is to dehumanize the Heart. Like Auden, Hawthorne believed that

'We must love one another or die.' The goal of the quest is the brotherhood of man, or in social terms the 'final triumph' of the republic; it will be reached not by reformers or builders but by a growth of self-awareness and vision.

The second situation is far more complex. It is a feminine version of the hero's quest, revealed in the tales of Circe, Pandora, and Proserpina. The protagonist of this narrative is the Dark Lady who has so fascinated Hawthorne's readers and critics. To begin with, as her fecund charms indicate, she is primarily a creature of the empirical realm, but she is also a creative 'force.' Where the hero creates ideas or works of art, she creates babies, and this creative act is linked with the realm of night. Like the questing hero, she has had her dark initiation in the moonlit world.

But for Hawthorne she is no more a figure of guilt than is the artist. The creative act, whether fiction or procreation, is fundamental to human nature; and man must accept his creativity rather than condemn it. Thus, though Circe appears as a vengeful enchantress who makes beasts of men, Hawthorne reveals that a man like Ulysses – armed with the imaginative talisman of Quicksilver – can meet her as a friendly master. She will bestialize him only if he lives for the senses and temporal things alone. Hawthorne's telling of this tale is coy, for unlike Homer he does not permit Ulysses to go on and 'enjoy' Circe for 'a full year.' But his interpretation of the story is clear: man is as responsible for evil as woman. The stories of Pandora and Proserpina make this view unmistakable. In Pandora's case, the Fall resulted from simple curiosity – a trait which Epimetheus (Adam) shared with her almost equally. In opening the box, Pandora did no more than obey the law of her nature. Evil, that is, is a *donnée*

I: The Shape of Hawthorne's Myth

which Hawthorne does not attempt to explain. He only knows that it exists and that woman is not a guilty creature who corrupts men. In the same way, Proserpina's 'fall' was caused by nothing more unnatural than extreme hunger – for seeds, significantly. And though Pluto initiated the action by abducting her, he is not a devil in the Christian sense. He is a representative of the night realm who hopes to warm his isolated heart with a little human love.

In the ideal myth, then, the Dark Lady is blameless. It is only in the Christian tradition that she has become a figure of fear, haunted by the spectre of a Black Man who will never let society forget that she knows the realm of night. Her Christian embodiments – Miriam, Zenobia, and Hester – detest the shadow which haunts them, but Calvinist men will never clear them of its opprobrium. The figure of the Dark Lady thus prepares us to enter the world of experience – the historical locale of Hawthorne's New England fiction.

For those, like Melville, who sensed the implications of Hawthorne's journey into the labyrinth of experience in America, his tales were sombre indeed. The Puritans had, with a breath-taking fortitude, gone on a long and perilous voyage from their tyrannical fatherland, and they were finally to escape its jealous power entirely. But their quest had somehow failed to produce the creative self-knowledge that crowned the adventures of Perseus and Bellerophon. Hawthorne saw them as men of iron and blazing sunlight, like the tyrants of the mythological tales – materialists who feared the night and the dark forests as the dwelling place of monstrous witches and demons. In the light of day they achieved triumphs of city-building, trade, and manufacturing, but

21

Young Goodman Brown, as his name suggests, was their representative young hero – a Calvinist Everyman. The ambiguity of Brown's night journey suggests that his quest was the universal descent which all men must make into the depths of their own nature.[13] But in contrast to the heroes of the ideal myth the outcome of Goodman Brown's quest is tragic: deprived of the help of Mercury and Minerva, and guided by a sinister 'black man,' he desperately calls on his Faith for help; but his 'Faith' seems committed to man's evil, too. And so Brown returns from the journey overshadowed by the thought that the night side of his nature, and of mankind's, is monstrous. This Puritan vision of evil blights his entire life, or at least makes it passive suffering, and even 'his dying hour was gloom.'

In its very beginnings, then, the New England quest was in some degree abortive. The Puritans' legalistic, rationalistic, 'heart-less' theology, as Hawthorne saw it, pre-doomed them to a kind of half-life. In this community 'The Gentle Boy' – a 'child of the skies' who reminds us of Bellerophon's young companion at the fountain of Pirene – could not survive; and his raven-haired mother, who proclaimed her 'inner light' against the Puritan insistence on law, was driven to a crazed, Medusa-like fanaticism. The Reverend Mr. Hooper's black veil served not only as the sign of the power of blackness but, in its power to isolate, as the very fact of evil.[14] Even Owen Warland, a late product of the Puritan society, did not escape

13 Perhaps the soundest article on this subject is David Levin's 'Shadows of Doubt: Specter Evidence in Hawthorne's "Young Goodman Brown," ' *American Literature*, xxxiv (November, 1962), 344–52.

14 W. Stacy Johnson, 'Sin and Salvation in Hawthorne,' *Hibbert Journal*, L (1951), 40. F. O. Matthiessen and Mr. Johnson are the most reliable analysts of Hawthorne's theology.

the paralyzing literalness of the Puritan 'watch-maker's' family. He was to see his beautiful butterfly ('psyche'), the achievement of long labours in the realm of night, crushed in childish hands; and Annie, his closest link with the empirical realm, turn from him to a vigorous 'iron man,' the local blacksmith.[15]

But if America's young heroes and heroic young America alike failed to achieve an ideal fulfilment of their quests, Calvinist theology was not entirely responsible, though it presented an initial difficulty. As Hawthorne turned from the terrors of Satan and the forest, he saw in every period of America's history promising heroes pursuing abortive quests which ended in isolation rather than in reconciliation of opposites and a new communion with their fellow men. The ultimate source of the failure was the denial of the values of the Heart – a denial often involuntary but nevertheless ending in cruel isolation. Thus Aylmer, brilliantly gifted in the practical knowledge of science, decided to eradicate the one blemish in his wife's nature; but in following an impossible ideal rather than accepting with Aminidab the knowledge of human imperfection, he destroyed her. Ethan Brand, one of the most powerful minds of the New England tales, committed the Unpardonable Sin – a pursuit of knowledge which finally regards its end as superior to the human beings which it should serve. For such men there was no 'return' from the quest, no application of their conquests to the needs of humanity, though Aylmer escapes Brand's final monstrousness because his motive, however misguided, was love. Roger

15 Millicent Bell's discussion of this tale is illuminating, but she does not emphasize sufficiently the historical period which limits Warland's possibilities as an artist.

Chillingworth, the 'doctor' of *The Scarlet Letter*, ends as a fiend, for he uses his knowledge coldly and deliberately to torture and destroy Dimmesdale rather than to heal him. At the opposite pole from the scientist, the inhuman artist of 'The Prophetic Pictures' commits the Unpardonable Sin in his icily detached inspection of the hearts of Walter and Elinor. When he asks Elinor why she did not heed his prophecy, she makes what to him must seem an inscrutable reply: 'But – I loved him!' (I, 209)

The night journey of Major Molyneux's young kinsman would suggest that, by the time of the pre-revolutionary era, the young American, freed of the need to seek help from his aristocratic European 'uncle,' had all the world before him to fashion into a great new community. But the new independence did not bring the fulfilment it seemed to promise. If Puritan America had denied the imaginative side of the self with the blind energy of terror, the new age similarly stressed the daylight, empirical side of experience; and in the face of this materialism, the man of vision was still suspect. As Hawthorne pondered this isolation, marriage became a symbol of his hero's reunion with the community. But in both Puritan and republican America, as Hawthorne saw them, the ways of true love were lethally stormy.

After the misstep of *Fanshawe*, which suggested that the sensitive hero's fate was to turn from the library to the tomb and allow the young materialists to take over, Hawthorne's first major analysis of the American situation was *The Scarlet Letter*. As Henry James perceived, Dimmesdale is – or should be – the hero of this narrative, although the story of the Dark Lady overshadows him. Today we would adjust this insight

24

and describe him, in Northrop Frye's terms, as an 'ironic hero.' In Boston, Dimmesdale had achieved the highest place that the Puritan community accorded its men of vision – the pulpit; and from this eminence it was his duty to fight the powers of blackness. To the end of his career, Dimmesdale was a believing Calvinist, but his nature – even stronger than his belief – attracted him irresistibly to the lush, temporal charms of Hester, with whom he created a 'Pearl,' 'the union of their two natures,' and then, because of his faith, became an easy prey to the unending torture of guilt. By the same token, his Dark Lady, Hester, whose temporal creativity could scarcely, under the circumstances, be concealed, was persecuted by a community which feared both carnal knowledge and the mystery of creativity except as confined within the narrow limits set by religion and law. To complicate this situation, the community unknowingly welcomed her husband, Roger Chillingworth, a deformed old scientist who had married Hester to warm the cold chamber of his heart, and who forces her to keep his identity a secret. In this repressive atmosphere he conveniently recalls 'his old faith' and becomes not a source of healing but a fiend who uses his knowledge of man's nature to torture the Puritan Dimmesdale to the point of death. But Hester privately refuses to accept the community's view of her nature as evil. Robbed of her real place in the town, she speculates boldly that human nature is naturally good. Finally, after meeting Dimmesdale on the scaffold at night and learning of his suffering, she refuses to keep Chillingworth's secret any longer, and in the 'natural' setting of the forest – as opposed to the legal forum of the marketplace – she offers Dimmesdale an escape to the wilderness or to Europe where she believes they can live by

25

the law of their natures alone. For a moment Dimmesdale accepts, but then a flood of carnal images reveals to him that man's nature, unregulated by any law but instinct, is as unthinkable as the repressive Puritan scheme. His solution to the dilemma, therefore, is to confess his full nature publicly. Hester's power has given him strength to be an integrated man at last; God, he hopes, will be a merciful judge.

Dimmesdale's confession of his full nature 'humanizes' his daughter Pearl. She is a complete person, even though the Puritans regard her as a demon. But Pearl cannot survive in New England any more than the ethereal Gentle Boy could. She escapes to Europe, endowed with Chillingworth's wealth – the chief 'good' that the Puritans produced. But, despite Dimmesdale's tragic death, the New England quest is not a complete failure, for Hester, the innocent Eve, finally returns to New England. Having hated her oppressors 'through seven long years,' she now repents of her unyielding pride and convinces them through gentleness and good works that she is not a temptress or witch but a nurse and benefactress. The Puritan austerity may be wrong, but man's imperfect nature must be governed. Man's full nature – its pearl – she believes, will yet be accepted in America. And the blood-red emblem which Pearl personifies, the *A Gules*, will in another age become a symbol of honour: 'at some brighter period ... a new truth would be revealed, in order to establish the whole relation between man and woman on a surer ground of mutual happiness' (C, I, 263). For the *A*, as its position over the heart suggests, is the sign of the self – of the warm red bloodstream which mingles gifts that should be used, and frailties that are better recognized and controlled than scourged.

I: The Shape of Hawthorne's Myth

So ended this New England quest. Dimmesdale, like Perseus, had found his identity, but only at the point of death. Hester, the Dark Lady, learned to accept her unhappy lot and await the bright revelations of such artists as Nathaniel Hawthorne. This gifted pair, at the price of great suffering, passed beyond the Puritan vision of evil. With the truth of man's nature revealed, the Black Man Chillingworth, with 'no more devil's work to do,' shrivelled and died.

Subsequent imaginative heroes (mercurial, moon types) would perhaps be more vigorous than Dimmesdale. But if they were to be more aggressive, their partners would have to be less aggressive than Hester, for in the world of Hawthorne's mythology two 'active' forces do not marry. Thus in the next romances Hawthorne's myth elaborated itself in an important new character, the pretty and fecund, but passive, maiden, a delightfully domestic creature who, like Cadmus's wife Harmonia, would be her husband's creative link with the empirical realm (the glories and weaknesses of this 'golden girl' will be considered fully in subsequent chapters). By the same token, the passive moon hero, the Dimmesdale of the first nineteen chapters of *The Scarlet Letter*, was to be perpetuated as a proper complement to the Dark Lady, although neither of this pair was to triumph in the new American community.

Two centuries and seven long generations later, Hawthorne saw a happy fulfilment of the American quest in *The House of the Seven Gables*. This quest narrative involves a long struggle between two families: the imaginative craftsmen called Maule, the possessors of a beautiful piece of 'garden ground' with a clear, bubbling spring; and the Pyncheons, a family of Puritan materialists who regard the

27

Maules as witches and steal their land as the site for a great house. In revenge, the Maules secrete the title to a great tract of 'Eastern land,' turn the clear well brackish, curse the sensual Pyncheons with something that resembles apoplexy, and return to torment them in dreams. Nevertheless, the Pyncheons triumph and the Maules disappear from view. In the course of seven generations, however, a more sympathetic strain of the Pyncheon family gains control of the house. Hepzibah, associated with owls – as Minerva is – and her brother Clifford, a Quicksilver type who has been banished to the darkness of a prison by the sun-tyrant Jaffrey, are in uncertain control of the house. This pair represent the frail and passive imagination of the nineteenth-century Puritans; unfortunately, they are too old and too weak to dominate their materialistic cousin Jaffrey. They give shelter, however, to a young couple, Holgrave and Phoebe. Holgrave is the last of the Maules, a vigorous and imaginative Daguerreotypist who 'makes pictures out of sunlight' in his dark chamber. Phoebe, far from reproducing the grasping materialism of her family, is a sunny, domestic angel. And this pair, the young moon hero and the cheerful young sun maiden, the last descendants of their lines, finally unite the warring families in a new and productive 'marriage.' Unlike his forebear who had attempted to enmesh Alice Pyncheon in the magic of wizardry, Holgrave captures Phoebe in 'love's web of sorcery.' The curse of the Maules carries off the hard-living Jaffrey, and the new inheritors of the Pyncheon-Maule property move to a new house, carrying their benign elders with them. Significantly, the new house will be built of wood. No family can build for its heirs; each generation must construct its own house. But what of the Eastern Land which the Anglophile Pyncheons hoped to wrest from the native Maules and exploit? Holgrave discovered its charter easily in the old house, and Clifford Pyncheon had known about it all along. He had thought of it as a vision – an ideal – which was not to be 'owned' by anyone, let alone the domineering Pyncheons. In the end, the Eastern Land turns out to be a thriving colony; it is the part of New England (or America) which the Puritans' greed failed to engulf.

The plot of *Seven Gables*, then, whatever its relation to fairytale or Gothic romance, is not the 'tiresome nuisance' that critics have complained of. Its outcome is an almost pastoral version of Hawthorne's central quest narrative, though the early events of the history are very dark comedy indeed; in sum, the action dramatizes with great subtlety the long quest of the nation's visionary powers to find their place of honour in the community, and to keep the Puritan ethos from dominating the entire Eastern Land. More important, perhaps, this perception of the informing principle of the romance reveals that all of Hawthorne's comments on the past – the advantages of frame houses, progress, and so forth – are relevant parts of the complete structure rather than tedious, 'tacked-on' morals.

By the same token, *The Blithedale Romance*, whatever its limitations as mass entertainment, is a clear and coherent statement of Hawthorne's central myth. In addition, it is his most sophisticated and disillusioned book. Coverdale, the imaginative hero, hoped that the experiment of Blithedale – the vision of a knot of American idealists – would produce 'the one true system,' a community in which the full range of mankind's talents would be accepted and fulfilled. But this idyllic dream is a failure. The sun-blinded materialist of

Greek mythology and of the Puritan era now appears as the reformer, Hollingsworth, a former blacksmith who can see man's nature only as depraved and evil. Still worse, the Black Man of the colonial period still plagues the women of Blithedale, now in the guise of a charlatan mesmerist, Professor Westervelt. Coverdale recognizes that this detestable spectre is no more than 'a moral and physical humbug,' but the women's ties to him predate the beginning of Blithedale.

Again, Hawthorne's so-called Gothic trappings reveal themselves as organic elements of the action. Zenobia and Priscilla (the Dark Lady figure has now split into active and passive 'sisters') were sent to Blithedale by their father, a one-eyed vagrant who reminds us of Odin, the 'prime mover';[16] the father's one stipulation was that the sisters should be treated as equals. But the satanic Westervelt has been 'wedded' to Zenobia, and Priscilla has served as a medium at his seances. Priscilla, we realize, might emerge as the ideal American woman if Westervelt and Hollingsworth would allow her to;[17] indeed, her frail beauty blossoms so well in the community that she promises to be a second Phoebe Pyncheon. Zenobia's legend, 'The Silvery Veil,' however, suggests that if men are to win this virgin they must have faith, even without seeing her face, that she is 'a heavenly essence ... which might have been tamed down to human bliss,' rather than Eve or Medusa. But Hollingsworth thinks of her only as a weak and erring woman. He rejects Zenobia,

16 Q. D. Leavis, 'Hawthorne as Poet, II,' *Sewanee Review* (Summer, 1951), 442.

17 A. N. Kaul, ed., *Hawthorne: A Collection of Critical Essays* (New York, 1966). In his important essay on *The Blithedale Romance* in this collection Professor Kaul suggests (p. 159) that Hollingsworth and Westervelt represent 'the final degradation of the Puritan tradition.'

just as the Puritans had rejected Hester, and 'saves' Priscilla from her evil and makes her his mouse – a devoted nurse rather than the blooming young woman that Coverdale hoped to win.

Ruled by Hollingsworth, the community inevitably fails, and when Coverdale sees him last he is a melancholy figure who has understood too late that he 'murdered' Zenobia. The potential wealth of Blithedale – the potential talents of Zenobia, Coverdale, and Priscilla – have been tragically wasted. Coverdale confesses that he had loved Priscilla, but she chose the 'blind' reformer as her protector. And so, though Coverdale lives in comparative opulence, he feels that he has no real place in American society; his ideal hopes – the hero's reward in the ideal myth – have failed, and he must console himself with the role of dilettante. Yet the picture is not unrelievedly bleak: Coverdale does produce a bitter parable of his experience by telling his story; his novel, like the portentous 'Prophetic Pictures,' may warn America of its continuing failure to recognize and use creatively the full potential of its human resources.

In *The Marble Faun*, Hawthorne uses his European experience to compare the pattern of the old culture with that of the New World, but the forces or personalities of the myth are still the same, although the tyrannical father or uncle does not appear. In Rome, the tradition of woman's responsibility in the Fall still persists. The lush and brilliant Miriam is haunted by a spectre that suggests a dim past of sexual guilt. Donatello, an unreflective faun from the 'state of nature,' attempts to rid Miriam of her dark persecutor by the simple expedient of killing him. In doing so, he embraces the darkness of mankind's post-lapsarian state, and must, through

31

a long process of suffering, learn to recognize and accept humanity's imperfect nature. The spectre whom he believed he had murdered does not die in the usual way: it is connected with the institution of the church, and the lovers discover it the following day, on display at a Capucin monastery where it will, in effect, never be buried. But if the Roman church, so to speak, 'keeps the devil alive' – keeps reminding man of his fallen nature – it also, unlike the Puritan faith, offers him a means of working out his salvation. Donatello and Miriam must suffer sorely for their humanity, but in the end they will receive the blessing of a benign Father, symbolized by the statue of Pope Julius.

However, Hilda and Kenyon, the American observers, are not directly involved in this European pattern of sin and expiation. Though the shadow of evil falls upon them, they suffer no more than guilt-by-association. Both of them, it appears, have until this moment lived in the cold realm of art which, as Hawthorne confessed to Sophia, 'is but the thinnest substance of a dream, – till the heart be touched.' Their contact with the fallible humanity of Miriam and Donatello, therefore, is their initiation into the community of imperfect men. Yet their guilt is not that of their European friends. They are an immaculate pair, and their 'Fall' is symbolic rather than actual. Thus Hilda disappears into the darkness of a convent, just as Proserpina had spent six innocent months in Pluto's dark kingdom; and Kenyon must discover, in an ancient grave, a nude sculpture of Venus in which he recognizes 'womanhood ... without prejudice to its divinity.' Then, after undergoing a symbolic death in the timeless ritual of a Roman carnival, he regains his Hilda, appropriately dressed in a white domino. Their initiation has humanized them without involving them in the suffering of the European pattern. Their future is not clear, but Hilda sees 'light on the mountain-tops.' Kenyon, the imaginative man of vision, has found his contact with the community in the person of a pure, dove-like Venus in petticoats. America has escaped the guilt of Europe, and though the lovers strike us as priggish even yet, they may indicate a happy ending to the American quest.

The foregoing is perhaps enough to suggest that the 'principle of coherence' in Hawthorne's *œuvre* is a quest narrative – a myth in which the imaginative hero assumes that man can achieve happiness only in communion with his fellowmen; and that woman is not a slave of the Black Man but a creative complement to the hero – his point of contact with the material world. Because Hawthorne was an artist who saw clearly the phenomena of his social and intellectual tradition, he enriched this personal myth with a body of reflection and commentary that cannot be summarized at this stage of our investigation; nor can we consider until parts II and III the developments which finally caused his vision of the American fate to run hideously aground. For the moment, one question remains: What is the relation of the informing myth to the vast body of criticism which has documented Hawthorne's theology, moral philosophy, political views, and so forth?

The present study, I think, does not run counter to such analyses, although it may place some of them in a new perspective. As his mythological tales make clear – and as a number of students of his thought have long since argued – the exact centre of his thought is the human heart, the *A*, the self. When empirical forces rule, as they do in the tyrants of Greek myth, or in the mechanical law of the Puritans, the

33

rejected night side of the self may become monstrous or vengeful; it harasses the self with the wizardry of the Maules, the paralyzing gaze of the Gorgon Medusa, or the terrors of the Black Man and of witches. When imagination dominates, all is well; the community will progress to new heights. Evil, in these terms, is not to be explained; it is imperfection, the fundamental *donnée* of the human condition. And love is the force which redeems the mingled light and dark of the 'human realm.'

Given this basic view of experience, it becomes clear that, for Hawthorne, man's attempts to formulate schematically 'the one true system' are foreordained to failure. He could agree with Emerson that 'the law of my nature' should be recognized, but he could never agree that it must be followed undeviatingly, for unlike Emerson he believed that man's nature is imperfect. Hence, law and convention and ethical sanctions are a necessary part of life in society. But such laws and conventions should take into account the limitations of the men whom they govern. For these reasons, Hawthorne was a great democrat; he believed that, despite the self-aggrandizing motives of materialists, the interests of all men would finally triumph. Yet he scoffed at doctrinaire clergy, philanthropists, and reformers, including abolitionists. Like Emerson, he might have claimed: 'I have other slaves to free.' There would be no real abolition – no real end of man's inhumanity to man – until the realm of imagination achieved a place of authority in the affairs of the self, and hence of the community and the nation.

PART II

Greek Myths and New England 'Baby Stories'

CRITICISM HAS GENERALLY TAKEN IT FOR GRANTED THAT the tales from Greek mythology which Hawthorne told for his 'dear auditors' at Tanglewood are so simple that there could be no point in comparing his versions with the accounts in Hesiod, Ovid, Homer, or other classical writers. As a result, *A Wonder-Book for Girls and Boys* and *Tanglewood Tales* have usually been ignored altogether, or dismissed with a genial nod towards such homely anachronisms as King Midas's New England breakfast: 'Hot cakes, some nice little brook trout, roasted potatoes, fresh boiled eggs, and coffee.'[1] But if Hawthorne was serious when he advised readers to 'look through the whole range of his fictitious characters, good and evil, in order to detect any of his essential traits' (III, 386), then the twelve mythological tales deserve close attention. Because there has been no previous study of Hawthorne's first-hand sources for these tales,[2] this essay will be necessarily lengthy. It is, however, indispensable to a knowl-

1 Daniel Hoffman's essay 'Myth, Romance, and the Childhood of man,' in *Hawthorne Centenary Essays*, ed., Roy Harvey Pearce (Ohio State University Press, 1964), pp. 197–220, is a valuable discussion of Hawthorne's mythology. See also Richard D. Hathaway, 'Hawthorne and the Paradise of Children,' *Western Humanities Review*, xv (Spring 1961), 161–72.

2 Roger Penn Cuff has written a doctoral thesis titled 'A Study of the Classical Mythology in Hawthorne's Writings,' which collates his mythological allusions with classical sources, but without discovering Hawthorne's major first-hand source in Anthon. See *Abstract of Contribution to Education*, No. 180 (George Peabody College for Teachers, 1936).

edge of Hawthorne, for it examines his prefatory remarks on the uses of myth, records his use of his sources, notices the development of his story-telling technique, and considers the meaning of his personal interpretations of such classic personae as Perseus, Proserpina, Bellerophon, and Cadmus. The basic source study follows the published order of the tales; the subsequent discussion of their meaning treats them in thematic groups – the brotherhood of man, the Dark Lady, and the questing hero.

A Wonder-Book was written during June and July of 1851, less than two months after the publication of *Seven Gables*. Since Hawthorne disliked writing during the hot weather, he must have felt that the composition of a half-dozen nursery tales would be more pleasure than work. We know that he had been thinking over the literary possibilities of Greek myth for some time; and as F. O. Matthiessen makes clear, he shared the taste of an age that exclaimed delightedly over Flaxman's mythological drawings.[3] Moreover, as I have argued elsewhere, he must have had conveniently at hand as his major source of information on incident, spelling, and detail, Professor Charles Anthon's *Classical Dictionary*.[4] The writing, then, went easily. George Parsons Lathrop says of the *Wonder-Book* manuscript:

Scarcely a correction or an erasure occurs, from the beginning to the end; and wherever an alteration was made, the after-thought was evidently so swift that the author did not stop to blot, for the word

3 A notebook entry for 1838 reminds him briefly: 'Pandora's box for a child's story' (IX, 207). See Matthiessen, *American Renaissance*, pp. 208–10 on genteel taste; and Julian Hawthorne, *Nathaniel Hawthorne and His Wife*, 2 vols. (Boston, 1884), I, pp. 354, 381.

4 Hugo McPherson, 'Hawthorne's Major Source for His Mythological Tales,' *American Literature*, XXX (November 1958), 364–65.

II: Myths and 'Baby Stories'

first written is merely smeared into illegibility and another substituted for it. It appears to be certain that although Hawthorne meditated long over what he intended to do and came rather slowly to the point of publication, yet when the actual task of writing was begun, it proceeded rapidly and with very little correction. (IV, 11)

It is clear, however, that Hawthorne understood from the beginning that his apparently simple plots (even as moral *exempla*) were not purely ingenuous. In the Pandora story, for example, he could not resist adding awkward interpretive comments which are neither childlike nor classical in spirit. He was, in fact, changing the entire emphasis of the myth. This impulse to reinterpret his materials in a personal way became so acute that in the introductory sketch to *Tanglewood Tales* (1853) he dropped the banter about Eustace Bright's 'sophomoric erudition,' and wondered audibly how these morally 'abhorrent,' 'hideous,' 'melancholy and miserable' legends could be made into 'children's playthings': 'How were they to be purified? How was the blessed sunshine to be thrown into them?' In the preface to *A Wonder-Book* his answer had been that every age must clothe them 'with its own garniture of manners and sentiment, and ... imbue them with its own morality' (IV, 13). In *Tanglewood Tales*, however, Eustace Bright earnestly advances an ideal explanation. 'When the first poet or romancer told these marvellous legends,' he suggests, 'it was still the Golden Age,' the age of man's innocence:

Evil had never yet existed; and sorrow, misfortune, crime, were mere shadows which the mind fancifully created for itself, as a shelter against too sunny realities: or, at the most, but prophetic dreams, to which the dreamer himself did not lend a waking credence. Children are now the only representatives of the men and women of that happy

39

era; and therefore it is that *we must raise the intellect and fancy to the level of childhood, in order to re-create the original myths.* (IV, 209–10; my italics)

The most striking part of this statement is the affirmation, fancifully expressed though it is, of a dual reality: an unfallen world, now beyond the reach of all but children, and perhaps artists; and an empirical, fallen world which is the realm of historical process. Here, in a new image, we have exactly the dualism which F. O. Matthiessen has discerned in Hawthorne's religious thought.[5] This ideal realm is variously 'the better world' which Queen Telephassa enters at the end of her quest for Europa; Eden; 'the spiritual world'; or that inner region of the Heart which reproduces 'the flowers and sunny beauty of the entrance, but all perfect' – the region of 'eternal beauty.'[6] And the highest truth, Hawthorne believed, resides in this region of innocence.

The leading principle of adaptation and interpretation, then, is to see the myths as ideal forms. The second principle is to make them living, relevant truth. As Hawthorne reflects on the liberties that Eustace exercised, he concludes that they are justified only by the necessity of restoring the childlike vision, 'and that the inner life of the legends cannot be come at save by making them entirely one's own property' (IV, 210).

In the process of purification, Eustace proposed to strip away the 'parasitical growth' which had 'no essential connection with the original fable.' This meant, primarily, the omission of merely supernumerary detail such as the story of Danaë's girlhood and seduction by Jupiter, the tedious after-

5 *American Renaissance*, pp. 337–51.
6 Randall Stewart, ed., *The American Notebooks*, p. 98.

math of Theseus' quest, or the long columns of analysis and
guesswork written by 'old gray-bearded grandsires [who]
pore over them in musty volumes of Greek, and puzzle themselves with trying to find out when, and how, and for what
they were made' (IV, 19). Unfortunately, too, purification
meant bowdlerizing. Hawthorne himself, although he polished what he thought of as blunt language into what strikes
us as elegant variation, was neither scandalized nor repelled
by the crudities of life; when Una fell down, she fell on her
'bum' according to his journal.[7] For Sophia, however, who
believed ecstatically that 'to do the highest, wisest, loveliest
thing is not the least effort to him, any more than it is to a
baby to be innocent,'[8] purity of word was a romantic obsession. It was an obsession which Hawthorne, despite his apparent candour, seems to have shared in part at least. Hence
the thorough scouring of the 'moral stains' of mythology.
Had he needed any ulterior incentive to conformity in this
respect, he might have found it immediately at hand in the
preface to Peter Parley's *Tales About the Mythology of
Greece and Rome*: 'Much that is in Mythology requires
judicious modification before it can, with propriety, be presented to youth. I have scrupulously avoided the unchaste
allusions which are introduced into almost every book on
this subject, thinking it better to be silent than to give my
young friends information likely to do them an injury.'[9]

The second step in the process of revealing the 'usable
truth' of Greek myth was the large problem of giving it

7 See Matthiessen's excellent discussion of Hawthorne's diction, *American Renaissance*, pp. 211–14.
8 Quoted in Julian Hawthorne, *Hawthorne and His Wife*, I, p. 373.
9 (London, 1838), p. iv.

41

warmth and 'presentness.' This was not, for Hawthorne, merely a matter of performing *Hamlet* in modern dress; it meant making the myths relevant – a part of the personal experience of both author and reader. The importance of this aspect of art emerges clearly when we recall Hawthorne's fast belief that an artist must live for his own age, must be true to the reality which he sees about him. For all their beauty, Hawthorne almost wished 'that the Elgin Marbles and the frieze of the Parthenon were all burnt into lime ... and, in fine, that all the material relics of so many successive ages had disappeared with the generations that produced them.' 'The present,' he lamented, 'is burdened too much with the past. We have not time, in our earthly existence, to appreciate what is warm with life, and immediately around us ... I do not see how future ages are to stagger onward under all this dead weight, with the additions that will be continually made to it.' (VIII, 207) Hawthorne therefore informed his publisher, James T. Fields: 'I shall aim at substituting a tone in some degree Gothic or romantic, or any such one as may best please myself, instead of the classic coldness, which is as repellent as the touch of marble ... and, of course, I shall purge out all the old heathen wickedness, and put in a moral wherever practicable.'[10]

In the first collection this question of relevance was met in several ways. The setting which Hawthorne invented did two things: it brought the tales into relation with the contemporary scene by placing them against a living background; and it made the narrator more relaxed than he had ever been, for in Squash Flower, Primrose, Sweet Fern, and the others, he had the most responsive and definable audience he had

10 Quoted in Stewart, *Nathaniel Hawthorne*, p. 114.

ever known as an artist. Within the tales themselves, Hawthorne employed several technical devices to increase relevance. On a very simple level he made certain that his juvenile audience would understand fully the events and pictures displayed. Thus Anthon's description of the 'impenetrable scales' which covered Medusa becomes in Hawthorne 'scales, which, if not of iron, were something as hard and impenetrable' (IV, 24). For both children and adults he included explicit moral interpretations of the action – interpretations which, for an exacting reader, do not always rise naturally out of the action and, at worst, even ignore it.[11] He introduced, too, for the same broad audience, repeated anachronisms which are often humorous, and sometimes regrettably coy. Thus King Midas wears glasses and eats a New England farmer's breakfast and Mother Ceres affects a matronly Bostonian propriety. Still further, for adults alone, there is irony, sometimes as purely dramatic as the contrast between the temporal success and spiritual failure of Cadmus' brothers, and sometimes so allusive as to echo Swift.

Hawthorne invoked all of these devices in support of the principle of relevance. But how could the fundamental import or inner meaning of the myths be made apparent through the welter of incident, detail, allusion, and reflection presented on the surface? His solution to this key problem involves two familiar terms: he will aim, he says, at 'a tone in some degree *Gothic* or *romantic*' (my italics).

Exactly how Hawthorne would have defined these words we cannot say, but we can be certain that they were not the genre labels which modern literary history makes them. Snobbish Mr. Pringle charges that Eustace's imagination will

11 'The Three Golden Apples' is the worst offender on this count.

'inevitably Gothicize' everything it touches, and cites the portrait of Atlas in 'The Three Golden Apples' as Gothic – a 'huge disproportioned mass among the seemly outlines of Grecian fable.' Eustace admits that: 'the moment you put any warmth of heart, any passion or affection, any human or divine morality, into a classic mould, you make it quite another thing from what it was before' (IV, 135). In effect, the Gothic 'humanizes' the classic form by infusing it with feeling or emotional colour. At the same time, as Mr. Pringle points out, the Gothic mode exaggerates. The Atlas of antiquity has become, in Eustace's hands, an enormous figure of pain and endurance, at once exciting the feelings and arresting the eye. He is, to use the third term which Hawthorne joins to 'Gothic' and 'romantic,' *picturesque*. Like Burke's 'sublime,' the Gothic inspires with awe; it is mysterious, even supernatural; and it is related to the tender sentiments of nostalgia, affection, and pity.[12]

The 'romantic aspect' of the tales is, of course, related to Hawthorne's idea of 'the romance' as opposed to the realistic novel. Since *A Wonder-Book* follows *Seven Gables* in close order, it is not extravagant to suppose that the preface to this romance bears closely upon the technique of the mythological tales. The novel, Hawthorne suggests, aims 'at a very minute

12 Christopher Hussey, in *The Picturesque* (London, 1927), analyses fully the eighteenth-century concept of 'the picturesque' in painting, and shows how picturesque landscapes function as *particular* realizations of states of mind. Hawthorne, whose house at Lenox was decorated with prints by Claude and Salvatore (Julian Hawthorne, *Hawthorne and His Wife*, I, pp. 166, 372), understood the relevance of misted and exaggerated scenes as 'landscapes of the mind.' Even in such early works as *Fanshawe* he carefully arranges his prose landscapes so that they become 'directly' and powerfully expressive; in *The Marble Faun* this technique becomes a presiding, sometimes overpowering, symbolic device.

fidelity, not merely possible, but the probable and ordinary course of man's experience.' The author of a romance, on the contrary, 'has fairly a right to present that truth under circumstances, to a great extent, of the writer's own choosing or creation. If he think fit, also, he may so manage the atmospherical medium as to bring out or mellow the lights that deepen and enrich the shadows of the picture.' (C, II, 1) The writer may, as Hawthorne suggested playfully in another context, surround his creations with as much 'glorified fog' as he wishes. And the effect of this? As in a picturesque landscape, the mistiness will draw attention away from particulars and concentrate it upon the main outlines, the true form of the work. Hence the 'legend' of the Pyncheons and Maules will bring 'along with it some of its legendary mist, which the Reader, according to his pleasure, may either disregard, or allow ... to float imperceptibly about the characters and events, for the sake of a picturesque effect' (C, II, 2).

The particular details of romance, then, whatever their superficial interest, are the occasion of meaning, not the meaning itself. Of explicit 'morals,' moreover, Hawthorne says this:

When romances do really teach anything, or produce any effective operation, it is usually through a far more subtle process than the ostensible one. The Author has considered it hardly worth his while, therefore, relentlessly to impale the story with its moral as with an iron rod ... A high truth, indeed, fairly, finely, and skilfully wrought out, brightening at every step, and crowning the final development of a work of fiction, may add an artistic glory, but is never any truer, and seldom any more evident, at the last page than at the first. (C, II, 2–3)

The real truth of a romance, like the truth of poetry, is the work itself.

45

Hawthorne as Myth-Maker

With these ideas before us, it now becomes possible to explain the apparently tedious 'summer house' image of 'The Wayside,' the prefatory note to *Tanglewood Tales*. In this rustic ruin Hawthorne discussed with Eustace Bright the second volume of mythological tales:

It is a mere skeleton of slender, decaying tree-trunks with neither walls nor a roof; nothing but a tracery of branches and twigs, which the next wintry blast will be very likely to scatter in fragments along the terrace. It looks, and is, as evanescent as a dream: and yet, in its rustic net-work of boughs, it has somehow enclosed a hint of spiritual beauty, and has become a true emblem of the subtile and ethereal mind that planned it. I made Eustace Bright sit down on a snow-bank, which had heaped itself over the mossy seat, and gazing through the arched window opposite, he acknowledged that the scene at once grew picturesque.

'Simple as it looks,' said he, 'this little edifice seems to be the work of magic. It is full of suggestiveness, and, in its way, is as good as a cathedral' ... [And Hawthorne replies:] 'The summer house itself, so airy and so broken, is like one of those old [mythological] tales, imperfectly remembered; and these living branches of the Baldwin apple-tree thrusting themselves so rudely in, are like your unwarrantable interpolations.' (IV, 206–7)

In the obliquely poetic manner which marks Hawthorne's deepest thought, this trifling incident sums up his idea of the meaning of Greek myth. Like the rustic bower of the Delphic oracle, the 'ruined boughs' of the myths 'enclosed a hint of spiritual beauty.' But the bower is merely a wintry ruin without the support of intrusive, 'living branches' of an apple tree. Out of this intricate web of new and old, living and dead, emerges the simple oracle of truth. And the romantic, the Gothic, the picturesque, are the interpretive modes which take us out of Sophia's genteel parlour and nursery into the clear, ethereal atmosphere of the summer house.

46

II: A Wonder-Book

A WONDER-BOOK:
Sources and Adaptations

Such were Hawthorne's aims in recreating the Greek myths
for his own age. Before we can make any detailed judgments
about the nature of his interpretations, or their relation to the
larger body of his work, it will be necessary to show exactly
what he did with his sources in Anthon's *Classical Dictionary*.
How much of the source did he use? How much did he omit?
What changes did he make in events as given in the source?
How did he realize dramatically the bare narratives of events?
These are the questions which we shall try to answer for each
of the mythological tales. In two instances we shall find that
the Anthon source is not of great importance, and in one
instance we shall turn to another source altogether.

The Gorgon's Head: In this, the first story that Eustace
Bright told for the children at Tanglewood, Charles Anthon's
article on 'Perseus' provided the narrative core, supplemented
by detail from the articles on 'Danaë,' the 'Phorcydes,' and
the 'Gorgones,' all of which Anthon had conveniently cross-
referenced at appropriate points in the main article on Perseus.[13] Hawthorne decided, apparently, to confine himself to
Perseus' best-known exploit, the quest for the head of Gorgon
Medusa. As a result, his story begins with two paragraphs in

13 Since the Anthon *Dictionary* is alphabetically arranged, I shall not
include page references. In quoting from it I have generally omitted the
Greek originals which he inserts in support of his translations of various
names and terms; I have also omitted his very full references to classical
texts and his elaborate discussions of the meanings of the legends. Hawthorne disregarded most of these interpretations; I shall refer to them
where they seem to be pertinent. Like Hawthorne, I have omitted diph-
thongs in Latin names: e.g. Antæus becomes Antaeus in both source and
text.

which the history of Perseus is summarized: Danaë, his mother, was 'the daughter of a king'; when Perseus was very young, 'some wicked people' set mother and child afloat in a chest. At the island of Seriphus they were caught in the nets of a fisherman (brother of the reigning monarch, Polydectes) who sheltered them throughout Perseus's youth. Finally the wicked Polydectes 'resolved to send Perseus on a dangerous enterprise ... and then to do some great mischief to Danaë herself.' Therefore, after summoning Perseus and drawing from him an avowal of his gratitude, Polydectes sent him in quest of the Gorgon's head – 'The bridal gift which I have set my heart on presenting to the beautiful Hippodamia.' Up to this point Hawthorne uses Anthon's history of Danaë very sparingly. He omits any mention of Perseus' parentage (Jupiter, 'under the form of a golden shower,' had impregnated Danaë) or of Polydectes' pretext of marriage with Hippodamia, and adds a number of general remarks about the evil nature of Polydectes and his subjects.

The main action of the story uses Anthon's account fully. Hawthorne first describes the Gorgons:

They were three sisters, and seem to have borne some distant resemblance to women, but were really a very frightful and mischievous species of dragon ... Why, instead of locks of hair, if you can believe me, they had each of them a hundred enormous snakes growing on their heads, all alive, twisting, wriggling, curling and thrusting out their venomous tongues, with forked stings at the end! The teeth of the Gorgons were terribly long tusks; their hands were made of brass; and their bodies were all over scales, which, if not iron, were something as hard and impenetrable. They had wings, too, and exceedingly splendid ones, I can assure you; for every feather in them was pure, bright, glittering, burnished gold ... If once a poor mortal fixed his eyes full upon one of their faces, he was certain, that very instant, to be changed from warm flesh and blood into cold and lifeless stone! (IV, 24–25)

In Anthon the parallel passage in the 'Gorgones' is:

Three celebrated sisters, daughters of Phorcys and Ceto, whose names were Stheno, Euryale and Medusa, and who were all immortal except Medusa. According to the mythologists, their hairs were entwined with serpents, they had wings of gold, their hands were of brass, their body was covered with impenetrable scales, their teeth were as long as the tusks of a wild boar, and they turned to stone all those on whom they fixed their eyes.

Hawthorne's fidelity speaks for itself here. The detail of the immortality of Medusa's sisters is added later in Hawthorne's version.

Anthon's articles on Perseus, Phorcydes, and Danaë supply both the details and the exact order of events for the remainder of Hawthorne's tale. It will be most useful at this point to quote Anthon:

When Perseus had made his rash promise to Polydectes, by which he bound himself to bring the latter the Gorgon's head, full of grief, he retired to the extremity of the island of Scyros, where Mercury came to him, promising that he and Minerva would be his guides. Mercury brought him first to the Graiae [*sic*] (*Vid*. Phorcydes) ...

Anthon's article on the Graeac proceeds as follows:

The daughters of Phorcys and Ceto. They were hoary-haired from their birth, whence their other name of Graeae (*'the Gray Maids'*). They were two in number, 'well-robed' Pephredo (*Horrifier*), and 'yellow-robed' Enyo (*Shaker*) ... We find them always united with the Gorgons, whose guards they were, according to Aeschylus ... This poet described them as *three* long-lived maids, swan-formed, having one eye and one tooth in common, on whom neither the sun with his beams, nor the nightly moon ever looks ... Perseus, it is said, intercepted the eye as they were handing it from the one to the other, and having thus blinded the guards, was enabled to come on the

Gorgons unperceived. The name of the third sister given by the later writers is Deino (*Terrifier*).

The 'Perseus' article continues:

whose eye and tooth he stole, and would not restore these until they had furnished him with directions to the abode of the Nymphs, who were possessed of the winged shoes, the magic wallet, and the helmet of Pluto which made the wearer invisible. Having obtained from the Graeae the requisite information, he came unto the Nymphs, who gave him their precious possessions: he then flung the wallet over his shoulder, placed the helmet on his head, and fitted the shoes to his feet. Thus equipped, and grasping the short curved sword (*harpe*) which Mercury gave him, he mounted into the air, accompanied by the gods, and flew to the ocean, where he found the three Gorgons asleep. (*Vid.* Gorgones.) Fearing to gaze on their faces, which changed the beholder to stone, he looked on the head of Medusa as it was reflected on his shield, and Minerva guiding his hand, he severed it from her body. The blood gushed forth, and with it the winged steed Pegasus, and Chrysaor the father of Geryon, for Medusa was at that time pregnant by Neptune. Perseus took up the head, put it into his wallet, and set out on his return. The two sisters awoke, and pursued the fugitive; but, protected by the helmet of Pluto, he eluded their vision, and they were obliged to give over the bootless chase. Perseus pursued his aërial route, and after having, in the course of his journey, punished the inhospitality of Atlas by changing him into a rocky mountain (*Vid.* Atlas), he came to the country of the Aethiopians. Here he liberated Andromeda from the sea-monster, and then returned with the Gorgon's head to the island of Seriphus. This head he gave to Minerva, who set it in the middle of her shield. The remainder of his history, up to the death of Acrisius, is given elsewhere. (*Vid.* Danaë and Acrisius.)

The history continues in Anthon's article on Danaë:

When Perseus had succeeded, by the aid of Hermes, in destroying the Gorgon, he proceeded to Seriphus, where he found that his mother and Dictys had been obliged to fly to the protection of the altar from the violence of Polydectes. He immediately went to the royal residence; and when, at his desire, Polydectes had summoned thither all the people, to see the formidable head of the Gorgon, it was displayed, and each became a stone of the form and position which he exhibited at the moment of the transformation. Having established Dictys as king of Seriphus, Perseus returned with his mother to Argos, and, not finding Acrisius there, proceeded to Larissa in Thessaly, whither the latter had retired through fear of the fulfilment of the oracle. Here he inadvertently killed Acrisius.

So close is Hawthorne's application to the material of this source that Hermes' 'short curved sword' becomes Quicksilver's 'short and crooked sword'; the 'winged shoes, the magic wallet, and the helmet of Pluto which made the wearer invisible,' become 'the flying slippers, the magic wallet, and the helmet of darkness'; the Graeae, 'on whom neither the sun with his beams, nor the nightly moon ever looks,' in Hawthorne's version 'never show themselves by the light either of the sun or moon.'

A few changes, usually of a minor nature, are made. Hermes, or Mercury, who claims that he 'has more names than one,' reveals himself to the disconsolate Perseus as 'Quicksilver.' Hawthorne adds the incident in which Quicksilver lends his staff to Perseus, and describes Minerva but does not name her; she remains invisible throughout the tale, although she speaks to Perseus and directs him. She does not, as Anthon records, guide Perseus' hand in the blow which decapitates Medusa. In Hawthorne 'the Gray Maids' become the 'Three Gray Women'; they are renamed Scarecrow, Nightmare, and Shakejoint. The details of Medusa's pregnancy, and the birth of Pegasus and Chrysaor from her death-blood are omitted.

So much for the bare facts of Hawthorne's re-working of

his source material. His methods of realizing its dramatic possibilities – of giving it form and vitality – deserve close attention. At the outset it is clear that the narrator is doing something that he likes; he is telling a story to a group of children with whom he is relaxed, and whose demands on the speaker are direct and definable. His tone, then, is informal, even colloquial, and his imagination embellishes the framework of his story freely, but without complication or tediousness. His effect will depend not upon static situation or complex analysis of motive, but upon movement, talk, and incident. Even more, it will depend upon suspense.

The opening paragraphs which summarize Perseus' early history are filled with arresting events, but Hawthorne wastes no time in precipitating his audience into an interview between the handsome young Perseus and the wicked Polydectes. The structure of the story, in fact, is a series of conversation-action scenes bridged by short narrative or expository links which achieve their own dramatic status through the personality of the narrator. Thus Anthon's bare statement that Perseus, 'full of grief ... retired to the extremity of the island of Scyros, where Mercury came to him promising that he and Minerva would be his guides,' becomes a dramatic scene in which Quicksilver assures Perseus that he 'need not fear being a stone image yet a while.' At the climactic moments – the death of Medusa and the petrifying encounter at Polydectes' court – we recognize that Hawthorne was a master of suspense. He prepares for such climaxes, and introduces auxiliary questions that maintain immediate interest. Thus a paragraph on the fourth page, following Perseus' acceptance of the quest, describes the Gorgons in chilling detail. And in the first scene with Quicksilver, Perseus is directed to polish his shield 'till you can see your face in it as distinctly as in a mirror,' an operation whose purpose is not apparent until the attack on Medusa. In the next scene the Gray Women become a problem, and so on. As in the New England tales, moreover, Hawthorne prepares his readers gradually for supernatural events: thus, because we know that Minerva is mysteriously present from the beginning of the journey, we expect her to speak and to assist Perseus in his critical encounter. In the same way, the slender sentence which tells us that 'on his way homeward [Perseus] ... changed an enormous giant into a mountain of stone, merely by showing him the head of the Gorgon,' establishes well in advance an anticipation of the fate of Polydectes.

Two other noteworthy factors in Hawthorne's realization of the Perseus story are his elaboration of detail and his use of humour. The bulk of the detail which he adds to the original gives life to what is otherwise skeletal, either by making the commonplace vivid or by making the unfamiliar familiar; hence his elaborate picture of the Medusa as Perseus sees her reflected in his shield; his alteration of 'winged shoes' to 'flying slippers'; and his picture of the 'magic wallet' as 'a small purse, made of deer skin, and curiously embroidered.' Occasionally his elaboration is merely fanciful – a weakness that he never overcame entirely; but this, perhaps, is the price he paid for a similar kind of elaboration which adds a symbolic dimension to whatever it touches; thus the suggestion that the ethereal world is frigid, and the imagery of moonlight, mirrors, and vision associated with the exploit.

The appearance of humour in Hawthorne is always startling. In his own words, 'The Author's touches have often an effect of tameness; the merriest man can hardly contrive to laugh at his broadest humor' (I, 16). In 'The Gorgon's Head' the humour is sometimes grim: the spectacle of the Gray Women – three New England spinsters squabbling over a quizzing glass – or the irony of Polydectes commanding Perseus to show him the Gorgon's head 'This instant ... or you die!' There is unfortunate humour, too, such as the feeble pun in Perseus' claim that Medusa's head will 'fix the regards of all who look at it.' But the general tone is gay – even sprightly – with only occasional glimpses of that dark mirth which led Hawthorne to speak of 'the tragic power of laughter.'

My account of the Perseus story has been necessarily long, since it is a first encounter with this phase of Hawthorne's work. The stories which follow will be examined in less detail, except where they add new insights into his vision and technique.

The Golden Touch: Eustace Bright's second tale is based upon an anecdote from Anthon which Hawthorne developed into a charming fable. The legend of Midas' wealth is proverbial, but his history, as Anthon records it, is fragmentary and confused:

Midas, an ancient king of the Brygians in Thrace, son of Gordius, and whose name is connected with some of the earliest mythological legends of the Greeks. According to one account, he possessed, at the foot of Mount Bermion, a garden, in which grew spontaneously roses with sixty petals, and of extraordinary fragrance. (*Herod.*, 8, 138 ...) To this garden Silenus was in the habit of repairing; and Midas (*Pausan.*, 1. 4, 5) or his people, by pouring wine into the fount from which he was wont to drink, intoxicated him, and he was thus captured ... We have likewise another legend relative to Midas and Silenus, the scene of which is laid, not in Europe, but in Lower Asia. According to this account, as Bacchus was in Lydia, on his return from the conquest of the East, some of the country people met Silenus staggering about, and, binding him with his own garlands, led him to their king. Midas entertained him for ten days, and then conducted him to his foster-son [Bacchus], who, in his gratitude, desired the king to ask whatever gift he would. Midas craved that all he touched might turn to gold. His wish was granted; but when he found his very food converted to precious metal, and himself on the point of starving in the midst of wealth, he prayed the god to resume his fatal gift. Bacchus directed him to bathe in the Pactolus, and hence that river obtained golden sands. (*Ovid. Met.*, 11, 85 ...) There is a third legend relative to Midas. Pan, the god of shepherds, venturing to set his reed-music in opposition to the lyre of Apollo, was pronounced overcome by Mount Tmolus; and all present approved the decision except King Midas, whose ears were, for their obtuseness, lengthened by the victor to those of an ass ... The same monarch, in all probability, gave a favorable reception to the rites of Bacchus, then for the first time introduced into his dominions, and hence his success in the accumulation of riches may have been ascribed to the favour of the god. The later cycle of fable, however, appears to have changed the receiver and protector of the rites of Bacchus into a companion or follower of Bacchus himself. Hence we find Midas numbered among the Sileni and Satyrs, and, as such, having the usual accompaniment of goat's ears ... Now it would seem that the Attic poets, in their satyric dramas, made the story of Midas a frequent theme of travesty, and in this way we have the wealthy monarch converting everything into gold by his mere touch ... and again, the pricked-up ears of the goat-footed Satyr become changed by Attic wit into the ears of an ass.

It would seem that Hawthorne studied this material rather than any finished version of the Midas story, for he includes details from several of the sources summarized by Anthon: the legendary rose garden, the origin of the Pactolus river's golden sands. He even alludes to Anthon's dubiety by remarking that Midas 'was fond of music (in spite of the idle story about his ears, which were said to resemble those of an ass).'

Hawthorne is explicit, however, in his admission that a great deal of the story is his own invention. King Midas, says Eustace, 'Had a little daughter, whom nobody but myself ever heard of, and whose name I either never knew, or have entirely forgotten.' The Bacchic Silenus of the source is thus replaced by little Marygold who objectifies those simple, warm-hearted human values which Hawthorne makes Midas forget in his lust for gold; and Bacchus becomes an unnamed stranger, 'a young man, with a cheerful and ruddy face,' whose smile 'had a golden radiance in it.' Curiosity is Bacchus' sole motive in giving Midas the Golden Touch. Midas' experiences following the granting of his wish are, again, pure Hawthorne, as is the moral which gives the story its *raison d'être*.

What Hawthorne saw in the Midas legend was, primarily, the opportunity of showing the folly of striving for wealth to the exclusion of other values. Unlike 'The Gorgon's Head,' then, his dramatic realization of this material involves, more than anything else, the depiction of character. We learn of Midas' fault in the second paragraph: 'He thought, foolish man! that the best thing he could possibly do for this dear child would be to bequeath her the immensest pile of yellow, glistening coin, that had ever been heaped together since the world was made' (IV, 55). Hawthorne then devotes two pages to establishing him as a kindly but misguided man who becomes the slave of an obsession. The felicity of such touches as the following finds Hawthorne at his best. Midas, gloating over his wealth would

look at the funny image of his own face, as reflected in the burnished circumference of the cup; and whisper to himself, 'O Midas, rich king Midas, what a happy man art thou!' But it was laughable to see how the image of his face kept grinning at him, out of the polished surface of the cup. It seemed to be aware of his foolish behavior, and to have a naughty inclination to make fun of him. (IV, 57)

The touch here is light, but the grimacing mirror-image does not allow us to forget that world of absolute values upon which Hawthorne continually forces our reluctant scrutiny.

When the Golden Touch comes to Midas 'with the first sunbeam!' Hawthorne recounts a series of events that reveal – with delicate irony and a fine sense of climax – the progressive loss of those values to which Midas had become blind. First he loses the wisdom of books when a 'gilt-edged volume' becomes illegible gold leaf. Next – and this prepares us for the loss of Marygold – the handkerchief which his daughter had embroidered turns to gold. As Midas' spectacles turn to gold, the reader realizes that he was already spiritually blind; the loss of his spectacles is one of the steps in a process which teaches him to *see*. In the rose garden the flowers lose their colour and fragrance as Midas methodically transforms them. At breakfast his troubles increase until, with sardonic humour, Hawthorne has him cram his mouth with a hot potato.

With the crowning transformation of Marygold, 'wise King Midas' ' vision is restored: 'At last, when it was too late, he felt how infinitely a warm and tender heart, that loved him, exceeded in value all the wealth that could be piled up betwixt the earth and sky!' Hawthorne underlines the nature of this change by having the stranger severely catechize the King, whose heart, it appears, 'has not been entirely changed from flesh to gold.' Although the lightness of tone is maintained in the final scene, the imagery suggests that Midas' plunge in the river is a spiritual purgation: 'He was conscious, also, of a change within himself. A cold, hard, and heavy weight seemed to have gone out of his bosom. No doubt, his heart had been gradually losing its human substance, and transmuting itself into insensible metal, but had now softened back again into flesh.' (IV, 72) As the first object which the reborn Midas touches, Hawthorne chooses a violet, the most innocent and delicate of flowers. Marygold, when she is restored, is not told of what has happened, but Midas, when an old man, tells his grandchildren that ever since that morning he has 'hated the very sight' of all gold but the gold in their hair.

'The Golden Touch' is without doubt a minor masterpiece of story-telling. There are moments when we wish that the style were free of the seemingly artificial sentiment that colours the nineteenth-century novelist's talk with 'little men and women.' We wish, too, that Marygold sounded less like an adult playing at dolls. Nevertheless, Hawthorne develops his materials with such skill that the story becomes more expressive than any statement of its moral. Two points in the form of the tale deserve special notice. First, as in 'The Gorgon's Head,' Hawthorne has dispensed with the opening paragraphs of reflection and the concluding paragraphs of moralizing which characterized his early tales. Second, he has brought the materials of his source into relation with the images which attracted him in earlier works. Thus the story of Midas involves such images as the mirror, the hardened heart, and the sun-flame-gold cluster of images associated with the Puritan materialists. The implications of both of these matters will be discussed further; their function in giving both spontaneity and depth to the story should not, however, be overlooked at this point.

II: A Wonder-Book

The Paradise of Children: This, the third tale of *A Wonder-Book*, is another example of the very free adaptation of a brief incident in classical mythology. Since the story was probably available in any Greek school-book, and since Hawthorne mentioned it in 1838 as 'Pandora's Box' (not a 'jar' as in Hesiod, the version which Anthon supports), it is quite possible that Hawthorne did not avail himself of the material in Anthon's article. On the other hand, the basic details of Hawthorne's tale – as well as a commentary on the box-jar confusion and a refutation of Christian interpretations of the Pandora myth – are found in Anthon. It is therefore not extravagant to imagine that Hawthorne, with Anthon's work at hand, consulted this source.[14]

Anthon introduces Pandora (*'All-gifted'*) as: 'The first created female, and celebrated in one of the early legends of the Greeks as having been the cause of the introduction of evil into the world.' After summarizing Hesiod's account of her creation at the order of Zeus, he proceeds as follows:

Thus furnished, she was brought by Mercury to the dwelling of Epimetheus; who, though his brother Prometheus had warned him to be on his guard, and to receive no gifts from Jupiter, dazzled with her charms, took her into his house and made her his wife. The evil effects of this imprudent step were speedily felt. In the dwelling of Epimetheus stood a closed jar, which he had been forbidden to open. Pandora, under the influence of female curiosity, disregarding the injunction, raised the lid, and all the evils hitherto unknown to man

14 The very simplicity of the events, as Hawthorne gives them, would seem to support the idea that he used Anthon as the source of this tale. In Hesiod, for example, there is striking detail which Hawthorne might well have used had this been his source. Hesiod, moreover, treats Pandora as a creature expressly created as a *punishment* upon mankind. See Hesiod, *The Homeric Hymns and Homerica*, trans., Hugh G. Evelyn-White (London, 1914), pp. 121n, 123n.

poured out, and spread themselves over the earth. In terror at the sight of these monsters, she shut down the lid just in time to prevent the escape of Hope, which thus remained to man, his chief support and comfort ... The idea has been universal among the moderns, that she [Pandora] brought all the evils with her from heaven, shut up in a *box* ... The only way of accounting for this is, that at the restoration of learning, the narrative in Hesiod was misunderstood.

In Hawthorne's re-telling, the origins of Pandora and Epimetheus are not mentioned. She, like Epimetheus, is 'fatherless and motherless ... [and] was sent from a far country, to live with him, and be his playfellow and helpmate.' Just before her arrival, Quicksilver left the fatal box with Epimetheus, solemnly commanding him not to open it. Pandora's curiosity, however, overcame these strictures and she opened the box, releasing a swarm of winged troubles upon the world. Then, hearing Hope's faint cries, she and Epimetheus again lifted the lid and received, from the fairy-like creature that emerged, solace for their cares and the assurance of 'an infinite bliss hereafter!'

Hawthorne's framework, then, bears a skeletal relation to Anthon's account. But how different the eighteen-page adaptation which introduced Pandora to generations of school children! Again Hawthorne is explicit about his departures from authority. In 'Tanglewood Playroom,' the sketch which introduces Pandora's story, Eustace Bright tells the children that 'It shall be a story of what nobody but myself ever dreamed of, – a Paradise of children' (IV, 181). Pandora and Epimetheus are children of the earth's 'tender infancy.' And Pandora's first speech, after a seven-line introductory paragraph, is: 'Epimetheus, what have you in that box?' This is the crux of the story; the action is the growth of

II: A Wonder-Book

Pandora's curiosity (for eleven pages) and its sad consequences. Here, even more than in 'The Golden Touch,' the narrator's success will depend upon his ability to dramatize an internal condition. It must be said that in this instance Hawthorne, for all the subsequent celebrity of his story, fails to make it a coherent, expressive whole.

At moments the tale gives evidence of Hawthorne's technical assurance. He plunges immediately into the problem of his story, and as the tale proceeds he prepares us very subtly for the climactic revelation of the contents of the box. But this preparation is double. For adults who know the story, he nonchalantly makes such statements as this: 'Those ugly little winged monsters, called Troubles, which are now almost as numerous as mosquitoes, had never yet been seen on the earth. It is probable that the very greatest disquietude which a child had ever experienced was Pandora's vexation at not being able to discover the secret of the mysterious box.' (IV, 83) For children there is the more obvious: 'But it was a mischievous box, as we shall see, and deserved all it got.'

The description of the box itself is richly suggestive. Its polished surface is a mirror in which Pandora sees her face. Soon after, Hawthorne tells us that there is a face 'with a garland of flowers about its brow,' carved in the 'polished wood' in 'the centre of the lid.' This face, it seems, almost 'speaks' to Pandora. As her curiosity reaches fever peak, Hawthorne's old symbolic device of multiple choice is introduced for the first time in these stories to suggest that the contents of the box are really, perhaps, in Pandora's mind: 'Positively, there did seem to be a kind of stifled murmur within! Or was it merely the singing in Pandora's ears? Or could it be the beating of her heart?' (IV, 90)

61

A final felicitous touch is the introduction of another mirror image. Hope, Hawthorne suggests, throws a light wherever she goes. Then he adds: 'Have you never made the sunshine dance into dark corners, by reflecting it from a bit of looking glass?' Again the mirror image; again the glimpse of an ideal world.

On the debit side, a number of things which make Pandora's story less accomplished than 'The Golden Touch' must be noted. Hawthorne counted too heavily, perhaps, upon his ability to maintain our interest in the psychological phenomenon of Pandora's curiosity. Sustained effects of this sort were his forte, but his juvenile audience limited his range in both diction and thought; and he was unable to express Pandora's conflict through the kind of incident that made King Midas' development so meaningful. The strain shows seriously when, after working Pandora up to the point of opening the box, he abruptly shifts to 'But it is now time for us to see what Epimetheus was doing.' Epimetheus was, of course, picking figs. Even worse is an abrupt invocation of the pathetic fallacy: 'And here I must mention that a great black cloud had been gathering in the sky, for some time past.'

The underlying difficulty, however, is thematic: the children's paradise is a dull and lifeless place in which Epimetheus is reduced to such banalities as: 'Let us run out of doors, and have some nice play with the other children.' Even more serious is an apparent confusion on Hawthorne's part about the meaning of his tale. Despite Anthon's warning, he ends by introducing his own idea of the Fortunate Fall. Needless to say, if the children's paradise really was a Paradise, then it becomes absurd to say that 'Hope spiritualizes

62

the earth. ... Hope shows it to be only the shadow of an infinite bliss hereafter!' Perhaps Hawthorne simply meant that the paradise of children was a delightful but completely material and sensory world, and that 'children' would learn through suffering and Hope to recognize an ideal *spiritual* realm. But whatever he may have intended, the alliance between action and moralized meaning in this tale is at best uneasy.

The Three Golden Apples: This tale presents yet another variation on the task which Hawthorne set himself in *A Wonder-Book,* for his subject is not an anecdote but a saga that embraces most of the celebrated places and persons of Greek mythology; and his artistic problem is selection rather than invention. His decision to describe the eleventh labour of Hercules lends strong support to the belief that Anthon was his source, for, with the exception of two omitted incidents and one major interpolation, Hawthorne's tale is an exact copy, in spelling, detail and order of events, of Anthon's article on the 'Hesperides.'

One can imagine Hawthorne searching through Anthon's long article on Hercules, and discarding, for one reason or another, the various exploits: the account of Hercules' childhood involved 'impurities'; the Nemean lion incident lacked body; the Hydra story was altogether too gory; the chase of the stag lacked detail, and so on. But the eleventh labour, 'to obtain the apples from the garden of the Hesperides (*Vid.* Hesperides.)' offered an appealing 'giant story' ready-made.

Anthon's account of these maidens opens with a description of their origins and the information (which Hawthorne adopted) that 'Hesiod makes them to have dwelt "beyond the bright ocean," opposite to where Atlas stood supporting the heavens.' Anthon then recounts the story of Juno's interest in the garden and the dragon which she 'sent thither to guard the precious fruit. This monster was the offspring of Typhon and Echidna, and had a hundred heads, so that it never slept.' The narrative of Hercules follows:

One of the tasks imposed upon Hercules by Eurystheus was to bring him some of this golden fruit. On his way in quest of it, Hercules came to the river Eridanus, and to the nymphs, the daughters of Jupiter and Themis, and inquired of them where the apples were to be obtained. They directed him to Nereus, whom he found asleep; and in spite of his numerous changes of form, he bound and held him fast until he had mentioned where the golden apples were. Having obtained this information, Hercules went on to Tartessus, and, crossing over to Libya, proceeded on his way until he came to Irassa, near the lake Tritonis, where Antaeus reigned. After destroying this opponent (*Vid.* Antaeus) he visited Egypt, and slew Busiris, the monarch of that land. (*Vid.* Busiris.) He then roamed through Arabia, and after this over the mountains to Libya, which he cleared of savage beasts. Reaching then the eastern course of the ocean, he was accommodated, as in the adventure against Geryon, with the radiant cup of the Sun-god, in which he crossed to the opposite side. He now came to where Prometheus lay chained, and, moved by his entreaties, shot the bird that preyed upon his liver. Prometheus, out of gratitude, warned him not to go himself to take the golden apples, but to send Atlas for them, and, in the mean time, to support the heavens in his stead. The hero did as desired, and Atlas, at his request, went and obtained three apples from the Hesperides; but he said he would take them himself to Eurystheus, and that Hercules might continue to support the heavens. At the suggestion of Prometheus, the hero feigned assent, but begged Atlas to hold the heavens again until he had made a pad ... to put on his head. Atlas threw down the apples and resumed his burden, and Hercules picked them up and went his way.

II: A Wonder-Book

In adapting this source, Hawthorne begins, as Anthon does, with general information on the golden apples. He omits all mention of Juno and the Hesperides themselves, but describes the dragon 'with a hundred terrible heads, fifty of which were always on the watch, while the other fifty slept.' He then proceeds to a picture of Hercules, 'wandering through the pleasant land of Italy.' (If Hawthorne had needed the information, he might have learned from Anthon that the Eridanus was 'a river of Italy ... now the *Po*.') The details of Hercules' appearance follow Anthon's description in his article on Hercules. While the nymphs of Eridanus (who, like Anthon, Hawthorne does not name) regale Hercules with bread and grapes, he tells them 'the story of his life.' Again Hawthorne follows Anthon's account, though in highly abbreviated form. He adds fanciful touches of his own such as six-legged Geryon's 'waste of shoe-leather,' but the only point at which he appears to have availed himself of Anthon's cross-references is in the account of Hippolyta. Following this recital the nymphs hang wreaths on Hercules and entwine his 'ponderous club' with flowers in a scene whose unconscious eroticism would have been deliberate in Melville.

For his account of the Old Man of the Sea, Hawthorne must have consulted Anthon's article on Nereus, and the immediately preceding article on the Nereïdes. Hence the free adaptation of Anthon's name for Nereus – '*Sea-elder*' – and the close parallel with Anthon's picture of the Nereïdes:

Nymphs of the sea, daughters of Nereus and Doris. They are said by most ancient writers to have been fifty in number, but Propertius makes them a hundred ... The Nereïdes were originally represented as beautiful nymphs; but they were afterwards described as beings with green hair, and with the lower part of their body like that of a fish. (*Plin*[y]. 9, 4.)

[Hawthorne:] 'He has fifty daughters, whom some people call very beautiful; but we do not think it proper to be acquainted with them, because they have sea-green hair, and taper away like fishes.'[15]

The account of the Old Man of the Sea's transformations, however, seems to be Hawthorne's invention (he describes the stag, the bird, Cerberus, Geryon, and the snake of Hercules' early adventures), and the moral is characteristically his own: 'One of the hardest things in the world is, to see the difference between real dangers and imaginary ones.'

Again following Anthon's article on the Hesperides, Hawthorne summarizes Hercules' combats with Antaeus and Busiris (who is identified only as the king of Egypt) and describes Hercules' journey in the bowl which resembles 'the round, golden disk of the sun, when it rises or sets over the edge of the world.' Hawthorne does not mention Prometheus; therefore, the encounter with Atlas, in which Hercules solves his problems without advice, enlarges our conception of the hero's native intelligence. Hawthorne, moreover, is explicit about his unclassical treatment of Atlas. In the sketch which follows this tale, Mr. Pringle questions the propriety of thrusting this 'huge, disproportioned mass among the seemly outlines of Grecian fable.' In other respects, however, Hawthorne follows Anthon to the letter. In the closing incident of the story, Anthon's expression, 'Atlas threw down the apples

15 Anthon's meticulous habit of giving all the variants of a legend is wonderfully well suited to Hawthorne's artistic methods, for it gives him repeated opportunities, as in this example, of using his device of multiple choice. A passage such as this lends further weight to the view that Anthon was Hawthorne's source.

66

and resumed his burden,' is very close to Hawthorne's: 'He threw down the golden apples, and received back the sky, from the head and shoulders of Hercules.'

There is little new in Hawthorne's dramatic realization of these materials. Again, he precipitates his hero into a dramatic conversation-piece at the first opportunity. But the extent of the material which he chose to use prevents him from recreating with richness any of the incidents of the tale except the encounter with the Old Man of the Sea, from which he draws a moral, and the incidents with Atlas. Although he is right dramatically in assigning to Hercules the role played by Prometheus, he does not manage here to do more than draw another moral: 'What the sky was to the giant, such are the cares of earth to those who let themselves be weighted down by them. And whenever men undertake what is beyond the just measure of their abilities, they encounter precisely such a doom as had befallen this poor giant.' (IV, 126)

The adaptation thus operates not as an expressive action but as a moralized tale; and even as an adventure tale it is defective, for the dragon, described at the beginning, is never seen, and the suspense which the description arouses is not dramatically resolved. The nymphs, who admittedly afford a pleasant dramatic background for Hercules' long monologue, are not seen again. Most seriously at fault, however, is Hercules' cavalier treatment of Atlas. In the original legend this incident is merely picaresque, but Hawthorne's picture of the suffering colossus who had been battered by storms and had borne his burden until 'oak-trees, of six or seven centuries old, had sprung from the acorn, and forced themselves between his toes,' arouses our sympathy. Thus, although we realize that Hercules, who 'had a kind heart of his own,' did Atlas a favour in assuming his burden, still we know that Atlas did Hercules an equally great favour. We are not prepared, therefore, when Atlas has been tricked into reassuming his burden, for the narrator's callous comment: 'Ah, the thick-witted old rogue of a giant!' Hawthorne's effective romanticizing of the giant, that is, has so altered the emphasis of the tale that we are not wholly sympathetic with the absconding Hercules.

In the final analysis, 'The Three Golden Apples,' with its multiple morals and uneven characterization, fails to achieve a oneness of meaning and form. Hawthorne was unable, perhaps because of too much incident, to make his action a unity, and he did not find images which would serve poetically to bind these diverse materials.

The Miraculous Pitcher: Hawthorne's adaptation of the Philemon and Baucis legend is an example not of transformation but of pure elaboration of a source. Anthon's account is brief but complete: the only changes which Hawthorne makes are to move the location of the old couple's cottage from the village to the crest of a nearby hill; to change the wine-bowl to a more healthful Band of Temperance pitcher of milk; and to make the 'temple' with which Jupiter endowed them a marble 'palace.'

BAUCIS, an aged woman, who dwelt in a small town of Phrygia along with her husband Philemon. They were both extremely poor, and inhabited a humble cottage. Jupiter and Mercury came, on one occasion, in the form of men, to this same town. It was evening; they sought for hospitality, but every door was closed against them. At length they approached the abode of the aged pair, by whom they were gladly received. The quality of the guests was eventually revealed by the miracle of the wine-bowl being spontaneously replenished as fast as it was drained. They told their hosts that it was their intention to destroy the godless town, and desired them to leave their dwelling and ascend the adjacent hill. The aged couple obeyed: ere they reached the summit they turned round to look and beheld a lake where the town had stood. Their own house remained, and as they gazed and deplored the fate of their neighbors, it became a temple. On being desired by Jupiter to express their wishes, they prayed that they might be appointed to officiate in that temple, and that they might be united in death as in life. Their prayer was granted; and as they were one day standing before the temple, they were suddenly changed into an oak and a lime tree. (*Ovid, Met.*, 8, 620) – The reader will not fail to be struck with the resemblance between a part of this legend and the scripture account of the destruction of the cities of the plains.

Although Hawthorne made no change in the narrative order of events in this source, he exercised every technique at his command in realizing the dramatic possibilities of the story. Thus the bare facts of the legend become a mystery story in which, by careful foreshadowing and ambiguous suggestion, Hawthorne prepares his audience for the climactic events. The story opens with a picture of old Philemon and Baucis sitting before their cottage at sunset, hearing the barking of dogs and the rude shouts of children in the neighbouring village. Philemon, fearing that 'some terrible thing will happen to all the people in the village unless they mend their manners' to strangers, says piously: 'As for you and me, so long as Providence affords us a crust of bread, let us be ready to give half to any poor, homeless stranger, that may come along and need it' (IV, 140–41). A description of their poor but charitable existence follows, as well as the information that the village had once 'when the world was new,' been the bed of a lake. This leads to a long reflection upon the villagers who have forgotten that 'human beings owe a debt of love to one another'; they now 'cared much about the money that a stranger had in his pocket, and nothing whatever for the human soul, which lives equally in the beggar and the prince' (IV, 142).

Philemon welcomes the 'very humbly clad' wayfarers, the object of the villagers' rudeness. In the scenes which follow, the old couple witness a series of miraculous events and hear a series of foreboding speeches which make them suspect that their guests are 'no ordinary personage[s].' Hawthorne's invention in this long scene shows a fine knowledge of the characteristic manner of old people. We may wish that his fancy had not led him to allow the snakes on Quicksilver's staff to lap up the milk which Baucis spilt; we may wish, too, that Baucis hadn't been so maddeningly goody-goody with her: 'O husband! husband! why didn't we go without our supper?' Nevertheless, we are able to accept the picture of these simple people serving their guests a supper that turns out to be nectar and ambrosia.

The elder stranger, whose name they 'must ask the thunder to tell,' is, apparently, the master of the pathetic fallacy: when he frowned, 'the twilight seemed suddenly to grow darker,' and when he granted Philemon's wish that 'they should die, as they had lived, together ... the sunset clouds threw up a bright flash from the west, and kindled a sudden light in the sky' (IV, 147, 149). Finally the stranger tells the old couple, who 'gazed reverently into his face, as if they had been gazing at the sky,' that 'When men do not feel towards the humblest stranger as if he were a brother ... they are unworthy to exist on earth, which was created as the abode of a great human brotherhood!' Quicksilver rounds off this moral by informing his hosts that the villagers are now fish: 'There needed but little change, for they were already a scaly set of rascals, and the coldest-blooded beings in existence' (IV, 159).

Then, as the strangers disappear, Philemon and Baucis behold 'a tall edifice of white marble' which is the new site of their unending hospitality. When they have become intolerably old and good, they appear one morning as a venerable oak and a linden tree, with boughs intermarried, murmuring to each other constantly, 'Philemon! Baucis! Baucis! Philemon!' or, to the way-worn traveller, 'Welcome, welcome, dear traveller, welcome!'

The best that can be said of this adaptation is that it is a masterpiece of the kind of sentimental humanitarianism which made New England's genteel culture seem so spurious. It may, perhaps, possess a timeless appeal for tender children, but in adult terms, it belongs in the Victorian room of a wax museum. The tone and execution are faultless, cloying, and palpably obvious.

The Chimaera: Knowing, perhaps, that this was his best story, Hawthorne placed it at the end of *A Wonder-Book*. Although he treats his source material with great independence, it is clear that he used Anthon rather than any classical source, for the detail which his tale contains is scattered through Homer, Hesiod, Pindar, Apollodorus, and Pausanius. Anthon's account of Bellerophon pieces together all of the classical fragments in an awkward jigsaw. Since a summary of this material would be both tedious and irrelevant, it may be enough to cite those details which appear in Hawthorne's story.

Hawthorne as Myth-Maker

Ignoring the account of Bellerophon's origins and the confusing stories as to the motive for his quest, Hawthorne begins with the arrival of handsome young Bellerophon, with an enchanted, jewelled bridle in his hand, at the fountain of Pirene. Anthon's article on Bellerophon records that Minerva appeared to the hero in a dream, 'and, giving him the bridle, bade him sacrifice a bull to his sire Neptune-Damaeus (*the Tamer*) and present the bridle to the steed. On awakening, Bellerophon found the bridle lying beside him.' A maiden who is drawing water at the fountain informs Bellerophon that: 'My grandmother has told me that this clear fountain was once a beautiful woman; and when her son was killed by the arrows of the huntress Diana, she melted all away into tears' (IV, 168). Anthon's article on 'Pirene' is strikingly parallel:

A fountain near Corinth, on the route from the city to the harbour of Lechaeum ... This fountain is celebrated by the ancient poets as being sacred to the Muses, and here Bellerophon is said to have seized the winged horse Pegasus, preparatory to his enterprise against the Chimaera ... The fountain was fabled to have derived its name from the nymph Pirene, who was said to have dissolved in tears at the death of her son Cenchreas, accidentally slain by Diana.

Bellerophon then reveals that he is seeking Pegasus, who 'wise people' have informed him may be found at the fountain of Pirene. The poetic description of Pegasus which follows has no parallel in Anthon except for the information that the winged horse dwelt on Mount Helicon and frequented the fountain of Pirene. The onlookers at the fountain (the maid, an old man, a middle-aged country fellow, and a little boy) give varying opinions about Pegasus: the practical farmer denies his existence: the old man believes that he has seen

72

him, but doubts his memory; the maiden has seen him and been frightened; the child sees him frequently, reflected in the waters of the fountain. It is in the 'gentle child,' who becomes the companion of his vigil, that Bellerophon puts his faith.

Hawthorne now pauses to explain that Bellerophon was a guest of King Iobates of Lycia who 'proposed to him to go and fight the Chimaera.' These details, with an account of Iobates' motives that Hawthorne omits, are included in Anthon's article on Bellerophon. Hawthorne's picture of the Chimaera synthesizes the alternatives provided by Anthon:

[Hawthorne:] It had a tail like a boa-constrictor; its body was like I do not care what; and it had three separate heads, one of which was a lion's, the second a goat's, and the third an abominably great snake's. And a hot blast of fire came flaming out of each of its three mouths! (IV, 175)

[Anthon:] A fabulous monster, the offspring of Typhon and Echidna ... which ravaged the country of Lycia until slain by Bellerophon. It had the head and neck of a lion, the body of a goat ... and the tail of a serpent, and vomited forth fire. (*Hom*[er]. *Il*[iad]., 6, 181.) Hesiod's account is somewhat different from that of Homer since he gives the Chimaera three heads, one that of a lion, another a goat's, and a third a serpent's.

During the long watch with his young companion, Bellerophon reflects impatiently that 'If he could only succeed in putting the golden bit into the mouth of Pegasus, the winged horse would be submissive, and would own Bellerophon for his master.' (Anthon's account says: 'Pegasus at once yielded his mouth to the magic bit, and the hero, mounting him, achieved his adventures.') The child's faith keeps Bellerophon from returning to Lycia to fight the Chimaera single-handed. 'Nobody,' Hawthorne asserts, 'should ever try to

73

fight an earth-born Chimaera, unless he can first get upon the back of an aerial steed.'

Finally the child sees Pegasus' image in the water. It descends to drink and Bellerophon, seizing his chance while the horse is at play, leaps upon its back. Pegasus, in rage and wonder, puts on an extraordinary aerobatic display, but Bellerophon, feeling that it is almost a 'sin' to bridle such a superb creature, finally curbs him. Upon Pegasus' submission, Hawthorne comments: 'He was glad at heart, after so many lonely centuries, to have found a companion and a master. Thus it always is with winged horses, and with all such wild and solitary creatures. If you can catch and overcome them, it is the surest way to win their love.' (IV, 182)

Bellerophon, inspired by the beauty and spirit of Pegasus, offers the horse its freedom, but Pegasus returns of his own accord, and they live, sleep, and adventure together until, finally, they are ready to face 'the terrible Chimaera.' Hawthorne's picture of the battle owes nothing to Anthon; its debt, in imaginative terms, is to Spenser. Nowhere in Hawthorne is there such a rousing spectacle. At one point, after having lost two heads, the Chimaera opens 'its snake-jaws to such an abominable width, that Pegasus might almost, I was going to say, have flown right down its throat, rider and all! At their approach it shot out a tremendous blast of its firey breath, and enveloped Bellerophon and his steed in a perfect atmosphere of flame.' (IV, 191) Then the 'earth-born monster' grapples Pegasus and is 'borne upward, along with the creature of light and air.' Bellerophon, now understanding that 'the best way to fight a Chimaera is by getting as close to it as you can,' stabs it through the heart.

Transported with joy, the victorious hero returns to the

fountain of Pirene where he finds the same onlookers. The old man thinks that Pegasus is less handsome than formerly; the maid, 'who had always the luck to be afraid at the wrong time,' dropped her pitcher and ran away; but the little boy wept with joy. In his happiness, Bellerophon again offers Pegasus his freedom and is refused. He then bids farewell to the boy who, says Hawthorne, was destined for 'more honorable deeds than his friend's victory over the Chimaera. For, gentle and tender as he was, he grew to be a mighty poet.' (IV, 194)

Like 'The Golden Touch,' the tale of Bellerophon is wonderfully unselfconscious about its source. The reader feels that Hawthorne knew at the outset exactly what he wanted to do and that every detail serves his broad intent. He even foregoes the usual prefatory excuses about his freedom of interpretation. Like 'The Gorgon's Head,' the tale is constructed in conversation-action scenes (or stream-of-consciousness-action scenes) bridged by paragraphs of exposition or commentary. Hawthorne's invention and elaboration is everywhere felicitous. The rather stereotyped onlookers at the fountain, for example, are exactly what the narrator needs; they at once furnish dramatic variety and focus attention upon Pegasus rather than upon themselves. In the same way, the child is a character rather than a protagonist; he is a 'type' of the intuitive faith and courage which Bellerophon needs to overcome the Chimaera. With remarkable tact and subtlety, Hawthorne never allows the meanings of his images to become explicit, but controls with great firmness the relationships between child, pool-mirror, Pegasus-inspiration-air, and Chimaera-fear-earth. In Mallarmé's phrase, the *trainée de feu* which flashes along the powder train of these images reinforces our sense of the organic wholeness of the action. One final blessing: Hawthorne's involvement in his subject led him to drop most of the artificialities of 'childish' language.

TANGLEWOOD TALES:
Sources and Adaptations

Apart from Hawthorne's private assurance to R. H. Stoddard that 'I never did anything so well as these old baby stories,' and Eustace Bright's claim in the preface to *Tanglewood Tales* that his new stories are 'Better chosen, and better handled,' than those of *A Wonder-Book*, there is other evidence that Hawthorne felt a new assurance in writing the second volume. Instead of describing his method as 'clothing' the stories with modern manners and sentiment and 'imbuing' them with modern morality, as he had in *A Wonder-Book*, he allows Eustace to assert that 'The stories (not by any strained effort of the narrator's, but in harmony with their inherent germ) transform themselves, and reassume the shapes which they might be supposed to possess in the pure childhood of the world' (IV, 210). Hawthorne, that is, had a deepened sense of the shape or meaning of myth as a symbolic 'playing out' of the basic conflicts in man's experience. He was even able, much as he liked the framed tale, to dispense with the fore- and after-words which had brought the tales of the first collection into relation with contemporary life; this is not only a relief for his adult readers but an indication of his confidence that the meaning of the new tales was implicit in them.

A further internal indication of the new freedom which Hawthorne felt in writing *Tanglewood Tales*, is their length.

76

II: Tanglewood Tales

In *A Wonder-Book*, four of the tales are twenty-four pages or less in length. The other two, which Hawthorne placed at the beginning and end, were each twenty-seven pages in length. In *Tanglewood Tales*, however, the two shortest tales are twenty-four pages; two are thirty-five, and the last two are thirty-eight and forty-three respectively. This new amplitude will be kept in view in the source study that follows.

The Minotaur: Internal evidence makes it clear that this tale is based on Charles Anthon's *Classical Dictionary*. The exploits of Theseus are so widely diffused throughout classical literature that it is unlikely that Hawthorne could have assembled them from separate sources. His ordering of events, moreover, follows to the letter the structure of Anthon's article on Theseus, although the amount of detail which he incorporated would indicate that he used Anthon's cross-references extensively. One detail which is difficult to account for is that the brazen giant, Talus, figures prominently in Hawthorne's version, although he is not mentioned in the Theseus article. But here again, Hawthorne's picture of Talus contains only the simple details given in Anthon's article on Vulcanus. Had Hawthorne used another source, he would have known that 'when strangers approached [Crete, "Talos"] heated himself red hot and then embraced them, or threw showers of stones upon them.' Lacking this colourful information, Hawthorne invents a brass club for Talus and gives him 'clockwork' motive power.[16] The most

16 The most plausible explanation for Talus' appearance in 'The Minotaur' is that Hawthorne, when consulting the article on 'Vulcanus' was struck by the picture of Talus, and remembered it when he came to write 'The Minotaur.' Anthon's information is as follows: 'VULCANUS ... He gave to Minos, king of Crete, the brazen man Talus, who each day

77

convincing evidence, perhaps, is Hawthorne's inclusion of the conflicting accounts which Anthon gives of Ariadne's fate:

Now, some low-minded people, who pretend to tell this story of Theseus and Ariadne, have the face to say that this royal and honorable maiden did really flee away, under cover of night, with the young stranger whose life she had preserved. They say, too, that Prince Theseus ... ungratefully deserted Ariadne, on a solitary island, where the vessel touched on its voyage to Athens. But, had the noble Theseus heard these falsehoods, he would have served their slanderous authors as he served the Minotaur! (IV, 243)

Ariadne, like a genteel romantic heroine, remained in Crete with her cruel old father who had 'nobody but myself to love him.'

Cumbersome as Anthon's account of Theseus is, I shall quote it fully, since it affords a striking illustration, on a scale much larger than that of 'The Miraculous Pitcher,' of the way in which Hawthorne's source determined the narrative order of events and furnished the bulk of the detail:

THESEUS ... king of Athens, and son of Aegeus by Aethra, the daughter of Pittheus, monarch of Troezene, was one of the most celebrated heroes of antiquity. He was reared in the palace of his grandfather; and, when grown to the proper age, his mother led him to the rock under which his father had deposited his sword and sandals, and he removed it with ease and took them out. He was now to proceed to Athens, and present himself to Aegeus. As, however, the roads were infested by robbers, his grandfather Pittheus pressed

compassed his island three times to guard it from the invasion of strangers. (Apollod[orus]., [Bibliotheca,] 1, 9, 26.)' The other nineteenth-century mythological works consulted, consistently spell the giant's name 'Talos,' and recount the story of his murder by Medea. The additional information on 'Talos' quoted above comes from Harper's Dictionary of Classical Literature and Antiquities (New York, 1921).

him earnestly to take the shorter and safer way over the Saronic
Gulf; but the youth, feeling in himself the spirit and the soul of a
hero, resolved to signalize himself like Hercules, with whose fame all
Greece now rang, by destroying the evil-doers and the monsters that
oppressed and ravaged the country; and he determined on the more
perilous and adventurous journey by land. On his way to Athens he
met with many adventures, and destroyed Periphates, Sinis, Sciron,
Procustes, and also the monstrous sow Phaea, which ravaged the
country in the neighbourhood of Crommyon. Having overcome all
the perils of the road, Theseus at length reached Athens, where new
dangers awaited him. He found his father's court all in confusion.
The Pallantidae, or sons and grandsons of Pallas, the brother of
Aegeus, had long seen with jealousy the sceptre in the hands of an
old man, and now meditated wresting it from his feeble grasp.
Thinking, however, that his death could not be very remote, they
resolved to wait for that event; but they made no secret of their
intentions. The arrival of Theseus threatened to disconcert their plan.
They feared that if this young stranger should be received as a son
of the old king, he might find in him a protector and avenger; and
they resolved to poison his mind against him. Their plot so far
succeeded that Aegeus was on the point of sacrificing his son, when
he recognized him, and then acknowledged him in the presence of all
the people. The Pallantidae had recourse to arms, but Theseus de-
feated and slew them. Medea, it is also said, who was married to
Aegeus, fearing the loss of her influence when Theseus should have
been acknowledged by his father, resolved to anticipate that event;
and, moved by her calumnies, Aegeus was presenting a cup of poison
to his son, when the sight of the sword left with Aethra discovered to
him who he was. The bull which Hercules had brought from Crete
was now at Marathon, and the country was in terror of his ravages.
Theseus went in quest of him, overcame, and exhibited him in chains
to the astonished Athenians, and then sacrificed the animal to Apollo
Delphinius. The Athenians were at this period in deep affliction on
account of the tribute which they were forced to pay to Minos, king
of Crete. (*Vid.* Androgeus and Minotaurus.) Theseus resolved to
deliver them from this calamity, or die in the attempt. Accordingly,
when the third time of sending off this tribute came, and the youths

79

and maidens were, according to custom, drawn by lot to be sent, in spite of the entreaties of his father to the contrary he voluntarily offered himself as one of the victims. The ship departed, as usual, under black sails, which Theseus promised his father to change for white ones in case of his returning victorious. When they arrived in Crete, the youths and maidens were exhibited before Minos; and Ariadne, the daughter of the king, who was present, became deeply enamoured of Theseus, by whom her love was speedily returned. She furnished him with a clew of thread, which enabled him to penetrate in safety the windings of the labyrinth till he came to where the Minotaur lay, whom he caught by the hair and slew. He then got on board with his companions, and sailed for Athens. Ariadne accompanied his flight, but was abandoned by him on the isle of Dia or Naxos. (*Vid.* Ariadne). Before Theseus returned to Athens, he sailed to Delos to pay his vow; for, ere setting out on his perilous expedition, he had made a vow to send annually, if successful, to the sacred island a ship with gifts and sacrifices ... [Anthon lists the other events of Theseus' voyage.] On approaching the cost of Attica, Theseus forgot the signal appointed by his father, and returned under the same sails with which he had departed; and the old king, thinking he was deprived of his newly-found son, destroyed himself. (*Vid.* Aegeus). The hero now turned his thoughts to legislation ...

In addition to these materials, Hawthorne referred to the article on Aegeus for a fuller account of Theseus' youth (he ignored the account of his conception and the reasons for the separation of the parents), and for details of the old king's suicide. The record of Theseus' adventures en route to Athens is supplemented with information from the articles on Procrustes and Sciron. Periphates, whom Anthon does not anywhere identify, is omitted, and the encounter with the sow, Phaea, about which Anthon gives no detail, is elaborated from Hawthorne's imagination.[17]

17 Hawthorne omits the Sinis of Anthon's account and, perhaps by mischance, condenses Sinis and Sciron to 'Scinis,' to whom he applies the

II: Tanglewood Tales

In handling the events at Athens, Hawthorne again follows Anthon's narrative. He does not name the Pallantidae, but passes over Theseus' conquest of them with: 'I have quite forgotten what became of the king's nephews.' He playfully amplifies the account of Medea, however, with the details of her enchantments based upon Anthon's article on Medea, and with detail of her 'fiery chariot' and flight (possibly derived from the *Medea* of Euripides). The incident of the bull of Marathon is used in abbreviated form and the account of Theseus' departure from Crete is amplified with detail from the article on Minotaurus. The elaborate treatment of Talus has been discussed above, as has the romanticizing of Ariadne. Though continuing to follow Anthon's narrative, Hawthorne invents the description of the labyrinth and the struggle with the Minotaur. In this, for the first time, he asserts the kind of freedom from his source which characterizes his handling of 'The Chimaera.' To the conclusion of the tale Hawthorne adds a description of the drowning of Talus, but omits all mention of Theseus' visits to Naxos and Delos. The assertion that the new monarch 'sent for his mother to Athens' is not traditional.

In adapting this extensive body of material, it would appear that Hawthorne was very much in the hands of his source, but the general tone of the tale argues against this appearance: in a relaxed and deliberate way he embraces the kind of incident that struck us as mere time-wasting episode in 'The Three Golden Apples' and makes it dramatically expressive. Every one of Theseus' encounters is a meaningful, organic part of the action. The diction is simple,

information from Anthon's article on 'Sciron.' This, of course, is further circumstantial proof that Anthon was Hawthorne's source.

81

and has freed itself from most of the coy juvenilism of *A Wonder-Book*. Moreover, Hawthorne is less self-consciously interested in moralizing upon the events of his tale; the events will speak for themselves. When morals do appear, they strike an unhappily false note – for example: 'When a son takes his father into his warm heart, it renews the old man's youth in a better way than by the heat of Medea's magic cauldron.' Such lapses, fortunately, are uncharacteristic in this tale.

Apart from the changed tone, 'The Minotaur' adds nothing new to Hawthorne's techniques of adaptation. It shows the same concern for focus on central incident and the same dramatic presentation of events as were noted in the earlier tales. Two features of this story, however, deserve special notice: first, Hawthorne has again used images or image clusters in a way which suggests depths below the surface of the tale; second, he has altered the emphasis of his source so that the tale is, finally, quite different from Anthon's version.

As Hawthorne knew, the Minotaur was the monstrous off-spring of an encounter between Minos' queen and a bull – a bull which Minos had promised to sacrifice to Neptune. This monster Minos now kept in the heart of a labyrinth fashioned by Daedalus, and fed it with human flesh. In describing Theseus' encounter with this monster, Hawthorne takes us to a grove which is duskily lit by moonlight. Ariadne, by pressing 'one of her soft little fingers against a particular block of marble' discloses an entrance 'just wide enough to admit them.' In speaking of the 'cunningly contrived' maze, Hawthorne says: 'There can be nothing else so intricate, unless it were the brain of a man like Daedalus, who planned it, or the heart of any ordinary man; which last, to be sure, is ten times as great a mystery as the labyrinth of Crete' (IV, 238). But Ariadne gives Theseus a silken thread which, as he moves deeper into the maze, she occasionally twitches. 'Oh, indeed, I can assure you,' says the narrator, 'there was a vast deal of human sympathy running along that slender thread of silk.' In Freudian terms these details and images are sexually charged, but within the larger frame of Hawthorne's symbolism they are specifically linked to the imagery of the Heart, and they awake echoes that reverberate through the whole structure of his work.

The picture of the Minotaur itself adds further depth to this layer of suggestion. This monster, in its first rush against Theseus, breaks off one of its horns, so that the ensuing battle is 'fought sword to horn.' The narrator tells his youthful audience that they 'will perhaps see, one of these days, as I do now, that every human being who suffers anything evil to get into his nature, or to remain there, is a kind of Minotaur, an enemy of his fellow-creatures, and separated from all good companionship, as this poor monster was' (IV, 240). With the battle over, however, 'the moon shone out as brightly as if all the troubles of the world, and all the wickedness and ugliness that infest human life, were past and gone forever.'

Hawthorne has, as far as possible, *stated* the moral meaning of Theseus' contest. His change in the emphasis of the tale (the implicit meaning of the action) is a matter of structure. In the original myth both Aethra, his mother, and Ariadne, his lover, are of minor importance. Both drop out of sight. In Hawthorne's version, on the other hand, both end up in comfortable family relationships, Aethra with her son; Ariadne with her father. Hawthorne's development of Aethra as a major figure at the beginning of the tale is so elaborate

83

that we are happy to see her reunited with Theseus at the end. The movement of the action has come full circle. Ariadne's return to her lonely old father, moreover, functions as a sub-plot comment upon the larger action. Hawthorne's neat tying up of the threads of his tale is a striking departure from the source. The silken clew which led the young people out of the labyrinth has led them back to their loving parents. But this conclusion is, somehow, neither logically nor causally related to the struggle with the Minotaur; the tale in some measure fails to achieve the inner coherence of the Bellero-phon story. The significance of this ending will be considered at some length in the next section.

The Pygmies: The second of the *Tanglewood Tales*, though the last written by Hawthorne (see IX, 444), is the opera bouffa of the mythological tales. Again Anthon is the source, for Hawthorne reproduces the facts, gathered from a dozen classical sources, in close parallel to Anthon's ac-count. Anthon's narrative, cleared of its numerous references to Homer, Aristotle, Pliny, Apollodorus, Eustathius, Philo-stratus, and so on, is as follows:

PYGMAEI, a fabulous nation of dwarfs, placed by Aristotle near the sources of the Nile; by Ctesias, in India; and by Eustathius, amusingly enough, in *England*, over against Thule ... They were of a very diminutive size, being, according to one account, of the height merely of ... 20 fingers' breadth ... while others made them ... 27 inches in size ... The Pygmies are said to have lived under a salubrious sky and amid a perpetual spring, the northern blasts being kept off by lofty mountains ... An annual warfare was waged between them and the cranes ... and they are fabled to have advanced to battle against these birds, mounted on the backs of rams and goats, and armed with bows and arrows. They used also a kind of bells or rattles ... to scare them

II: Tanglewood Tales

away ... Every spring they came down in warlike array to the sea-shore, for the purpose of destroying the eggs and young of the cranes, since otherwise they would have been overpowered by the number of their feathered antagonists ... Their dwellings were constructed of clay, feathers, and the shells of eggs. Aristotle, however, makes them to have lived in caves, like Troglodytes, and to have come out at harvest-time with hatchets to cut down the corn, as if to fell a forest ... Philostratus relates, that Hercules once fell asleep in the deserts of Africa after he had conquered Antaeus, and that he was suddenly awakened by an attack which had been made upon his body by an army of these Lilliputians, who professed to be the avengers of Antaeus, since they were his brethren, and earth-born like himself. A simultaneous onset was made upon his head, hands, and feet. Arrows were discharged at him, his hair was ignited, spades were thrust into his eyes, and coverings or doors ... were applied to his mouth and nostrils to prevent respiration. The hero awoke in the midst of the warfare, and was so much pleased with the courage displayed by his tiny foes, that he gathered them all into his lion skin and brought them to Eurystheus.

This, with the addition of two sentences from Anthon's article on Antaeus is the material which Hawthorne expanded into a twenty-four page tale. In the first paragraph he intro-duces the earth-born giant, Antaeus, and the earth-born race of Pygmies: 'This Giant and these Pygmies being children of the same mother (that is to say, our good old Grandmother Earth), were all brethren and dwelt together in a very friendly and affectionate manner, far, far off, in the middle of hot Africa' (IV, 247). This is followed by a fanciful picture of their kingdom and dwellings (their houses were made 'out of straw, feathers, eggshells, and other small bits of stuff, with stiff clay instead of mortar') and by an interminable account of their friendship with Antaeus and their wars with the cranes. Hawthorne does not give the reason for these wars,

85

but pauses for a whimsical aside on the Pygmies' steeds: 'According to some historians, the Pygmies used to go to the battle, mounted on the backs of goats and rams; but such animals as these must have been far too big for Pygmies to ride upon; so that, I rather suppose, they rode on Squirrel-back or rabbit-back, or rat-back' (IV, 253). Big brother Antaeus, of course, was always on hand to see that his little friends (who, like Swift's Lilliputians, were only six inches high) did not come off too badly in the conflict.

Hawthorne then gives an imaginative account of the battle between Antaeus and Hercules,[18] the moral of which recalls the last phase of Bellerophon's battle with the Chimaera: 'These earth-born creatures are only difficult to conquer on their own ground, but may easily be managed if we can contrive to lift them into a loftier and purer region' (IV, 262). The final third of the narrative, the story of the Pygmies' attack upon the sleeping Hercules, again follows Anthon, although Hawthorne believes that writers who say 'that Hercules gathered up the whole race of Pygmies in his lion's skin, and carried them home to Greece,' are mistaken: the Pygmies remained in their African kingdom where they may yet be alive.

Perhaps Hawthorne, nearing the end of his twelve mythological labours, was both weary and short of good material; whatever the reason, the thin little anecdote about the Pygmies fails on many counts as a work of art. Its artistic inspiration, undoubtedly, is Swift's *A Voyage to Lilliput*,

18 There is no basis in Anthon for Hawthorne's statement that Antaeus had a single large eye in the centre of his forehead, or for his equivocation about whether Antaeus' strength became twice as great or ten times as great each time he touched the earth.

but where Swift's clean matter-of-factness gives his irony an autonomous surprise and bite, Hawthorne's whimsy and rhetoric makes his ironies over-inflated and trivial; where Swift relies on low-key realism, Hawthorne creates the ingenious picturesqueness of 'let's pretend' land. Even the mock-epic tone of the Pygmy champion's speech – 'Tall Pygmies and mighty little men!' – is disappointingly over-done. As comic opera the tale is equally unfortunate, for it is neither elegantly artificial nor uproariously clownish; such backwoods joshing as 'Let me hit you but one box on the ear, and you'll never have the headache again,' merely evokes the humourless raconteur.

At the same time, despite its clear-cut, three-part structure, the tale lacks any real coherence of idea, image, or action. Antaeus, who is a generous and paternal big brother to the Pygmies in the first part of the story, becomes 'this numbskull of a Giant ... huge, earth-born monster that he was,' in the second part. And Hercules, the demigod hero who conquers his earth-born foes in that 'loftier and purer region,' the air, is moved by the valour which, a few pages earlier, has been mocked in the Pygmy champion's speech. 'The Pygmies,' then, is that rare thing in Hawthorne, a tale which, though it illustrates two important ideas, possesses no further depth or resonance.

The Dragon's Teeth: In this tale Hawthorne used two related narratives which, despite Anthon's contention that they did not belong together, he was able to fuse into a single, coherent work. In the articles on Europa and Cadmus, he found the following material:

EUROPA ... A daughter of Agenor (called by some Phoenix) king of

87

Hawthorne as Myth-Maker

Phoenicia. Jupiter, becoming enamoured of her, according to the old legend, changed himself into a beautiful white bull, and approached her, 'breathing saffron from his mouth,' as she was gathering flowers with her companions in a mead near the seashore. Europa, delighted with the tameness of the animal, caressed him, crowned him with flowers, and at length ventured to mount on his back. The disguised god immediately made off with his lovely burden, plunged into the sea, and swam with Europa to the Island of Crete, landing not far from Gortyna. Here he resumed his own form, and beneath a plane-tree caressed the trembling maid. The offspring of their union were Minos, Thadamanthus, and Sarpedon. Asterius, king of Crete, espoused Europa subsequently, and reared her sons.

CADMUS ... son of Agenor, king of Phoenicia, by Telephassa, was sent by his father, along with his brothers Phoenix and Cilix, in quest of their sister Europa, who had been carried off by Jupiter, and they were ordered not to return until they had found her. The brothers were accompanied by their mother, and by Thasus, a son of Neptune. Their search was to no purpose: they could get no intelligence of their sister; and, fearing the indignation of their father, they resolved to settle in various countries. Phoenix thereupon established himself in Phoenicia, Cilix in Cilicia, and Cadmus and his mother went to Thrace, where Thasus founded a town also named after himself ... After the death of his mother, Cadmus went to Delphi, to inquire of the oracle respecting Europa. The god desired him to cease from troubling himself about her, but to follow a cow as his guide, and to build a city where she should lie down. On leaving the temple, he went through Phocis, and meeting a cow belonging to the herds of Pelagon, he followed her. She went through Boeotia till she came to where Thebes afterward stood, and there lay down. Wishing to sacrifice her to Minerva, Cadmus sent his companions to fetch water from the fountain of Mars, but the fount was guarded by a serpent, who killed the greater part of them. Cadmus then engaged and destroyed the serpent. By the direction of Minerva he sowed its teeth, and immediately a crop of armed men sprang up, who slew each other, either quarrelling or through ignorance; for it is said that when Cadmus saw them rising he flung stones at them; and they thinking

88

it was done by some of themselves, fell upon and slew each other.
Five only survived ... These were called the *Sown* ... and they joined
with Cadmus to build the city. For killing the sacred serpent Cadmus
was obliged to spend a year in servitude to Mars. At the expiration
of that period, Minerva herself prepared for him a palace, and Jupiter
gave him Harmonia, the daughter of Mars and Venus, in marriage.
All the gods, quitting Olympus, celebrated the nuptials in the Cad-
mea, the palace of Cadmus. The bride-groom presented his bride with
a magnificent robe, and a collar, the work of Vulcan, given to him,
it is said, by the divine artist himself. Harmonia became the mother
of four daughters, Semele, Antonoë, Ino, and Agave, and one son
Polydorus. After the various misfortunes which befell their children,
Cadmus and his wife quitted Thebes, now grown odious to them, and
migrated to the country of the Enchelians. The ancient tradition was,
that Cadmus brought sixteen letters from Phoenicia to Greece, to
which Palamedes added subsequently four more ... and Simonides,
at a still later period, four others.

This, with two details borrowed from Anthon's article on
Delphi, constitutes not only the narrative but also most of the
detail of 'The Dragon's Teeth.' In the opening scene, Europa's
brothers are off in pursuit of a butterfly when the little girl
first sees the 'snow-white bull.' Although Hawthorne does no
more than imply the supernatural nature of this animal, and
gives it a rose-bud or clover-blossom breath, he follows the
remainder of Anthon's account in detail. Europa's subsequent
history is omitted.

In the scenes that follow, Hawthorne develops Anthon's
account in dramatic form. As Phoenix, Cilix, and Thasus
(whom Hawthorne describes as 'the son of a seafaring person') in turn abandon the quest, he describes the bowers
which the pilgrims build for each, and gives a short account
of the cities which grow up around them. The dying Telephassa then begs Cadmus to relinquish the search and consult

the Delphic oracle. Availing himself of Anthon's article on Delphi, Hawthorne describes this shrine as a picturesquely 'rustic bower' on the slope of Mount Parnassus, 'the very mid-most spot of the whole world.' When the cow, which the oracle directs Cadmus to follow, finally lies down, the companions who have joined him go to get water from a spring. They are all devoured by a dragon which guards the spot. Cadmus, 'enraged at the destruction of his friends,' leaps down the dragon's throat and stabs it to death. In this part of the story, Hawthorne omits the proposed sacrifice of the cow and the year's expiation which Cadmus is required to pay to Mars; he does not name the fountain of Mars, or the voice which directs Cadmus to sow the dragon's teeth, or the five soldiers who help him build the city. He departs from his source in asserting that all of Cadmus' companions were devoured, rather than 'the greater part of them' and invents the account of the dragon's death. In the last incident, again in the interests of simplicity, he does not explain the appearance of Cadmus' magical palace or the origins of Harmonia. Instead, he suggests that Cadmus mistakes Harmonia for Europa until 'the voice' informs him that this is 'a daughter of the sky,' who will be to him everything that brother, sister, friend, and mother have been. Then, without describing Cadmus' young children, Hawthorne concludes by remarking that the hero invented the alphabet for them, 'lest there should be too much of the dragon's tooth in [their] ... disposition.'

Like 'The Gorgon's Head,' and 'The Minotaur,' the story of Cadmus gives us no feeling that Hawthorne is inhibited by his highly detailed source. He seems, in fact, deliberately to stretch his material and to include more passages of reflection than we find in any of the other tales. This, it appears, contributes to an effect which Hawthorne consciously seeks – a new device in the artistic adaptation of myth which may be called 'ritual repetition,' the repetition of a pattern not for its interest as action but for its intrinsic expressiveness. Thus 'The Dragon's Teeth,' though the record of a quest, places less emphasis on rousing action than on cyclical pattern. The history of Cadmus' quest is simply a series of long journeys punctuated by the successive withdrawals of Phoenix, Cilix, Thasus, and Telephassa. In each case the pattern is similar, except that the 'home' which Telephassa finds is beyond life. The final cycle is a resolution – an end of the quest.

Hawthorne's use of imagery heightens our awareness of pattern and repetition in this quest. In general, the colours of the story are drab and subdued; therefore the bright spots which he introduces stand out strongly. To return to the beginning, we recall that Phoenix, Cilix, and Cadmus are pursuing a 'splendid butterfly' when Europa is carried away by the white bull. Europa had been dozing among the flowers when the bull appeared, so that her experience is, in a sense, a dream, and – with its final 'Goodbye' – death. The very real fact of her disappearance, however, forces all of Agenor's family to embark on a perilous night journey. At first Telephassa is seen dressed in her crown and royal robes, a picture which implies that the quest must be of transcendent importance to draw a queen away from her throne. The queen and her sons soon cast off these 'tatters,' however, for such 'mean attire as ordinary people wore.' And they all learn to give assistance to others without asking recompense.

Hawthorne treats with great delicacy the repeated incidents in which one of the party drops the quest. Phoenix believes that the search is 'a foolish waste of life.' By giving up he gains a temporal kingdom, with 'purple robe' and 'golden crown.' His 'conscience never quite ceased to trouble him,' however, for his first royal decree was that Europa, should she be seen, should be kindly treated and brought immediately to the palace. Cilix gives up because he believes that 'we are like people in a dream. There is no substance in the life which we are leading.' He, too, gets 'a long purple robe ... with a jewelled crown upon his head,' but sends a mission to 'the principal kingdoms of the earth' in search of Europa, for he 'secretly blamed himself for giving up the search.' Thasus, who has been truer than Phoenix and Cilix, gives up because of a physical injury. Because he was 'an upright, true-hearted, and courageous man,' he wins a purple robe, a sceptre, and a crown. But later on, he lays aside these pomps and makes another pilgrimage in search of 'some hoof-mark of the snow-white bull.' Upon his return he keeps a table set against Europa's appearance, a table at which poor travellers often dine.

Cadmus alone insists that the quest 'is no dream ... Everything else is a dream, save that.' When Telephassa ends *her* journey, he is 'convinced that, at her very first step into the better world, she ... caught Europa in her arms.' Although it is difficult to define the progression of Hawthorne's images and repetitions, it is clear that the quest for Europa is now a much more momentous affair than it originally seemed. The seekers, whatever worldly pomp they achieve, are melancholy at not having realized their 'dream.' The queen, apparently, ends her quest happily, though not in life.

We are prepared, then, for an extraordinary end, *in* life, to Cadmus' quest. Oddly enough, he now follows a cow which leads him to a dragon that he kills by leaping into its very inside. The end of Cadmus' quest, then, is a kind of death and rebirth. He is now able to extract the destroying teeth of the monster and use them creatively. Magically, the reward of his perseverance is a beautiful woman – not his sister Europa, as he imagined for a moment, but a 'daughter of the sky' called Harmonia, who becomes the centre and soul of his life. Hawthorne's theme, we realize, is a complete and coherent action, an action whose significance has been communicated to the reader not by rational statements or by moralizing (though the tale contains several explicit morals) but by a poetic adjustment of image to incident.

In this low-keyed but deeply expressive tale, the artificialities of style noted elsewhere are blessedly absent. There are minor flaws: for example, Thasus' 'sprained ankle' is an unimaginative injury for one so noble; but the tale, as a work, has been sensitively 'felt through.'

Circe's Palace: For this, the second last of the children's tales in date of writing, it seems likely that Hawthorne began his research by referring to Anthon, but ended, when Anthon proved inadequate, by turning to the original in Homer's *Odyssey* and following it in great detail. This is the only one of the mythological tales for which there is conclusive evidence that a primary classical source was used. Anthon's article on 'Ulysses' contains only a brief reference to the Circe episode. The article on 'Circe' summarizes, with some inaccuracy, Homer's account of Ulysses' adventure with Circe, but still there is no substantial detail. The reader is referred to '*Od*[yssey]., 10, 35 *seqq.*'; in addition, he learns that Circe 'had been married to King Picus, whom, by her magic, she changed into a bird.' This, in the article on Picus, is expanded as follows:

A fabulous king of Latium, son of Saturn, and celebrated for his beauty and his love of steeds ... One day Picus went forth to the chase clad in a purple cloak, bound round his neck with gold. He entered the wood where Circe happened to be at that time gathering magic herbs. She was instantly struck with love, and implored the prince to respond to her passion. Picus, faithful to his beloved Canens, indignantly spurned her advances, and Circe, in revenge, struck him with her wand, and instantly he was changed into a bird with purple plumage and a yellow ring around its neck. This bird was called by his name *Picus*, 'the woodpecker.'

Hawthorne's procedure with this material was to turn to book ten of the *Odyssey* for the framework of his narrative and supplement that with Anthon's information on Picus, and with invention of his own. It has not been possible to ascertain whose translation of the *Odyssey* Hawthorne used, but there can be little doubt that he did use a translation, for his Greek must have been, like Mr. Pringle's, 'as rusty as an old case-knife by this time' (IV, 107).[19]

The tale opens with the arrival of Ulysses' bark at the 'green and pleasant' island. Hawthorne then describes briefly the disastrous hurricane which resulted from the sailors' curiosity about the 'leather bags' of tempests given Ulysses by King Aeolus. The still more disastrous loss of Ulysses' fleet at Laestrygonia is briefly noted. Neither the diction nor detail

19 The translation of Homer used for this study is S. H. Butcher, *The Odyssey of Homer Done Into English Prose* (London, 1879, 1919). A comparison of Hawthorne's diction with the translations by Pope and Butcher makes it clear that Hawthorne used a prose version, or at least an extremely literal translation.

reveal whether Hawthorne used Anthon or Homer for these episodes, but the description of Aeolus' 'brazen-walled island' is found only in Anthon. What follows is Homer – embellished. Both the fidelity and the elaboration of Hawthorne's adaptation is well illustrated by the following parallel passages:

[Hawthorne:] 'But,' continued the wise Ulysses, 'you must remember, my good friends, our misadventure in the cavern of one-eyed Polyphemus, the Cyclops! Instead of his ordinary milk diet, did he not eat up two of our comrades for his supper, and a couple more for breakfast, and two at his supper again? Methinks I see him yet, the hideous monster, scanning us with that great red eye, in the middle of his forehead, to single out the fattest. And then again only a few days ago, did we not fall into the hands of the king of the Laestrygons, and those other horrible giants, his subjects, who devoured a great many more of us than are now left? ... My proposal is, therefore, that we divide ourselves into two equal parties, and ascertain, by drawing lots, which of the two shall go to the palace, and beg for food and assisance. If these can be obtained, all is well. If not, and if the inhabitants prove as inhospitable as Polyphemus, or the Laestrygons, then there will but half of us perish, and the remainder may set sail and escape.'

As nobody objected to this scheme, Ulysses proceeded to count the whole band, and found that there were forty-six men including himself. He then numbered off twenty-two of them, and put Eurylochus (who was one of his chief officers, and second only to himself in sagacity) at their head. Ulysses took command of the remaining twenty-two men, in person. Then, taking off his helmet, he put two shells into it, on one of which was written, 'Go,' and on the other 'Stay.' Another person now held the helmet, while Ulysses and Eurylochus drew out each a shell; and the word 'Go' was found written on that which Eurylochus had drawn. In this manner, it was decided that Ulysses and his twenty-two men were to remain at the seaside until the other party should have found out what sort of treatment they might expect at the mysterious palace. As there was no help for it, Eurylochus immediately set forth at the head of his twenty-two followers, who went off in a very melancholy state of mind, leaving their friends in hardly better spirits than themselves. (IV, 311–13)

[Homer:] 'Even so I spake, but their spirit within them was broken, as they remembered the deeds of Antiphates the Laestrygonian, and all the evil violence of the haughty Cyclops, the man-eater. So they wept aloud shedding big tears. Howbeit no avail came of their weeping.

'Then I numbered my goodly greaved company in two bands, and appointed a leader for each, and I myself took the command of the one part, and godlike Eurylochus of the other. And anon we shook the lots in a brazen-fitted helmet, and out leapt the lot of proud Eurylochus. So he went on his way, and with him two and twenty of my fellowship all weeping; and we were left behind making lament.'[20]

The principal departures which Hawthorne makes from his source are: first, the inclusion of a great deal of swinish lip-smacking on the part of Ulysses' crew; and second, the introduction of a melancholy purple and gold bird which repeatedly attempts to prevent the mariners from approaching Circe's palace by crying 'Peep, peep, pe – weep!' Hawthorne also elaborates considerably the account of the visit of Eurylochus' party to Circe's palace. On the 'broad pathway' which leads towards the palace, the men drink from a very un-Homeric spring which distorts their images so that each appears 'to be laughing at himself and all his companions.' The fawning animals of Homer's account meet them in the palace courtyard, but the fountain within the foyer, which changes from the shape of a man to that of 'a hog, wallowing in the marble basin,' is Hawthorne's invention.

20 Butcher, trans., *The Odyssey*, pp. 159–60.

II: Tanglewood Tales

In the same way, the account of Circe's entertainment which occupies twenty-six lines in Butcher's translation of the *Odyssey*, swells to nine pages in Hawthorne's adaptation. In Homer, the four handmaidens, 'born of the wells and of the woods and of the holy rivers, that flow forward into the salt sea,' do not appear until Circe's honourable seduction of Ulysses; in Hawthorne, the maidens assist Circe from the first: 'They were only less beautiful than the lady who seemed to be their mistress. Yet Eurylochus fancied that one of them had sea-green hair, and that the close-fitting bodice of a second looked like the bark of a tree, and that both the others had something odd in their aspect.' (IV, 320) Similarly, Homer's plain information that Circe 'set them upon chairs and high seats, and made them a mess of cheese and barley-meal and yellow honey with Pramnian wine, and mixed harmful drugs with the food' is embroidered by Hawthorne into an 'oval saloon' with 'two-and-twenty' canopied thrones, four-and-forty servitors, and so on.

When Ulysses, determined to rescue his men, meets Quicksilver, we get Hawthorne's usual fanciful picture of this young man. As in Homer, Quicksilver informs him of Circe's enchantments and (Hawthorne's addition) explains the meaning of the purple and gold bird. Although Hawthorne repeats the full panoply of the original reception for Ulysses, he stops short of his blunt inquiry to Circe: 'requirest me to pass within thy chamber and so up into thy bed, that so thou mayest make me a dastard and unmanned when thou hast me naked?' Instead, Hawthorne's Ulysses virtuously ignores Circe's offer 'to show true hospitality and even give myself to be thy slave,' and demands the restoration of his men whom, he knows, 'are hardly worth the trouble of changing ... into the human form again.' He also forces Circe to restore Picus to his original state, and then, with his entire crew, makes himself comfortable in Circe's enchanted palace, 'until quite rested and refreshed from the toils and hardships of [the] ... voyage' (IV, 340).

In Hawthorne's hands the Circe episode has become a parable – a thirty-five page moral tale whose lesson, echoing the closing pages of *Gulliver's Travels*, is: 'When men once turn to brutes, the trifle of man's wit that remains in them adds tenfold to their brutality' (IV, 337). In children's terms, perhaps, the story has been told with graphic opulence. Certainly, too, the element of suspense is cleverly handled: the omens of the birds; the distorting mirror of the spring; the fawning-fierce animals; the fountain with its water-sculpture; and the tapestry upon which Circe unfolds man's history. All point effectively towards the climax. For adults, also, there are features to be admired: there is charm in Hawthorne's subtle use of incremental repetition, such as the repeated description of the hand-maidens; and there is real acerbity in the picture of the restored mariners again wallowing after a handful of acorns scattered by the malicious hamadryad. But the final impression is disappointment, for the means are almost outrageously in excess of the end; moreover, the *mélange* of purple prose and talk about 'bacon' and 'dainty little porkers' is disconcerting, and the humour – such as Ulysses' reflection that 'For my own part, neither the most careful fattening nor the daintiest of cookery would reconcile me to being dished at last' – is dubious at best.

The underlying difficulty, however, is the fundamental shift in emphasis which Hawthorne imposes on the story. In the original, Ulysses is the kind of vigorous personage who, opposed by Eurylochus, admits that: 'I mused in my heart whether to draw my long hanger from my stout thigh, and therewith smite off his head and bring it to the dust, albeit he was very near of kin to me.' Ulysses' fear is that Circe will make him unmanly, or impotent.

Once he has asserted his own terms, he enjoys her for a full year. His followers, released from her spell, 'became men again, younger than before they were, and goodlier far, and taller to behold,' so that even 'the goddess herself was moved with compassion.' In Hawthorne's version, Ulysses exchanges this masculine status for the role of a moralist: it is his crew's self-indulgence that worries him, not the fact that Circe tyrannizes over the men who succumb to her 'enchantments.' The action of this episode, then, is anything but Homeric; the forces represented by hero and villainess are, finally, more closely allied than those of the hero and his followers. This strange paradox will be discussed in detail in the next section when we turn to Hawthorne's Dark Ladies.

The Pomegranate Seeds: This, the first piece that Hawthorne wrote for *Tanglewood Tales,* has long been celebrated in school readers. It is a nature myth, an account of how the seasons came to be, and by implication a version of the story of Eden. Hawthorne could have referred here to the second Homeric Hymn, 'Demeter,' but the language, the kind and quality of detail which he uses, and the fact that Hecate is not described in the hymn, make it likely that he relied on the simple but exhaustive account given in Anthon under 'Ceres' and the brief article on Hecate.[21] Using all of the narrative

21 See Hugh G. Evelyn-White, *Hesiod, the Homeric Hymns,* pp. 288–323, for text and translation of the original Homeric hymn.

and dramatic devices which we have noted previously, Hawthorne expands his thousand-word source to thirty-five pages, but does not once depart from Anthon's narrative order.

The story opens with the description of Ceres which Anthon appends to his narrative. Hawthorne's moralizing habit leads him on the first page to allow Ceres to remark: 'Young girls, without their mothers to take care of them, are very apt to get into mischief.' Without availing himself of the multiple choice offered by Anthon – Venus, Minerva, Diana, the Sirens, or the ocean-nymphs – Hawthorne gives us a scene in which Proserpina, playing with the 'sea-nymphs,' runs off in search of flowers with which to garland them. The hundred-flowered plant which she finds is not a narcissus (as in Anthon) but a glossy shrub with flowers of different, jewel-like colours, much like the plant which Beatrice Rappaccini calls her 'sister.' More vigorous than Anthon's Grecian heroine who merely 'stretched forth her hand to seize the wondrous flower,' this New England Proserpina uproots the plant. Then, as in Anthon, Pluto appears in his golden chariot, and whirls the 'child' (goddess, in the source) away. In Hawthorne's imaginative account of their journey to the underworld, we get a description of Cerberus and of Lethe. It is the narrator's opinion 'that even King Pluto had never been happy in his palace, and that this was the true reason why he had stolen away Proserpina, in order that he might have something to love, instead of cheating his heart any longer with this tiresome magnificence' (IV, 351).

Ceres, hearing the last shriek of her child, rushes home. Then, forgetting her dragon-drawn chariot, she sets out on foot, carrying an inextinguishable torch, in search of her daughter. In the nine days of her search (here Hawthorne greatly elaborates a single sentence of his source) she enquires of people, of dryads and water-sprites, of fauns and satyrs, and even of Pan. On the tenth day she meets Hecate, whose dog-face and crown of serpents are described in Anthon's article, 'Hecate.' Together they go to Phoebus – an effeminate musical aesthete as Hawthorne describes him – and learn that Proserpina has been carried away by Pluto. Ceres' mordant farewell to this high personage is 'Ah, Phoebus ... you have a harp instead of a heart.'

In the following pages Hawthorne omits the fact that Ceres 'abandoned the society of the gods' because Jupiter had connived at Proserpina's abduction. He describes Ceres' distracted wandering among men, however, and gives a wholly faithful account of her stay in the house of King Celeus and Metanira. He omits the conclusion of this incident – Ceres' decree that the Elusinians should erect a temple in which she will dwell in seclusion – and simply states that the goddess resolved that nothing should be 'suffered to grow until her daughter were restored.' Then, without explaining the first attempts of the gods to mollify Ceres, Hawthorne reports that 'Quicksilver was sent post haste to King Pluto, in hopes that he might be persuaded to undo the mischief he had done.' Proserpina, who is able to tell Pluto that she 'loves him a little,' is restored to her mother. For the six pomegranate seeds which she swallowed, while Pluto's prisoner, she must spend half of each year with the King of Darkness. In choosing six as the number of months of confinement, Hawthorne is perhaps choosing a median between seven and four, both mentioned in his source, or simply using a number that North Americans understand only too well as winter.

In adapting this tale for children, Hawthorne creates a

coherent structure, an action which – again through its images – suggests a good deal more than the simple cycle of the seasons. Firelight, jewels, gloom, magnificence, and artificiality are associated with Pluto in opposition to the images of sunlight, flowers, happiness, simplicity, and organic life which cluster about Ceres. In these terms, the most objectionable people in the story are Phoebus (all sun) and Hecate (all darkness). Pluto wants and needs love: Ceres learns the real value of love by losing it. And Proserpina, after her long sojourn in Hades, learns that the underworld is not wholly objectionable, if for no other reason than that it sharpens her understanding of sunny realities.

Hawthorne, we note, does not attempt to draw a comprehensive moral to this tale. Because he has succeeded in making an expressive form, he does not need to explain, as he does in 'The Paradise of Children.' He has even made us see that the long digression on Demophoön, Metanira's son, serves as a kind of sub-plot comment upon the larger action. Nothing, then, is wasted in 'The Pomegranate Seeds'; it is solidly constructed and simply told, though not wholly free from the weaknesses of Hawthorne's 'juvenile' style.

The Golden Fleece: If length is any index to interest, Hawthorne must have liked this forty-three page adaptation which he placed at the end of *Tanglewood Tales*. It is more than double the length of 'The Paradise of Children,' and contains more classical names and detail than any of the other mythological tales. As with 'The Minotaur,' and 'The Three Golden Apples,' the source is much too elaborate and scattered to be reproduced here. Internal evidence makes it certain that Hawthorne used Anthon, for the detail of his story is drawn from Apollodorus, Hesiod, Pindar, Ovid, and many other classical writers whose accounts Anthon has pieced together. The narrative structure of Hawthorne's version is, with a few exceptions, faithful to Anthon's articles on Jason and the 'Argonautae' which together give the full story of Jason's youth and his celebrated quest. The tale contains detail, however, from the following brief articles to which, in all but a few cases, Anthon refers the reader: Argo, Argus, Atalanta, Boreas, Chiron, Cyzicus, Harpyiae, Juno, Lynceus, Medea, Orpheus, Phineus, and Zetes. The description of the young Jason reveals how closely, on occasion, Hawthorne followed his source:

[Anthon:] He bore, says the Theban poet, two spears; he wore the close-fitting Magnesian dress, and a pard skin to throw off the rain, and his long unshorn locks waved on his back.

[Hawthorne:] He took a spear in each hand, and threw a leopard's skin over his shoulders, to keep off the rain, and set forth on his travels, with his long yellow ringlets waving in the wind (IV, 381).

Although it will not be possible in a summary to indicate the skill with which Hawthorne introduces essential information at appropriate points, we may note his principal departures from his source, and additions to it. The story develops in Hawthorne's characteristic fashion in a series of scenes bridged by narrative summary or reflective comment. It opens with a description of Chiron and his 'school for heroes,' and then tells of Jason's origins and enforced flight from the wicked King Pelias, his uncle. Adding considerable detail from Anthon's article on Juno, Hawthorne then dramatizes Jason's act of kindness in carrying her (an unnamed old woman) across a swollen (unnamed) river. This incident is

103

used skilfully as preparation for the meeting with Pelias in which Hawthorne combines, for dramatic effect, two versions given by Anthon. His principal omission here is the account of Jason's reunion with his family. The next episode, in which Jason consults the Talking Oak of Dodona, is Hawthorne's own invention, an imaginative retrospect based on Anthon's statement that Minerva 'aided the Architect' in the construction of the Argo 'and set in the prow a piece of timber cut from the speaking oak of Dodona, and which had the power of giving oracles.' Minerva is not named, but the branch which Jason cuts from the sacred oak is carved into a figure-head in her likeness; and this figure gives advice on critical occasions.

Hawthorne greatly abbreviates Anthon's account of the Argonautae, but adds supplementary information on a few of the heroes: Orpheus, Lynceus, Atalanta, and Zetes, whom he calls the 'son of the North Wind' (Boreas). Then, in summarizing the Argonauts' adventures, he introduces supplementary material from Anthon on Cyzicus, Phineus, and the Harpies. He omits such details as the Argonauts' virile repeopling of the island of Samothrace and the loss of Hercules at Mysia. When, guided by the sons of Phrixus who have been added to the company during the voyage, the Argonauts reach Colchis, Jason prepares for his exploit. Here Hawthorne, as well as elaborating the account of Jason's contest, makes two important departures from his source. First, Jason does not fall in love with Medea but merely responds to her proffered aid with: 'I promise to be grateful to you my whole life long.' Medea, Jason feels, is one of those serpent-like persons whose motives can never be trusted. Second, Medea does not embark with the victorious

104

II: Tanglewood Tales

Argonauts. She is left unaccounted for, and the horrible story of the dismemberment of her young brother, whose limbs, cast in the sea, impede the pursuing Aeetes, is omitted. The story ends with the breathless escape of the Argonauts as Orpheus sings 'a song of triumph.'

The amplitude of Hawthorne's adaptation of this story indicates that he felt very much at home with it. The style, which is again free in large degree of the juvenilisms of 'The Pygmies,' is simple, but Hawthorne does not strive to simplify names or antecedent action for his young audience. His narrative technique is at its best. On the first page he gives a rational explanation of Chiron's appearance by suggesting that, 'being a kind-hearted and merry old fellow, he was in the habit of making believe that he was a horse, and scrambling about the schoolroom on all fours, and letting the little boys ride upon his back.' This explanation, however, prepares us gently to accept greater marvels which are explained with only 'apparent' rationality: 'Jason bethought himself that the image [the figurehead of the Argo] had been carved out of the wood of the Talking Oak, and that, therefore, it was really no wonder, but on the contrary, the most natural thing in the world, that it should possess the faculty of speech' (IV, 394). Techniques of foreshadowing events and implying supernatural forces create a continuous current of suspense. Thus the old woman who causes Jason to lose a sandal in carrying her across the flood says: 'Only let King Pelias get a glimpse of that bare foot, and you shall see him turn as pale as ashes, I promise you.' And later, when Jason approaches Iolchos, the citizens whisper: 'The man with one sandal! Here he is at last! Whence has he come? What does he mean to do?' In the same way, Jason notices a strangeness in the old woman whom he has aided: 'Whether the light of her beautiful brown eyes threw a glory round about her, or whatever the cause might be, Jason fancied that there was something very noble and majestic in her figure after all, and that, though her gait seemed to be a rheumatic hobble, yet she moved with as much grace and dignity as any queen on earth' (IV, 386).

The action of the story is fully coherent: Hawthorne uses cause and effect in developing incident; he carefully relates past event to present situation; and he uses images poetically. The logic of events, perhaps, needs no comment, but the relation of past and present should be noticed. The story, we recall, begins with school-master Chiron. Later, it is Chiron's teaching which prompts Jason to say that Pelias should send a dangerous enemy on the quest for the Golden Fleece. Still later, it is again Chiron's training that prompts the hero's uncompromising behaviour towards King Aeetes. The repeated references to Jason's schooling suggest obliquely that his quest is in some sense an internal voyage.

Hawthorne's use of images gives depth to this idea. Jason's training, the imagery implies, assists at inward battles as well as at physical struggles in the empirical world. The most direct statement of this idea is Jason's speech to the sons of Phrixus: 'You have grown up from infancy in fear of this monster, and therefore still regard him with the awe that children feel for the bugbears and hobgoblins which their nurses have talked to them about' (IV, 403–4). The monster is, in a sense, an affair of fantasy or dreams. Even for King Pelias, the imagery implies, the struggle is psychological: 'Wicked old Pelias ... stood on a promontory, scowling at her [the Argo], and wishing that he could blow out of his lungs the tempest of wrath that was in his heart, and so sink the galley with all on board' (IV, 398). Jason, moreover, (although the source does not specify this) meets Medea at midnight and, like Perseus and Theseus, fights his battles by moonlight. Thus when King Aeetes says, 'Your eyes look heavy, Prince Jason ... you appear to have spent a sleepless night,' Jason is able to reply that the fiery bulls are already yoked and the dragon's teeth planted.

There are many other expressive touches of the same sort in this story. It is marred, however, by two things. Hawthorne does not escape the fatal temptation to be merely whimsical or humorous: he wonders 'what the blacksmith charged [Chiron] ... for a set of iron shoes'; and he describes Castor and Pollux as 'the twin brothers, who were never accused of being chicken-hearted, although they had been hatched out of an egg.' A more serious flaw is the moral problem presented by Medea. Hawthorne suggests that she is a dangerous enchantress; thus Jason is in the position either of using this evil means to achieve his quest, or of callously deserting a maiden who has deserved his highest regard. This problem is not resolved, and though it does not irrevocably mar the skilfully developed story of the quest, it leaves us with a tension which can scarcely be understood within the context of the tale itself.

Hawthorne's 'Ideal' Myth

At this point, having explored Hawthorne's aims, his use of sources, and his principles of adaptation in the mythological tales, we come to the question of meaning – a problem which finally expands beyond the tales themselves to the whole range of Hawthorne's work. The most satisfactory approach here will be to discuss first the relation between explicit moral, narrative action, and clusters or patterns of imagery in the tales, and then to generalize as far as the materials warrant upon the themes and ideas thus revealed.

The foregoing source study has perhaps made it clear that Hawthorne uses myth not as an anthropologist or archeologist might, but as a vehicle for expressing a personal vision. He leaves to the limbo of history the crabbed controversies of 'gray-bearded grandsires' over the historical interpretation of myth. His preoccupation is a fundamental interest in the operations of the human heart – 'what is common to human nature.' Like Freud and Jung, he sees myths as narratives which reveal the deepest sources and patterns of human action. But his choice of subjects and his rendering of them is entirely his own; there is no Oedipus or Electra in his vision; no 'anima' or 'shadow'; instead there are mercurial heroes, dark ladies, and tyrannical materialists whose stories have to do with the discovery of self, the problem of evil, and the brotherhood of man.

The theme of brotherhood and sympathy – the needs of the Heart – appears incidentally in almost all of the mythological tales, and is dominant in 'The Miraculous Pitcher,' 'The Pygmies,' and 'The Golden Touch.' The parable of Baucis and Philemon in 'The Miraculous Pitcher' is a direct plea to treat one's fellowmen with sympathy and love. Unfortunately, much of the moralizing appears gratuitous, since the action is expressive in itself; and Baucis and her spouse are so folksy and sentimental in their goodness that the chain of sympathy which should bind men together feels not unlike a rope of toffee.

108

II: Hawthorne's Ideal Myth

But if the theme of this dangerously genteel tale is all too explicit, one interesting item emerges. Quicksilver, the ubiquitous messenger of the gods is a very special figure for Hawthorne. Like the Hermes of mythology he is light-hearted, clever, and sly. He is able to help Perseus against Medusa, though he cannot perform the deed himself; he arms Ulysses against the enticements of Circe; he mediates between Pluto and Ceres, and delivers the box of troubles which are Pandora's, and mankind's, undoing. So consistent is his character and appearance in all of the tales in which he figures that we neither doubt his importance for Hawthorne nor fail to see that his mercurial, magical qualities are in part the qualities which Hawthorne associates with mirrors, fountains, moonlight, and imagination.

'The Pygmies,' with less formal wholeness and coherence than 'The Miraculous Pitcher,' restates the idea of the bond of affection which binds earth-born creatures together. Here the relation between action and idea is so loosely anecdotal that the tale ends by saying something almost contradictory to the original statement. Antaeus, in the first episode, lives on terms of friendly tolerance with his little brothers – a happy exemplification of the harmony which ought to infuse the relations of the most diverse creatures. In the second episode he becomes an 'earth-born monster' whom Hercules conquers by raising into that 'loftier and purer region,' the air. Here we have another of Hawthorne's presiding ideas: the troubles of this world are often illusory – monsters and demons that men create out of their private fears. In the spiritual realm the hollowness of such illusions is revealed. Unfortunately this idea receives so little support from either the action or imagery of 'The Pygmies' that it can scarcely be

109

distinguished from such other 'morals' as the narrator's comment upon the Pygmies' decision to set fire to Hercules' hair: 'A Pygmy, you know, though so very small, might set the world on fire, just as easily as a giant could' (IV, 268).

On the same theme, a much more successful though thoroughly unpretentious tale is 'The Golden Touch.' Here the moral 'iron rod' which is used so ineptly in 'The Pygmies' becomes an organic structural element, the occasion for a full exploration of the meaning of the Golden Touch. As in Hawthorne's best work, the action itself is a dramatic realization of the idea, and the imagery, like the 'Drummond light' of Melville's symbolism, 'rays out' and illuminates areas which would not be revealed in a prose statement of the moral. In Hawthorne's version, Bacchus, the giver of the Golden Touch, is a smiling, golden stranger who enters on a sunbeam and offers Midas his wish, 'Merely for the curiosity of the thing.' Appropriately, the magical power arrives 'with the first sunbeam,' and Midas rushes about converting everything he sees – flowers, books, food, and even his blonde daughter Marygold – into hard, worthless gold. As these images pile up, the reader realizes that Hawthorne has established some kind of an equation between gold, greed, sunlight, and material things; the Golden Touch is an emblem of the crass materialism that destroys the values of the Heart. Midas is unable to see that the reflection in the sun-like goblet mirror mocks him, or that the blaze of gold blinds the beholder. The deliberate anachronism of the solid gold spectacles wonderfully underlines his state of spiritual blindness. Midas' salvation becomes possible only when he renounces forever the materialistic brilliance of sun-gold; the god then makes possible the recovery of his humanity in a ritual of purification and rebirth. But what is the *value* to which Midas is reborn? Still within the terms of his imagery, Hawthorne makes this clear: it is colour and life – the delicacy of violets – which is valuable; it is love and vision; it is the gold of children's hair.

Within the very narrow limits of this tale, Hawthorne has made a complex statement. Man lives in the temporal world, and in this sunlit realm gold is important; but if it 'blinds' him to the needs of the Heart then he ends in anguished isolation. Midas, fortunately, recovers the power to 'see'; and his immersion (again the water-mirror image) softens his hardened heart and restores him to the human family.

Less obvious in theme and richer in treatment than 'The Miraculous Pitcher' and 'The Pygmies' are three tales in which women – Circe, Pandora, and Proserpina – are central characters. I have labelled them 'Dark Lady' stories, for though Pandora and Proserpina are portrayed as children, they were fully nubile in Hawthorne's source, and his interpretation of their stories connects them with Eve and the legend of the Fall. Here, in Hawthorne's ideal myth, are the forebears of Hester, Zenobia, and Miriam.

The most perplexing of the three tales is 'Circe's Palace,' for Hawthorne interprets it in entirely un-Homeric terms. Circe, as all the imagery of sunlight, gold, and material splendour suggests, represents the temporal realm of physical pleasure. But she is not, as in Homer, entirely wicked. She is served by nymphs who represent the sea, the forest, brooks, and fountains; and she is supreme mistress of the domestic arts of weaving, decoration, cooking. Hawthorne does not explain the source of her magic powers, but it becomes clear

111

that she uses them to punish men who have fallen short of her ideal of manliness. Thus she transforms her vain husband, King Picus, into a brightly-plumed bird, and Ulysses' gormandizing crew into swine.

Ulysses escapes a similar fate by heeding the advice of Quicksilver, the messenger of the moonlight realm; he holds Quicksilver's gift, a 'snow-white flower' to his nostrils and inhales 'so long a breath that his lungs were quite filled with its pure and simple fragrance.' Thus armed with mercurial power, he drinks Circe's wine, 'a liquid as bright as gold ... which kept sparkling upward, and throwing a sunny spray over the brim' (IV, 334–35), without harmful effects. Indeed it would appear that the senses can be safely enjoyed if the individual is guided by Mercury's vision – the talismanic white flower, and the warning images in the pool and the fountain.

Ulysses remains a man of vision, and forces Circe to restore King Picus, who has learned his lesson so well that 'he felt himself merely the upper servant of his people, and that it must be his lifelong labor to make them better and happier.' The implication is that Circe will cease her vengeful enchantments when men overcome their vanities and gross sensual indulgences. Ulysses feels that some of the beasts in the palace courtyard are irredeemable, and leaves them in their animal form. He is so disgusted with his followers that he redeems them not because they are men and deserve a better fate, but because 'their bad example ... [might] corrupt the other hogs.'

Hawthorne's reading of the Circe legend, then, becomes a parable about the need for the sensual side of human nature to be guided by the clear vision of the spiritual realm.

II: Hawthorne's Ideal Myth

Ulysses allies himself with Circe as a moralist. He does not approve of her mode of revenge, but it is important to note that he does not see her as a guilty temptress. Woman's 'enchantments' and beauties, as the nymphs who attend Circe indicate, are a part of nature; and man's grossness is more blameworthy than woman's seductiveness. In Hawthorne's 'ideal' myth, such exotic Dark Ladies as Circe are not the cause of evil. They become vengeful when their rich physical gifts are abused by men.

'The Paradise of Children' explores further the question of woman's guilt. At the surface level it is a simple parable which proves that idle curiosity produces trouble. The appearance of Hope as the consort of trouble, however, forces us to look at the tale as a myth of the Fall in which Hope takes the place of a more orthodox Faith. Pandora and Epimetheus are the mythological prototypes of Adam and Eve, and the box which they open is a secular counterpart of the fatal apple tree. But this analogy is not valid, for the childish pair are not alone in their Paradise, and they have entered no contract to worship their God. Their Eden, moreover, is a dull place: 'When life is all sport, toil is the real play. There was absolutely nothing to do.' (IV, 88) For Hawthorne the conception of an earthly Paradise was repugnant; thus the loss of Paradise was really a piece of good luck, for 'that lovely and lightsome little figure of Hope' accompanied the swarm of Troubles and promised the children 'an infinite bliss hereafter!'

This is as palatable, no doubt, as any other account of the Fortunate Fall. But Hawthorne forces us to place a little too much trust in the efficacy of Hope – the mosquito lotion which is preferable to the absence of mosquitoes. Read in these

113

terms the tale is a somewhat artificial but quite innocuous parable.

The imagery of the story, however, suggests still another dimension of meaning. The polished wood of the box is a mirror in which Pandora sees her own face. Hawthorne even implies, through his use of multiple choice, that the sounds which seem to come from the box really come from Pandora's mind. In these terms, Pandora is a type of mankind itself, and the 'troubles' are the dark promptings of man's inner nature which ought to be kept boxed up. But no. Perhaps it is best that we allow such perverse imps to appear – that we face our full nature and learn to live with it. Meanwhile the mirror of Hope will confirm our belief in a world that transcends human imperfection. In philosophical terms this is thin stuff, but the ambiguity which hints that Pandora's problem is a discovery of self which every man must go through gives us a glimpse of Hawthorne's consistent moral attitude. The chimaeras and monsters of the Heart must be faced courageously, for only by confronting them can man overcome or control them.

Unfortunately the implications of the tale are so loosely controlled that it falls short of artistic coherence. One thing, however, is unmistakable. Pandora is not the blameworthy 'mother of mankind' that we find in Milton's Eve; or, at least, Hawthorne does not *blame* her for obeying the promptings of her nature. He makes it clear, in fact, that 'too sunny realities' (the purely material life) are not enough for man. The dark side of human nature may be in many respects a burden, but the reflected light of a mirror reveals to earth-bound humans an ideal realm.

Like Pandora's story, 'The Pomegranate Seeds' is a basic

myth – this time an explanation of the seasons. For Hawthorne, who seeks to make the stories 'entirely one's own property,' it is also a myth of the self and of the Fall; the cycle of the seasons is never mentioned explicitly. The most striking thing about the structure of this tale is the apparently irrelevant three-page interpolation of Ceres' interlude with Queen Metanira and the infant prince Demophoön. Demophoön is a sickly baby whom Mother Ceres restores to abundant health by the bizarre therapy of nightly sleep in a bed of hot coals. When the easily perturbed Metanira discovers this practice, she shrieks in outrage. Ceres rebukes her sternly: 'Foolish woman ... You little know the mischief you have done him. Had you left him to my care, he would have grown up like a child of celestial birth, endowed with superhuman strength and intelligence, and would have lived forever. Do you imagine that earthly children are to become immortal without being tempered to it in the fiercest heat of the fire?' (IV, 367–68)

This digression is particularly striking because it bears no apparent relation to the central action of the tale. For Hawthorne, however, it must have had meaning as a sub-plot comment on the main action. The irony of Ceres' treatment of Demophoön is that she benignly subjects him to repeated death by fire (a process which will make him, like the sun, immortal), but fails to realize that this is analogous to the ordeal which her beloved daughter is suffering in Hades.[22] The whole point of the incident would be lost, of course, if it were known that Proserpina is already a goddess. This information Hawthorne suppresses. She is, for his purposes, a

22 The relation of Demophoön to the puny winter sun which slowly grows towards vernal rebirth is not implied by Hawthorne.

115

mortal; and even more important, she is a child. Woman, then, must go through an initiation into the night world just as man must go through a death-rebirth experience, an exploration of the dark, in order to discover or win his mature authority.

The nature of Proserpina's ordeal is defined in large part by Hawthorne's handling of imagery. In her innocent life with Mother Ceres, she knows no responsibility but the promptings of her nature towards beauty and affection. She gathers flowers to make garlands for sea-nymphs. About this aspect of her life Hawthorne clusters images of sunlight, happiness, flowers, simplicity, and organic life. Her experiences with Pluto – and we should not overlook the erotic overtones of the wild chariot ride to the underworld – produces a contrasting series of images. Sunlight is replaced by burning naphtha; happiness becomes pervasive gloom; jewels replace flowers; simplicity becomes 'tiresome magnificence'; and plain food is replaced by artfully contrived dishes. But the King of Darkness, proud, isolated, and unhappy, needs Proserpina as much as her mother Ceres does. At length Proserpina does learn to love him a little: 'He has some very good qualities,' she says; 'There is some comfort in making him so happy' (IV, 378). Proserpina, then, was anything but a guilty Eve; her dark initiation gives her for the first time a sense of responsibility towards another individual; and it gives her a self-conscious awareness of the happiness which her mother's realm represents. Like Pandora she has lost a paradise, but she has discovered her selfhood.

As in 'The Golden Touch,' Hawthorne has managed to invest a simple action with dimensions of meaning that extend far beyond the original story. He has made his material

116

II: Hawthorne's Ideal Myth

expressive in exactly the way that – as Q. D. Leavis argues –
he made New England history luminous. Proserpina's adventure is a parable of the seasons of the soul which at once
describes the process of growing up and defines the forces
that contend for dominion in the human heart. The golden
blaze of Apollo is as objectionable an extreme as the un-
relieved blackness of Hecate. The characteristically human
values occupy that realm of sun and shade in which absolutes,
though conceivable, are best avoided.

There now remain Hawthorne's adaptations of six mythological quests – five against monsters and one in search of a
lost sister. In these tales, which resemble in spirit such earlier
works as 'My Kinsman, Major Molyneux' and 'Young Goodman Brown,' Hawthorne generally allows the action, sup-
ported by images, to speak for itself, though he occasionally
pauses to moralize on a particular incident or event. The
present analysis will therefore consider the relation between
explicit ideas, actions, and images within each tale and
discuss the recurrence of these elements in the tales as a
group.

The prime materials of these narratives are as follows: in
each a young man undertakes a dangerous quest; except in
the Theseus story, the quest is undertaken at the prompting
or command of a king who is usually old and jealous; the
fulfilment of each exploit involves the killing of a monster;
and the hero's reward (except for Bellerophon and Hercules)
is kingship. Three of the adventures take place at night
(Perseus, Theseus, Jason); the fourth begins as a long, night
journey (Cadmus); in the fifth the hero (Bellerophon)
'started as from a dream' at the sight of the monster; in the

117

sixth the hero (Hercules) performs a feat of strength while Atlas completes the mission. In four of the tales – again Bellerophon and Hercules are the exceptions – a woman is involved in the conclusion of the quest, but only one of the heroes marries: Perseus rescues his mother from the menace of Polydectes; Theseus goes home to his mother while Ariadne returns to her father; Jason mistrusts Medea and leaves her in Crete; Cadmus marries Harmonia, 'a daughter of the sky.'

Hawthorne's handling of these materials – with the single exception of Hercules – relates them, by both specific statement and poetic image, to the self or to the imagination. The quests, it appears, are in some sense spiritual or psychological; the monsters conquered resemble the 'monsters of diverse kinds' which Hawthorne places in the Heart itself;[23] and the reward of kingship is related to the individual's achievement of dominion over himself. Up to a point, then, it is possible to understand the 'actions' of these tales as Hawthorne's serious exploration into the workings of the heart. Beyond this point – when we come to consider, for example, just what Medusa or the Minotaur really is – we begin to conjecture about matters of which Hawthorne himself may not have been fully conscious. I do not propose to violate the artistic status of such 'monsters' by adopting the psychologist's reductive method and relating them to the artist's personal psychology. Adequate explanations, I believe, can be discerned in the works themselves.

The Cadmus myth, in terms of poetic or symbolic meaning, is the most revealing of the tales which explore the nature of the self. The atmosphere of the story is dreamlike,

23 Stewart, *American Notebooks*, p. 98.

almost from the beginning, and the highly stylized use of repetition gives it a ritual quality which makes the step from the actual to the symbolic very easy. King Agenor is a tyrannical father-figure who banishes his sons to search for their princess-sister Europa. These young men will never supplant the father, never inherit his power, until their torch-lit journey through the night is fulfilled.

As has been noted earlier, the object of their quest gradually becomes a spiritual image. Europa is, above all, a figure of childlike innocence and beauty. One by one the searchers relinquish the quest, but the resulting acquisition of temporal power and glory never makes up for the loss of innocence represented by Europa. The arrangement of imagery here reminds us strongly of the contrast between King Pluto and Proserpina. Without Europa, the accoutrements of kingship are mere pomps. Telephassa, in death, finds Europa again, but Cadmus persists in his quest to find her *in life*.

His labyrinthine wanderings in pursuit of the oracular cow lead him, finally, to a fountain in a grove guarded by a serpent. In an astonishing scene which is Hawthorne's own invention, Cadmus leaps down the throat of this monster and destroys it; he then transforms its destructive teeth into a virile company who end his exile by creating a new community. His exploit, moreover, is so acceptable to the gods that, although they do not (as in Anthon) attend his wedding they give him a 'daughter of the sky' called Harmonia, as a reward. Harmonia, Hawthorne suggests, not only resembles Europa, but also comprehends for Cadmus the affection of mother, sister, friend, and brother.

Although stopping short of the fully explicit, Hawthorne makes it clear that Cadmus' ordeal is a spiritual rebirth. His

119

symbolic death in the serpent's jaws results not in a rediscovery of the lost innocence of Europa, but in an ability to organize the destructive, warring forces of the self, and use them creatively in the community of human beings. But this, in variant form, is the experience of Midas whose symbolic death by water saved him from the isolation and loneliness of his obsession and restored to him the human values of love and sympathy. It is also the experience of Proserpina whose descent into the underworld transformed her irresponsible life of play into a mature life of qualified pleasures. Jason, too, experienced a symbolic death when the fiery bulls enveloped him in flame; and Bellerophon and Pegasus flew, at least figuratively, into the snaky jaws of the Chimaera. In Hawthorne's ideal myth, the hero or heroine undergoes an ordeal which enables him or her to become a complete or integrated person.

One further detail of Cadmus' experience that requires comment is the divine gift of Harmonia. Hawthorne is at pains to suggest that this beautiful creature is immaculate – free from the guilt of Eve, despite her very 'natural' fecundity. The love which Cadmus finds is at once spiritual and sexual, sharply distinguished from the tenderness he feels for mother and sister, and transcending both. Those who read with Hawthorne in one hand and Freud in the other may point out triumphantly that the fountain in the grove, guarded by the terrible serpent is the female pudenda protected by the incest taboo related to mother and sister, and by projection to all real women; and such dragons or monsters symbolize Hawthorne's personal and obsessive sexual fears. However accurate this may be as a guess at Hawthorne's personal psychology, it is less than faithful to the terms of the Cadmus story. The magical reward of Cadmus' descent into the self is 'harmony' – a balanced control of the threatening spectres which haunt the individual in his troubled journey between childish innocence and self-conscious manhood or kingship. Hawthorne follows Spenser in portraying the experience allegorically, and like Spenser he saw it as a much more complex process than Freudian orthodoxy would allow, for it involves the full range of the individual's faculties and sensibilities.[24]

As suggested above, the quests of Jason, Theseus, and Perseus are variants of the Cadmus theme. The common feature of the monsters in each is that they are unnatural – isolated. The fiery bulls of 'The Golden Fleece' can scarcely eat because they destroy their natural food by fire, and the dragon which guards the Golden Fleece has devoured 'many heroes ... [who] longed to behold' the prize. The Gorgons 'turn to stone' those who gaze upon them, and the Minotaur is a carnivorous creature 'with no society, no companion, no kind of a mate, living only to do mischief, and incapable of knowing what affection means.' The conquest of these monsters, moreover, usually takes place in moonlight rather than in the prosaic light of common day, for as Hawthorne

24 Frederick C. Crews, Hawthorne's most recent analyst, states with questionable rhetoric: 'either we are entitled to use Freudianism retroactively or we must say that it is false' (*The Sins of the Fathers*, p. 259). Freudians, no doubt, are entitled to use their theories in any way they wish; but a theory which regards art as neurotic sublimation is not likely to help very much in discussing an author who regards it as supreme vision. One wonders why psychoanalysts persist in regarding their insights as superior to the vision of art. To read literature as data in the case-histories of dead writers may provide analysts with an amusing 'clinic without walls,' but this procedure is peripheral to the central concerns of literary criticism.

121

repeatedly implies, they are creatures of the imagination like the 'bugbears and hobgoblins' with which nurses frighten children.

Given such similarities of action and image, we may expect to discover that the *dramatis personae* of the quests are also analogous; the hero, tyrannical king, mother-sister, dragon-monster, and wife-reward elements of the Cadmus story appear in variant forms in the other quests. In 'The Golden Fleece,' the heroic Jason is menaced by two kings, Pelias and Aeetes; and he must master a pair of fiery bulls before confronting the dragon. Aeetes' daughter Medea combines in herself the qualities of wisdom, beauty, and treachery. In short, she may be like Minerva or Ariadne or Medusa. As Hawthorne describes her, Medea is 'One of those persons whose eyes are full of mystery; so that, while looking into them, you seem to see a very great way, as into a deep well, yet can never be certain whether you see into the farthest depths, or whether there be not something else hidden at the bottom ... for, beautiful as she now looked, she might, the very next instant, become as terrible as the dragon that kept watch over the Golden Fleece.' (IV, 407) Jason, who has been aided by Juno and the many-gifted Argonauts, accepts Medea's assistance with gratitude, but finds her 'ill-natured.' Indeed she is apparently mistress of the dragon and does not allow Jason to destroy it, for 'One always finds a use for these mischievous creatures, sooner or later.' Jason's reward, then, is not Medea's hand, as in Anthon. He will claim Pelias' throne but be spared further involvement with this enchantress, who is the one truly evil Dark Lady of the mythological tales.

In 'The Minotaur' the tyrannical king, Minos, is contrasted

II: Hawthorne's Ideal Myth

with Theseus' benignly ineffective father Aegeus; the benign
mother Aethra has lost her place to Medea, Aegeus' second
wife. The monster is the Minotaur, and the hero's helper is
the tender and innocent princess, Ariadne. Ironically enough,
Aegeus has been partly responsible for the death of Minos'
son, Androgeus (a detail not mentioned by Hawthorne) so
that Minos' rage at Theseus is not unmotivated. Again, a wife
is not part of the hero's reward: Ariadne remains with her
father, and Theseus 'sent for his dear mother to Athens.' In
'The Gorgon's Head' Polydectes is the tyrannical king; his
benign brother, the unnamed Dictys, befriends Perseus and
his mother. Danaë and Minerva, the devoted females, have
their evil counterpart in Medusa, whose 'lifelike representa-
tion' is the device on Minerva's shield (IV, 393). In Hercules'
quest for the three golden apples we have the jealous relative
who provokes the quest, and the monster which must be
overcome. But in other respects the tale is untypical. The
reason may be that Hercules is a sun hero, a rather complacent strong-man in whose adventure Hawthorne sees more
evidence of cunning than of vision. As a result, the narrative
is merely episodic, and though Hawthorne states his belief in
the efficacy of the imagination, and the illusory nature of
many worldly troubles, there is no coherent dramatic rendering of these ideas.

In one view, these quest tales, with their recurring patterns
of character and incident, may be seen as no more than
garbled versions of Greek myths. But Hawthorne's choices
of subject and his reworking of them are surely deliberate;
and in that case the meaning of the quest stories is something
like this. In order to become a man (a king), a hero must
first recognize the menacing nature of the father-figure's

123

empirical power. The father, in rage or jealousy, sends the young man on a quest in which he must conquer supernatural monsters. The crucial encounter with the monster takes place at night, or in a dusky atmosphere; fortunately the hero finds magical friends in this dangerous realm and through their help accomplishes his mission. In some respects, indeed, the monsters appear to be no more than imaginary creatures: one is called a 'chimaera'; another is seen only in a mirror; and all of them haunt dark caves or labyrinths, away from the light of day. Having overcome these monsters, the hero returns to society to claim a place of honour. He need not supplant the father (Cadmus, for example, founds his own city), but he must govern; the quest, in sum, is an exploration and conquest of the self, and its 'inestimable prize' is self-knowledge, and the creative power which self-knowledge brings. Hawthorne typifies this power variously as the ability to rule generously rather than selfishly, the power of procreation, and the power of 'vision.'

There can be little doubt that Hawthorne read Charles Anthon's long paragraphs of speculation about the meaning of the myths which we have just discussed. He probably knew, for example, that Minerva, the goddess who is most helpful to his heroes, is a moon goddess, and that the moon is at once a productive and destructive force whose destructive power is symbolized by the impure and hateful Gorgons (Anthon, 1007). But even without Anthon's information, Hawthorne had a fully developed idea of the significance of moonlight. In the introduction to *The Scarlet Letter* he describes the ideal atmosphere for the perception of artistic truth as a mirror-image in which the cold spirituality of moonlight mingles with the warm glow of the hearth (C, I,

II: Hawthorne's Ideal Myth

36). Again, in the damning revelation of the nature of the dead Governor Pyncheon, Hawthorne remarks: 'We were betrayed into this brief extravagance by the quiver of the moonbeams; they dance hand-in-hand with shadows, and are reflected in the looking-glass, which, you are aware, is always a kind of window or doorway into the spiritual world' (C, II, 281). And Perseus destroys the Medusa in moonlight, regarding her image in the mirror-like surface of a shield loaned him by Mercury; in effect, the Medusa is an illusion.

This explanation does not account fully for the complexity of Hawthorne's images, however. If Minerva, Medusa, and the moon are closely related, the imagery of quicksilvered mirrors and Perseus' mirror-shield link them to Mercury, Minerva's brother. The power which enables Perseus to overcome the terrible female enchantress is thus symbolized not only by moonlight-mirror but also by a male-female relation, at once as ubiquitous and bright as Quicksilver, and as wise and impersonal as Minerva. This power is so attractive that Perseus finds it, for a moment, more desirable than earth; but he realizes that it is divorced from the human realm of the affections, just as the blaze of noon, in its crass way, can be blindingly inhuman:

It was now deep night. Perseus looked upward, and saw the round, bright, silvery moon, and thought that he should desire nothing better than to soar up thither, and spend his life there. Then he looked downward again, and saw the earth, with its seas and lakes, and the silver courses of its rivers, and its snowy mountain-peaks, and the breadth of its fields, and the dark cluster of its woods, and its cities of white marble; and, with the moonshine sleeping over the whole scene, it was as beautiful as the moon or any star could be. And, among other objects, he saw the island of Seriphus, where his dear mother was. (IV, 40)

The moon, for all its beauty, is cold and inhumanly remote; but its qualities are incorporated in nature – in silvery rivers, snow, and marble – with great beauty. The hero, having learned that the night realm is a region of vision rather than petrifying evil, will return to his destiny in the human realm.

In 'The Chimaera' Hawthorne triumphantly reveals the highest realization of the power which Perseus won. The symbolic action with its supporting imagery is everywhere felicitous in this tale. Hawthorne postpones until the end his explicit statement of the analogy between Bellerophon's adventure with Pegasus and the equally inspiring adventure of poetic creation. The essential qualities of the poet – Bellerophon's qualities – are tenderness, steadfastness, and childlike simplicity.

The analogous adventure of Perseus makes possible a fuller interpretation of the action of 'The Chimaera,' for even though Bellerophon's exploit is a daylight adventure, the images which Hawthorne uses are variations of the Perseus images. Pegasus, as Hawthorne must have read in Anthon, is the magnificent steed which was released, fullgrown, from the bloodstream of the overpowered Medusa. This relation to the moon goddess is not mentioned in the tale, but we sense Pegasus' significance in the picture of his 'snowy or silvery wings' and in the fact that he is first seen as a tiny gleam, infinitely high in the sky, reflected in the mirror of the fountain. The hint of Medusa's power is strong in the child's statement: 'I dare only look at its image in the water.' Unlike Medusa, and despite his untamed energy, Pegasus is a benign force. After the wild tumult of his first ride, Bellerophon learns by practice how to control his impulsive steed. Then, 'when he had become accustomed to feats of horsemanship

126

in the air, and could manage Pegasus with the least motion of his hand, and had taught him to obey his voice, he determined to attempt the performance of this perilous adventure' (IV, 184). The mere possession of a winged horse is not the goal of the quest. Bellerophon cannot live indefinitely in the ethereal world of the sky any more than Perseus can; he must descend into the deathlike valley of Lycia and purify it of its fiery cave-dwelling monster, the Chimaera. As the battle develops, he realizes that 'the best way to fight a Chimaera is by getting as close to it as you can.' It is only when the earth-born monster, borne aloft by Pegasus, envelops both horse and rider in 'a perfect atmosphere of flame,' that Bellerophon is able to end its life.

Like Jason and Cadmus, Bellerophon experiences a symbolic death and rebirth, but his quest is not, like theirs, an adventure which allows him to become a temporal king. The high reward of his quest is the articulate self-awareness of the poet – a power which gives him mastery over the chimaeras that harry mankind.

The foregoing discussion has suggested in detail the function of the mythological tales as serious formulations of Hawthorne's understanding of the drama of the self, the power of the imagination, and the concrete rewards which a conquest of the night realm brings to the hero. In this 'pure' myth the hero is always successful. This does not mean that he is superhuman but simply that he achieves the goals which a man of vision should achieve; he has enlisted the magical powers of the moonlit world in a struggle against night monsters and power-greedy tyrants of the daylight world. At the same time, Hawthorne has made the point that the hero's gifts, whether of gold or silver, sun or moon, are valueless if they do not bring him into creative union with his community. And finally, the tales have made it clear that woman, in her different way, is a gifted, creative figure. She can threaten the man of vision, but she is not any more responsible for human imperfection than man himself.

My next concern will be to relate this new material to the corpus of Hawthorne's other works. As Randall Stewart, Malcolm Cowley, and others have shown, Hawthorne deals repeatedly with a few situations, differently garbed. In the same way, he uses again and again the same patterns of imagery and makes the same explicit statements. Moonlight and mirrors, for example, play an important part in works as diverse as *Seven Gables* and 'Feathertop.' There can be no doubt, therefore, that the conflicts of the mythological tales are related to those of Hawthorne's New England heroes, and that the patterns of the 'baby stories' will throw light on the New England tales of experience. For Hawthorne, like his ideal heroes, underwent a long and painful quest in the shadows of his 'haunted chamber'; he returned from it with a talisman – an uncannily fashioned Mirror for Puritans.

PART III

The New England Myth: A Mirror for Puritans

A CENTURY OF CRITICISM HAS FIRMLY ESTABLISHED Hawthorne's position as a classic, a position which is enhanced from year to year by our growing awareness of the influence he has had on subsequent writers. Even T. S. Eliot, to whom much in Hawthorne's thought must have been uncongenial, expressed his grateful awareness of this debt:

Neither Emerson nor any of the others was a real observer of the moral life. Hawthorne was, and was a realist ... In consequence, the observation of moral life in *The Scarlet Letter*, in *The House of the Seven Gables*, and even in some of the tales and sketches, has solidity, has permanence, the permanence of art. It will always be of use: the essays of Emerson are already an encumbrance. The work of Hawthorne is truly a criticism – true because a fidelity of the artist and not a mere conviction of the man – of the Puritan morality, of the Transcendentalist morality, and of the world which Hawthorne knew. It is a criticism as Henry James' work is a criticism of the America of his times, and as the work of Turgenev and Flaubert is a criticism of the Russia and the France of theirs.[1]

Many contemporary critics would echo this praise, but few have seen Hawthorne's major romances as a true criticism in Eliot's sense, 'true because a fidelity of the artist and not a mere conviction of the man.' In some respects Hawthorne was indeed no more than an opinionated man, but Eliot was surely thinking of his power to commit his imagination fully to experience, to plumb its depths intuitively, and to record his insights in symbolic narratives. But what *are* the essential

1 Quoted in Matthiessen, *American Renaissance*, p. 193.

131

narratives in Hawthorne's tales of New England experience? Are they related to each other? Are they related to the idealized patterns of the Greek tales? Despite many excellent readings of individual tales and romances, and such sensitive discussions as we find in F. O. Matthiessen's *American Renaissance* and A. N. Kaul's *The American Vision*, our answers to these questions remain tentative. What follows will certainly not close the subject, but in the light of the new material studied in part II I shall attempt to delve beneath the various discursive themes of Hawthorne's major romances to discover a radical coherence in their narrative structure and statement, and to relate these works to his larger vision – his 'life of allegory.' Since it will be impossible to examine the entire canon in detail (an adequate study of the tales and sketches would require a volume in itself), the discussion will concentrate on the four major romances and two of the later works. The relevance of the tales to the complete *œuvre* will be indicated somewhat schematically in the final essay.

THE HOUSE OF THE SEVEN GABLES

The House of the Seven Gables was the most popular of Hawthorne's romances during his lifetime, and has proved one of the most baffling to modern critics.[2] It was written during Hawthorne's idyllic and productive year at Lenox,

2 Q. D. Leavis finds Seven Gables 'quite uninteresting, illogical in conception and frequently trivial in execution.' Clark Griffith, in 'Substance and Shadow: Language and Meaning in "The House of the Seven Gables," ' *Modern Philology*, LI (February 1953), 194, finds the plot 'strained, hackneyed, and, as Austin Warren has remarked, a tiresome nuisance.'

and was followed very closely by *A Wonder Book*; hence my choice of it as a point of departure. The relation between the *Seven Gables* preface and the mythological tales has been observed at the beginning of part II above. This preface – in company with the preface to *The Snow-Image* and the remarks on 'romance' in 'The Custom House' – ranks as Hawthorne's central statement about the meaning of romance. Its two major doctrines are, first, that a moral tale is its own meaning, and second, that this meaning is revealed through picturesque mistiness of setting, Gothic exaggeration, and romantic heightening of lights and shadows. Since both *Seven Gables* and *A Wonder-Book* ought to exemplify these ideas, we may for the moment disregard the plethora of specific statement in *Seven Gables* and concentrate upon its narrative line and imagery.

Arranged in chronological order, the action of *Seven Gables* is seen to be a long struggle between two families, the Maules and the Pyncheons, over a piece of ground which is made valuable by a 'natural spring of soft and pleasant water' – Maule's Well. The original owner of this property, Matthew Maule, is executed as a witch, at the instigation of the Puritan colonist, Colonel Pyncheon, who then seizes the property and engages Matthew's son to construct a mansion upon it. The water of the well turns brackish, and the Colonel, on the christening day of his house, dies mysteriously – the victim, perhaps, of wizard Maule's curse: 'God will give him blood to drink!' Just before the Colonel's death, the builder of the house hides a document in a secret compartment which he has constructed in the central chimney behind the portrait of the Colonel. This document is the Colonel's deed to a vast tract of 'Eastern land' which he hopes will make his wealth

133

equal to that of European monarchs. In a subsequent generation, the reigning Pyncheon (now an irritating pseudo-
European called Gervayse) offers to return the house and
well to the current Matthew Maule in exchange for the deed
to the 'Eastern land.' This bargain involves the subjection of
Alice, the owner's foreign-educated, ethereal daughter, to the
will of the artisan Maule; but Alice's mesmeric vision merely
discloses that the Maule wizards are preventing the old
Colonel from revealing the hiding place of the deed.

In a still later generation, the guilty conscience of the
reigning Pyncheon (this time a bachelor) prompts him to
return the property to the rightful owners, or to leave it to
Clifford, his imaginative nephew (Hawthorne's story is
deliberately vague on this point). A grasping nephew, Jaffrey,
the reincarnation of the old Colonel, prevents this event by
frightening the bachelor to death, destroying the will in
favour of Clifford and sending this naive cousin to a thirty-
year imprisonment for the murder of his benign uncle.

The main action of the romance – like the action of Greek
tragedy – deals with the final phase of this long struggle. The
murderous nephew, Jaffrey, has become a prosperous judge
and prospective governor, while his cousins, the old crone
Hepzibah and the recently paroled but utterly crushed
Clifford, occupy the family mansion. The decay of the house,
however, is somewhat arrested by the presence of two young
people – sunny-natured, plebian Phoebe Pyncheon (the last
of the family) and artist-artisan Holgrave (the last of the
Maules). The Judge, believing that Clifford possesses the
secret of the Pyncheon wealth, dies of apoplexy – again the
blood-drinking curse – while attempting to wrest this knowledge from his victim. Clifford and Hepzibah flee from the

III: The House of the Seven Gables

House of the Seven Gables, and Phoebe and Holgrave return and confess their love and mutual understanding. The young couple who thus resolve in their love the age-old conflict of Pyncheon and Maule, move from the ancient house to a less permanent structure of wood, strong enough to last for one generation only. Clifford, Hepzibah, and the handyman-philosopher Uncle Venner accompany them to their new abode to spend a happy old age. Maule's Well, now freed of the curse, throws up 'a succession of kaleidoscopic pictures in which a gifted eye might have seen foreshadowed the coming fortunes of Hepzibah and Clifford, and the descendant of the legendary wizard, and the village maiden, over whom he had thrown *love's* web of sorcery' (C, II, 319, my italics).

At the surface level (and stripped of its logical statements about old houses and the evils of the past) this is a tale whose Gothic contrivances and coincidences recall the wonders of *The Castle of Otranto*. What, the reader asks, ever happened to the Eastern land? How do we know that Maule's curse is really revoked?

If we assume for purposes of exploration that the imagery of the mythological tales is essentially the imagery of the *Seven Gables*, we find that the mythological tales are helpful in answering these questions. *Seven Gables* as a whole suggests that Greek myth was deeply alive in Hawthorne's imagination, whatever debts of detail he owed to Anthon; for example, when the Judge dies, the Pyncheon elm produces a golden bough which, 'presented at the door' by the next in line, 'would have been a symbol of his right to enter.' The old king is dead and the new is about to enter into his heritage. Again, Phoebe Pyncheon is a domesticated, humanized relative of the dazzling Phoebus-Apollo of 'The Pomegranate

Seeds.' The house itself is a dusky 'labyrinth,' and the well a mysterious mirror. Hawthorne's quest tales and this New England romance, it would appear, are linked by images as well as by date of composition.

The central image is the house itself, with its well, and the plot of ground upon which it stands. The nature of this property, as Hawthorne describes it, is double: on the one hand it is a simple cottage lot with a flowing spring, reminding us of the fountains, springs, and gardens that belong to Minerva and Quicksilver; on the other it is an oppressive labyrinth with a brackish well – not unlike the forbidding castle and maze of King Minos. It is, in short, an ambivalent property which reflects the opposed characteristics of the simple, creative Maules and the ambitious, money-mad Pyncheons – plebians and patricians, natives and Europeans, dreamers and pragmatists. But Seven Gables is not a happy house, for one group who have a claim upon it have been suppressed or banished, while the other group, the Pyncheons, guard it jealously.

Judge Pyncheon (whose son is appropriately luxuriating in Paris) is the representative of the Pyncheon claim to the Maule property. His characteristics are a combination of the traits of greedy Midas, lustful Polydectes, and black-hearted Pelias. He is the figure of the tyrannical father; though everything about him radiates sun and benignity, he is cruel, repressive and hard-hearted. Hawthorne is everywhere explicit about these qualities in the Judge and the old Colonel: 'Endowed with common sense as massive and hard as blocks of granite, fastened together by stern rigidity of purpose, as with iron clamps, [the Colonel] ... followed out his original design, probably without so much as imagining an objection to it. On the score of delicacy ... the Colonel, like most of his breed and generation, was impenetrable' (C, II, 9). The Judge, living in a more prosperous generation than his ancestor's, 'had lost the ruddy hue that showed its warmth through all the duskiness of the Colonel's weather-beaten cheek, and had taken a sallow shade, the established complexion of his countrymen.' He had also developed 'a certain quality of nervousness,' the result of the 'refining process' of progress. Nevertheless he was the sunny image of his ancestor:

For example: tradition affirmed that the Puritan had been greedy of wealth; the Judge, too, with all the show of liberal expenditure, was said to be as close-fisted as if his grip were of iron. The ancestor had clothed himself in a grim assumption of kindliness, a rough heartiness of word and manner, which most people took to be the genuine warmth of nature, making its way through the thick and inflexible hide of a manly character. His descendant, in compliance with the requirements of a nicer age, had etherealized this rude benevolence into that broad benignity of smile, wherewith he shone like a noonday sun along the streets, or glowed like a household fire in the drawing-rooms of his private acquaintance. The Puritan – if not belied by some singular stories, murmured, even at this day, under the narrator's breath – had fallen into certain transgressions to which men of his great animal development, whatever their faith or principles, must continue liable, until they put off impurity, along with the gross earthly substance that involves it. (C, II, 122)

The Judge, in a word, is the typical Pyncheon: his images are sun and gold; he is iron-hearted, a lover of wealth, power, and the physical things of life; he is the man who, above all, gets things done.

In pursuit of power the Pyncheons have crushed everything that stood in their way. They have erected the emblem

137

of their success, the House of the Seven Gables, upon the site of their enemy's stronghold – Maule's Well – though the reward has been the bitter taste of the water and the loss of the Eastern land. The Maules, likewise, living for their bitter curse, seem to have failed; in fact they have disappeared. They are, however, as ever-present as their well; they haunt the Pyncheons in dreams and even crop up, it would appear, in the closed stream of the Pyncheon blood: hence the ethereal Alice who becomes the victim of carpenter Matthew Maule; the mercurial, epicene Clifford 'for whose character [the Judge] ... had at once a contempt and repugnance' (C, II, 312); and the poor old bachelor, Clifford's uncle, who was murdered for his un-Pyncheonlike remorse.

Again the imagery of the myths helps us; the Maules, it suggests, are essentially moon people like Minerva and Mercury – the people of wells and fountains and mirrors – the people of the imagination, spiritual opponents of the empirical Pyncheons. When suppressed they become wizards or, in Puritan terms, witches. Thus Alice Pyncheon (the spirit of European art, not its commercial artifact) becomes subject to the more vigorous will of artisan Matthew Maule. Her second or third cousin, Clifford – a lover of beauty – is confined to a dungeon by the rampant commercial spirit of Jaffrey Pyncheon, the secularized nineteenth-century Puritan.

But what is the meaning of Hepzibah, the warm-hearted old crone who keeps alive, or almost alive, the House of the Seven Gables? She is the most complex figure of the romance. On the one hand she is a Pyncheon. Like her ancestor, Alice, she wants to be a 'lady' – the female representative of the power of wealth and prestige and art (although as a native-born member of the family she was never allowed to play Alice's imported harpsichord). On the other hand she is forced to emerge from her dusky world, in which she resembles the Gorgon Medusa more than the wise Minerva, and cope with the sunlit realities of keeping a cent-shop. She does this, of course, because the effeminate Clifford is completely incapable, after his long, dark banishment, of facing the world at all. Her effort, however, makes her more a *woman* (C, II, 45) than she has ever been. She becomes, instead of an ineffectual Gorgon, a protectress and mother who shields Clifford from contact with the sunny world, especially the scorching sunniness of Judge Pyncheon's 'philanthropy.'[3]

Hawthorne rings every possible change on this picture of Clifford and Hepzibah as the ineffectual proprietors of the House of the Seven Gables, the generation which is at once inadequately 'old' and inadequately 'new.' Hepzibah's scowl results from her need to face the sunshiny world of things. When she and Clifford finally escape from the house they are two owls (sacred to Minerva) who leap drunkenly on the train, the steam-fiend of progress. At first, in the exhilaration of his escape, Clifford takes command. His liberation fills him with the intoxication of power. Then Hepzibah, whose enterprise is feeble (her experience has been limited to keeping a cent-shop for one day), decides that they must return to their secluded home, whatever its terrors. The pair of them, both moon-people, are ironic representatives of the powers of Minerva and her brother Mercury. Because of the long domination of their materialistic relatives, their powers

3 Note the subtlety of Hawthorne's description of Clifford's first breakfast at home. Hepzibah directs Phoebe to 'draw the curtain a little, so that the shadow may fall across his side of the table' (C, II, 102).

are atrophied and decrepit. Although they are the legal inheritors of the house, they are not capable of giving it new life; their era is not the era of trains and factories. As Hawthorne says, 'Clifford was indeed the most inveterate of conservatives' (C, II, 161).

The resolution of the action thus descends upon Phoebe and Holgrave, the last representatives of the two families. The Judge's attempt to extract Clifford's supposed secret is the last gasp of the Pyncheon-sun tyranny. Holgrave's 'magazine story' about Alice Pyncheon (chapter XIII), is the last gasp of the Maule-moon wizardry. A new and changed generation – a 'new breed,' almost – will now have its way. These youngsters, we realize, typify their forebears in a new guise. The sunniness of Phoebe is the Pyncheon sunniness in gentle, feminine form. Her concerns are domestic, even angelic. She is pure, thrifty, and as warm-hearted as the blaze of a domestic fire; she is more like the Maules in her creativity than like the Pyncheons. Holgrave, for his part, softens the Maule's artisan-wizard virility with the intellectuality and love of art of Alice Pyncheon. Though his career has been checkered and impulsive, he emerges as 'the cool observer'; his talent is not house-building but 'making pictures' out of sunshine with a camera – an up-to-date version of the mirror.

The resolution of the conflict of the *Seven Gables* thus involves a change in sex of the protagonists. The blazing sun-gold masculinity of the old Colonel and the Judge become the domesticated sunshine of Phoebe's cheerful spirit; the dreamy music of Alice's harpsichord and the ineffectually effeminate love of beauty in Clifford join in the cool mascu-

III: The House of the Seven Gables

linity of Holgrave. Like the sun and moon of mythology, the strains of Pyncheon and Maule reveal opposed but related dangers. The sun-money-power-flame cluster of images produces the tyrant-father figure; the moon-talent-intellect-dream cluster produces the Maule wizards. The benign integration of these motifs – which is the integration of the self – is subtly summed up in a description which implies that the house and the Heart are closely related:

The moon, too, which had long been climbing overhead ... now began to shine out, broad and oval, in its middle pathway. These silvery beams were already powerful enough to change the character of the lingering daylight. They softened and embellished the aspect of the old house: although the shadows fell deeper into the angles of its many gables, and lay brooding under the projecting story, and within the half-open door. With the lapse of every moment, the garden grew more picturesque; the fruit-trees, shrubbery, and flower-bushes had a dark obscurity among them. The commonplace characteristics – which, at noontide, it seemed to have taken a century of sordid life to accumulate – were now transfigured by a charm of romance. A hundred mysterious years were whispering among the leaves, whenever the slight sea-breeze found its way thither and stirred them. Through the foliage that roofed the little summer-house the moonlight flickered to and fro, and fell silvery white on the dark floor, the table, and the circular bench, with a continual shift and play, according as the chinks and wayward crevices among the twigs admitted or shut out the glimmer.

So sweetly cool was the atmosphere, after all the feverish day, that the summer eve might be fancied as sprinkling dews and liquid moonlight, with a dash of icy temper in them, out of a silver vase. Here and there, a few drops of this freshness were scattered on a human heart, and gave it youth again, and sympathy with the eternal youth of nature. The artist chanced to be one on whom the reviving influence fell. It made him feel – what he sometimes almost forgot,

141

thrust so early as he had been into the rude struggle of man with man – how youthful he still was. (C, II, 254–55)

The pattern of *Seven Gables*, then, is fundamentally related to the quest pattern of the mythological tales, though here the conflict extends over a period of seven generations before the mercurial hero can claim his authority in the material world. The prize is clearly Holgrave's and Phoebe's matrimonial understanding, which resembles the innocent love of a new Adam and Eve. The endowment of the Eastern land is inconsequential, as we shall see below; and Holgrave has renounced the wizard's web of magic for a human magic – the sorcery of Love.

But what is the meaning of Uncle Venner and his farm, and what about the vast tract of Eastern land? Uncle Venner, in terms of Hawthorne's mythological symbolism, is the benign aspect of the tyrant-father – the deposed father who, like King Aegeus, gives all to youth. He is the venerable father figure who says to Phoebe: 'I thought of you both, as we came down the street, and beheld Alice's Posies in full bloom. And so the flower of Eden has bloomed, likewise, in this old, darksome house to-day.' (C, II, 308)[4]

And the Eastern land? It is, apparently, America, or the part of New England that escaped Puritan domination – at once the lavish dream of the Pyncheons and the secret which the Maules withheld until the European aristocrats were

4 At the close of the romance, Phoebe insists that Uncle Venner share his old age with herself and Holgrave, Clifford and Hepzibah. In this New England myth he is an inconsequential figure because he denies all of the iron Puritan virtues. As we expect, he is dear to Clifford, for he is the only person 'whose wisdom has not a drop of bitter essence at the bottom!' (C, II, 317).

levelled and ready to accept it. This problem suggests the second meaning of the romance. Hawthorne is at pains to make clear that the old Colonel is in close touch with Protestant King William. He is an Englishman who will exploit the Eastern land ruthlessly. Gervayse Pyncheon, although an American, affects a European name. He wants the Eastern land only for its wealth. He is even willing to sacrifice his daughter's imaginative gifts to the vengeful Maules for the gold which will enable him to rival European gentlemen. Significantly, Gervayse is an eighteenth-century colonial whose only claim upon European high society is his wealth. When his hopes of extravagant wealth are frustrated, he gives place to his hideous and money-grubbing grand-nephew, Jaffrey, the spirit of nineteenth-century New England (the domestic baron whose family dissipates abroad). But Jaffrey, Hawthorne implies, is no more capable of possessing the Eastern land than was Gervayse, for the Eastern land is now in the possession of a sturdy society of native Americans, and the wealth which Jaffrey might hope to gain from it is an illusion – a *reality* in the best sense – of Clifford's imagination (C, II, 242). Clifford has discovered long since the secret of the concealed chamber behind the Colonel's portrait. Ironically, he fails to regard the deed as commercially valuable; for him it is an imaginative land of castles and dominions, the antithesis of the commercial empire for which the Colonel hoped (C, II, 316). Holgrave too, in a practical but unavaricious way, knows the secret. The Pyncheons 'bartered their Eastern territory' for a bitter supremacy over Maule's 'garden-ground.' The mystery of the Eastern land is thus seen to be the conflict of European 'colonialism' – which wished to hold the so-called 'East

Indian' territory in vassalage – with the native creativity of humble colonists who wished to make it a 'garden-ground.' The Puritans and their eighteenth-century commercial heirs failed to appreciate the indigenous value of the place: the natives, over all opposition and tyranny, finally made it their own. In these terms, the 'secret' of the Eastern land disappears in the achieved dream of democracy; it is a free land over which the now united Pyncheons and Maules will not struggle.

One question remains: how is the House of the Seven Gables itself the 'monster' or central problem of the romance? Why is there so much talk about stone houses as opposed to wooden houses or birds' nests? Why, for example, does Clifford deliver his oracular discourse on houses during his train trip (his momentary identification with progress)? Here, it is clear, we have Hawthorne's most complex poetic statement about three things: the self, the relation of past and present, and the relation of England and America. Each self, as we have seen in the mythological tales, must supplant and re-integrate the forces of the parents – not by overthrowing the father but by superseding him, as Cadmus does. The individual must, moreover, discover, as Holgrave the artist does, the meaning of the past – of his own posterity of seven generations – and make this meaning relevant to the problems of the present.[5]

For Hawthorne, this discovery inevitably involved an

5 That is, the dead past is *dead* until the imagination comprehends its relevance. This is exactly the problem which Hawthorne set himself in the mythological tales. The 'seven' gables of the New England house suggest the same need to overcome a long past by understanding it.

understanding of the relation of America to England. In the colonial phase of the *Seven Gables* story this meant the inflexible, greedy opposition of Colonel Pyncheon and Matthew Maule; in eighteenth-century dress it meant the Europeanized fop's bartering away of all spiritual value for the crass, not-to-be-spoken-of wealth which would buy his European success; in the nineteenth century it meant the abandonment of all European pretensions and the marriage of the forces of wealth and power to the now educated native imagination. The marriage of Holgrave and Phoebe, then, is America's attainment of mature independence. The opposition of Maule's Well and the Pyncheon mansion have merged in the democratic unity of the descendants of two lines, native and foreign, and the Eastern land has become the reality of the new republic. The House of the Seven Gables, dark symbol of English (and Puritan) repression of the native imagination (Maule's Well) is abandoned for a new residence – a residence which will last not for seven but for one generation. In this new era America will rediscover itself from generation to generation.

This is Hawthorne's seven-gabled myth of the self, of progress, and of America. It is not to be repeated. In artistic terms we may find it badly over-written – gauded out with rhetoric and inflated with unnecessary repetitions. But its meaning, despite its involution, is coherent. Hawthorne said what he wanted to say. The aftermath of this statement is recorded in *The Blithedale Romance* and *The Marble Faun*; its foreword is *The Scarlet Letter*. We shall now turn to *The Blithedale Romance*, the tale which came between Hawthorne's two excursions into the realms of Greek mythology.

Hawthorne as Myth-Maker

THE BLITHEDALE ROMANCE

The Blithedale Romance is the most ambitious and sophisticated of Hawthorne's major romances, and apparently the least successful. Critics have found its narrative pattern so difficult that in the *Hawthorne Centenary Essays* Robert C. Elliott writes: 'it has seemed to most readers that *The Blithedale Romance* suffers from a radical incoherence. Even the greatest ingenuity cannot bring into meaningful relation the Veiled Lady-Fauntleroy-Westervelt business with the thematic interests of the work.'[6] The difficulty, perhaps, is that critics have not taken seriously Hawthorne's statement in the Preface that he is not writing about Brook Farm, and that he has not the 'slightest pretensions' to study socialism or pass judgment on it. He has used Blithedale 'merely to establish a theatre ... where the creatures of his brain may play their phantasmagorical antics'; he hopes to produce 'an atmosphere of strange enchantment, beheld through which the inhabitants have a propriety of their own' (C, III, 1). *Blithedale*, in short, is a symbolic work, an American myth.

Hawthorne repeatedly draws attention to the mythical aspect of the narrative: Zenobia talks of the 'pastoral' which the colonists are 'playing out'; Coverdale speaks of himself as an 'allegorical figure,' or as the 'chorus' in a tragedy; and he and Hollingsworth are 'mythical personages.' Zenobia is a queen or princess; Priscilla is diaphanous and ethereal – a sprite, a nymph, or a wraith; and Old Moodie, whose face is rarely seen directly, is a shadow who appears and vanishes unaccountably. Moreover, Hawthorne's technique adds to the 'atmosphere of strange enchantment.' He pre-

6 P. 113.

146

sents a May Day pageant, an autumn masque, a seance, and two interpolated tales – the legends of the Veiled Lady and Fauntleroy – which are as integral to the action as the story of Alice Pyncheon is to the action of *Seven Gables*. Again and again the episodes of the action are described as 'scenes' or 'tableaux.' And, finally, the whole action is set in the past: twelve years after the event the ineffectual soldier, 'Miles' Coverdale, tells the story of an abortive quest to establish 'the one true system' – a quest from which there is no triumphant return, and no prize but the hero's sombre awareness that: 'the good we aim at will not be attained. People never do get just the good they seek. If it come at all, it is something elsc, which they never dreamed of, and did not particularly want.' (C, III, 75–76)

Before studying in detail the events which bring Coverdale to this stoical role of tragic witness, we must consider the overt themes or subjects of the romance. First, as in Hawthorne's other romances, the title image is most important: Blithedale is to be a utopian community, planned by 'a knot of visionaries,' in which people of all convictions and talents will find a new life – a life in which social classes do not exist, in which all will be united by a common bond of toil, and all rewarded by mutually shared pleasures. It is a political experiment, and as A. N. Kaul has pointed out, it involves 'an extension of the Puritan tradition';[7] in *The Scarlet Letter* and a number of the historical tales Hawthorne described the failure of the pilgrims' utopian quest; but that quest was renewed in political form with the establishment of the republic. Blithedale, then, with its 'written constitution,' is an image of the ideal hopes of the

7 *Hawthorne: A Collection of Critical Essays*, pp. 153–154.

founding fathers for a regenerate community. The action of the romance deals with the crumbling of those hopes, in part because the Puritan tradition – now secular and materialistic – thinks of the state not as an instrument for social regeneration but as an institution for the reform of criminals. But such utopian enterprises, however unsuccessful, are in Coverdale's view essential:

> let us acknowledge it wiser, if not more sagacious, to follow one's day-dream to its natural consummation, although, if the vision have been worth the having, it is certain never to be consummated otherwise than by a failure. And what of that? Its airiest fragments, impalpable as they may be, will possess a value that lurks not in the most ponderous realities of any practicable scheme ... therefore, let it be reckoned neither among my sins nor follies that I once had faith and force enough to form generous hopes of the world's destiny, – yes! – and to what in me lay for their accomplishment. (C, III, 10)

We must follow our dreams even though human imperfection may always put their realization beyond reach.

But there are specific problems which contribute to Blithedale's failure. Hawthorne's second theme or subject is misguided reformers and philanthropists. The man who sacrifices all to a single purpose or *idée fixe* is a danger to society, not its benefactor. As Coverdale tells Hollingsworth: ' "The besetting sin of a philanthropist, it appears to me, is apt to be moral obliquity ... He is tempted to palter with the right, and can scarcely forbear persuading himself that the importance of his public ends renders it allowable to throw aside his private conscience." ' (C, III, 132) Third, Hawthorne gives us a variety of direct statements on the rights or place of women in society. These range from

148

III: The Blithedale Romance

Zenobia's passionate feminism to Priscilla's extreme sub-
servience; and from Hollingsworth's Miltonic concept –
' "Her place is at man's side. Her office, that of sympathizer;
the unreserved, unquestioning believer" ' (C, III, 122) – to
Coverdale's liberal view: ' "I would give her all she asks,
and add a great deal more, which she will not be the party
to demand, but which men, if they were generous and wise,
would grant of their own free motion" ' (C, III, 121).

These materials – the political concept of Blithedale, the
question of reform, and the subject of women's rights – are
easily accessible. But what of the action itself? When
Coverdale sees Priscilla, Zenobia, and Westervelt in Boston,
he reflects: 'There now needed only Hollingsworth and Old
Moodie to complete the knot of characters, whom a real
intricacy of events, greatly assisted by my method of in-
sulating them from other relations, had kept so long upon
my mental stage, as actors in a drama' (C, III, 156). The
best approach to understanding this 'intricacy of events' is
to retell the story in chronological order, and to stand far
enough back from the characters to see them as representative or typical forces which 'play out' the drama of Blithedale. Again, the image patterns of the Greek myths will be
helpful in suggesting the meaning of Hawthorne's maskers.

The history begins with Fauntleroy, a shallow millionaire
from 'a Middle State' who sires a very beautiful daughter,
Zenobia (the name means 'having life from Jupiter'). At
that period his life 'seemed to have crystallized itself into an
external splendor, wherewith he glittered in the eyes of the
world, and had no other life than upon this gaudy surface'
(C, III, 182). But Fauntleroy lost his wealth, committed
a crime involving money, and fled north to New England:

149

'Being a mere image, an optical delusion, created by the sunshine of prosperity, it was his law to vanish into the shadow of the first intervening cloud' (C, III, 183). Zenobia, a wilful, over-indulged child, though greatly gifted, was adopted by a wealthy 'uncle,' and was rumoured to have made an imprudent marriage. In Boston the much-chastened, poverty-stricken Fauntleroy, now known as Old Moodie, remarries and produces a second child, the ethereal and clairvoyant Priscilla, the solace and support of his old age. Father and daughter are alike shadowy figures; Moodie wears an eye-patch, and seldom seems to speak directly to anybody. He tells the frail Priscilla long tales of her glorious half-sister, and Priscilla, whose 'life was one of love,' dreams of nothing but meeting this beautiful heiress.

A few months before the events of chapter I, a sinister but handsome stranger visits Old Moodie's quarters in the mansion of a former colonial governor, and in a short time this wizard begins a series of public seances with a Veiled Lady, Priscilla, now 'inthralled in an intolerable bondage, from which she must either free herself or perish.' The wizard is Westervelt, and Coverdale learns in one of his moments of eavesdropping that Zenobia is linked to him in some 'miserable bond' – perhaps marriage.

On the eve of Coverdale's departure for Blithedale, Old Moodie approaches him to ask a favour, but decides that 'some older gentleman' or a lady might serve his purpose better. Coverdale recommends Hollingsworth. The favour, we learn later on, was to conduct Priscilla to Blithedale, and to protect her there. But Moodie wants further guarantees of Priscilla's safety; he summons Zenobia to the city, hints that he might claim all her wealth as his brother's rightful heir, but concludes: 'Keep all your wealth, but with only this one condition: Be kind – be no less kind than sisters are – to my poor Priscilla!' Weeks later, when Moodie visits the colony, he sees that Zenobia and Priscilla are less like sisters than like lady and servant, and shakes his staff threateningly.

Why, one wonders, should Hawthorne have created such an elaborate background for Zenobia and Priscilla? And why should he have presented it in the mysterious and oblique manner of chapters I and XXII? The answer is either that he was not in control of his materials, or that he was deliberately sketching in a symbolic or mythical background which he regarded as essential to his 'drama.' The second answer, I believe, is demonstrably the correct one. As myth, the pattern of events summarized above suggests that Fauntleroy-Moodie is a kind of god, and that Hawthorne, as in the Pandora story, is constructing a special version of the Creation and the Fall. Q. D. Leavis has identified Moodie with Odin, the 'prime mover,' complete with eye-patch and staff; but this 'deity' is peculiarly western and modern. Perhaps enough has been said above about the immateriality of this double-faced spirit who lives in a blaze of sunshine or in deep New England shadow. In his first incarnation in another time and place he lived for the senses and material things alone, and created the exotic Zenobia. Hawthorne compares her to a gorgeously nude Eve (C, III, 17), and to the primal woman, Pandora, 'fresh from Vulcan's workshop, and full of the celestial warmth by dint of which he had tempered and moulded her' (C, III, 24).

Her talisman is an exotic jewelled flower, reminiscent of
Beatrice Rappaccini's 'sister' flowers and the peculiar, jewel-
like blossoms that Proserpina plucked; her quality in Coverdale's summation is 'a passionate intensity' (C, III, 102).
Fauntleroy, in short, is a pagan spirit, and his first daughter,
conceived and loved in pride, is wilful but not evil. Moodie,
by contrast, is a much-diminished spirit dwelling in the
ruins of the colonial governor's house with a purely spiritual
second daughter conceived in love and sorrow; this 'angel,'
far from living in the wealth and splendour of Zenobia,
fashions beautifully embroidered little purses, the emblem
or talisman of her poverty.

But these two women have been plagued by a Black Man
who long ago enslaved the Eve-like Zenobia, and now
attempts in the modern guise of mesmerist to corrupt the
immaculate Priscilla. A leading issue of the drama, then, is
whether the 'snow-maiden' Priscilla can be saved. And can
Zenobia be set free of her ancient guilt? The great opportunity for their salvation which Moodie seizes upon is to
send Priscilla to Blithedale where she and Zenobia will be
true and loving sisters. That is, the god Fauntleroy-Moodie,
will endow the new society (the ideal American republic)
with one woman who represents the gifts of wealth, beauty,
passion, and intellect, and another who represents purity,
simplicity, naturalness, and love. How will they be received
in the utopian community?

The events that grow out of this background constitute
the main action of *The Blithedale Romance*. Before turning
to them, however, we must consider Coverdale and Hollingsworth, the two other actors or 'forces' who join the
Blithedale experiment. Coverdale is the only one of Haw-

thorne's major heroes who tells his own story; as his name suggests, he is aloof and even mysterious – an intellectual, mercurial figure who thought the prize of Blithedale worth the winning. He possesses the masculine clairvoyance and artistic temperament of Holgrave to whom he is imaginatively related; he moves about in search of the truth of events, observing but often unobserved; and he fears that his activities may 'unhumanize' his heart. Coverdale's brave hopes are frustrated in part by Hollingsworth, whom Hawthorne presents quite explicitly as the nineteenth-century incarnation of his Puritan ancestors. The money-sun-flame-iron images which cluster about such mythological figures as Pelias, Polydectes, Aeetes – and 'Governor' Jaffrey Pyncheon – are very much his images, though in nursing Coverdale he reveals a tenderness and sympathy that the tyrant fathers lack. Before coming to Blithedale he was a blacksmith, and though not an orthodox Puritan he believes that man's nature is criminal and depraved – a view which finally persuades him that Blithedale should become an institution for criminal reform.

Against all evil omens, Coverdale set out in a 'pitiless snow-storm' which brought him to Blithedale, a world that 'looked like a lifeless copy of the world in marble' (C, III, 38). The shock of this change resulted in a serious cold from which he was at length reborn into a May-Day world of glowing hope. A leading reason for his optimism is Priscilla's acceptance in the community. Zenobia, at first cool, offers to be 'a duenna' to her (C, III, 77), and the child becomes exuberantly sunny, tanned, and joyful. The colonists even make her their May-queen (C, III, 61). Priscilla, it is clear, may be transformed from a pale and almost bodiless spirit into a woman with the domestic charm and gaiety of Phoebe Pyncheon. Hence Coverdale's nascent affection for her: her smile is 'a wondrous novelty'; her shortcomings affect him 'with a kind of playful pathos, which was as absolutely bewitching a sensation as ever I experienced.' Priscilla is the potentially sunny and creative personality who could give the coolly observant artist the contact with humanity that he so sorely needs.

But Coverdale will not gain this flesh-and-blood Harmonia, for fundamental oppositions developed at Blithedale. In a scene at Eliot's Pulpit, Zenobia argues that Priscilla, in her passivity, is ' "the type of womanhood, such as man has spent centuries in making," ' and that man ' "is never content unless he can degrade himself by stooping towards what he loves." ' Hollingsworth replies that ' "woman is a monster – and, thank Heaven, an almost impossible and hitherto imaginary monster [like Medusa?] – without man as her acknowledged principal!" ' This view, Coverdale feels, betrays an egotism that 'centered everything in itself, and deprived woman of her very soul ... Hollingsworth had boldly uttered what he, and millions of despots like him, really felt.' And astonishingly, Zenobia, for the moment at least, accepts Hollingsworth's verdict.

Later, ironically while mending a stone wall, Coverdale and Hollingsworth reveal the fundamental opposition of their views. Hollingsworth discloses his contempt for the 'wretched, unsubstantial scheme' of Blithedale (C, III, 130). He attempts to enlist Coverdale in his philanthropic programme, but Coverdale rejects the monomaniac's plan: 'I saw in his scheme of philanthropy nothing but what was odious. A loathsomeness that was to be forever in my daily work! A great black ugliness of sin, which he proposed to collect out of a thousand human hearts, and that we should spend our lives in an experiment of transmuting it into virtue!' (C, III, 134)

Equally disastrous are the mysterious events involving Westervelt. It appears that this Black Man who has haunted woman throughout Christian history cannot be kept out of Blithedale. He meets Zenobia in the community's Arcadian forest and demands that she fling Priscilla off, but Zenobia replies: 'she loves me, and I will not fail her.' Westervelt then threatens Zenobia, but whatever the threat, Coverdale decides to keep it secret. Shortly after, Zenobia tells her legend of the Veiled Lady. This tale, in the anecdote of Theodore, makes the point that men must have perfect faith in the purity and goodness of woman's nature if they are to win her. It also hints that the Veiled Lady is the 'maiden, pale and shadowy, [who] rose up amid a knot of visionary people, who were seeking for the better life'; the Veiled Lady is Priscilla. And finally the legend suggests that this gentle creature will blight all of Zenobia's prospects, 'In love, in worldly fortune, in all ... pursuit of happiness,' unless she returns to Westervelt's service.

That Priscilla does indeed return to Westervelt is the most perplexing of all the events of the romance, for we know that she is terrified of him: at the end of 'The Silvery Veil' story she almost faints away; and when Coverdale asks whether she came to town of her own free will she replies: 'I never have any free will.' She soon discloses, however, when asked whether Hollingsworth knows of her whereabouts, that 'He bade me come.' But what could Hollingsworth's motives have been, as Priscilla's avowed

155

protector? And how could Zenobia have connived at the betrayal? The best evidence we have to go on appears in the last great scene between the three ('The Three Together'); again Hawthorne is oblique, but the following reconstruction is possible. Zenobia, infatuated with the reformer, agrees to support his projected community for the reform of criminals; but she fears Priscilla's submissive charm, and perhaps fears equally that Westervelt will reveal the past that lies behind her pseudonym 'Zenobia.' In the blindness of passion, then, she decides to deliver up Priscilla to Westervelt; and Hollingsworth shares her terrible guilt by sanctioning the betrayal and directing Priscilla to go. He has placed his selfish dream of power above his sacred moral duty. Then, gnawed by conscience, he traces Westervelt and rescues his Veiled Lady. The ubiquitous Coverdale witnesses this scene, and believes religiously that 'she had kept ... her virgin reserve and sanctity of soul throughout it all' (C, III, 203).

When Coverdale discovers the three together (chapter xxv), Zenobia tells him that she has just been on trial for her life. Hollingsworth, looking like 'the grim portrait of a Puritan magistrate holding inquest of life and death in a case of witchcraft,' has apparently condemned her self-righteously for betraying Priscilla. And since Zenobia has just lost her fortune (did the angry Moodie claim it after all?) the reformer is casting her off altogether. In one of the best passages in all of Hawthorne, she asks her tormentor: ' "Are you a man, No; but a monster! A cold, heartless, self-beginning and self-ending piece of mechanism!" ' Then she continues: ' "It is all self! ... Nothing else; nothing but self, self, self! The fiend, I doubt not, has made his choicest mirth of you these seven years past, and especially in the

mad summer which we have spent together." ' (C, III, 218)
In her view, Hollingsworth is the real criminal: he has
'aimed a death-blow ... at this scheme of a purer and higher
life'; he has ruthlessly thrown away Coverdale; he now
discards Zenobia, 'a broken tool'; but his blackest sin is that
he stifled down his inmost consciousness – ' "you were ready
to sacrifice this girl, whom, if God ever visibly showed a
purpose, He put into your charge, and through whom He
was striving to redeem you!" ' Zenobia, even in her extremity, is able to admit that Hollingsworth was not always
evil; instead, ' "a great and rich heart has been ruined in
your breast." ' Of her own guilt, she can only say to Priscilla: ' "I never wished you harm. You stood between me
and an end which I desired. I wanted a clear path. No
matter what I meant. It is over now. Do you forgive me?" '
(C, III, 220)

Priscilla *can* forgive, but the dream of Blithedale is over;
there is no prize to be won in this quest, for the Puritan
egotism has effectively rejected both the passionate gifts of
one of Old Moodie's daughters, and the mercurial gifts of
insight possessed by Coverdale. Wedded to the guilt-ridden
man of iron, there is little chance that Priscilla will fulfil
the sunny promise of her first weeks at Blithedale. The
season has come to autumn, and Coverdale, the nineteenth-
century dilettante-poet can only stand by to witness, as
Hamlet does, the tragedy of the human condition.

But perhaps the ending of this history of the American
experiment in its post-revolutionary phase is not entirely
gloomy. In Priscilla a new kind of woman has emerged –
an immaculate, spiritual woman, untainted by the Black
Man; and she has inherited Zenobia's talismanic flower.

157

Hawthorne's new heroine, then, will possess both passion and spirituality; she will be an American Harmonia. And Coverdale, though he does not win Priscilla, has not lost all faith in quests. He hopes for a 'cause' that will command his measured enthusiasm – in Hungary, in Africa – anywhere, though he is unlikely to embark on the quest as a younger hero might. But meanwhile he has accomplished one important thing: he has written a true account of Blithedale. At the close of *The Scarlet Letter* Dimmesdale was able to reveal his vision of the human condition, though only at the point of death, and to an audience that failed to comprehend his meaning. In nineteenth-century America Coverdale is free to tell his story and publish it. Again, perhaps, his audience will not comprehend, but the artist has at least spoken. It may be for this reason that Hawthorne chose a first-person narrator. Everybody ridicules Coverdale, including himself, but he is finally the one who gets at the truth; his romance is a 'criticism' in the sense that T. S. Eliot has used that word in comparing Hawthorne with Emerson.

THE MARBLE FAUN

I shall be less prolix over *The Marble Faun*, the romance which troubled Hawthorne and mystified its early readers. Between large chunks of guide-book description, unremitting moralizing, and exfoliating emblematic symbolism, the romance is so over-blown that Harry Levin discusses it in *Hawthorne Centenary Essays* in tones of faint mockery. Certainly Hawthorne's notebook material is used immoderately, though not irrelevantly: instead of finding a few apposite pictures which he can use as meaningfully as

III: The Marble Faun

he does Coverdale's 'hermitage' or Westervelt's wood-path at Blithedale, he multiplies descriptions in a manner that obscures rather than deepens his statement. In the same way, such vivid emblems as Zenobia's exotic flower decline here to endless allusions to Hilda's doves and tower – images which function organically in the tale, but strike us at once as laboured, ornate, and obtrusive. Yet, whatever its awkwardness, the book is true to Hawthorne's personal myth: he knew what he had to say and said it, however asymetrically and obliquely.

Hawthorne specifically relates the story of Miriam and Donatello to the fall of Adam and Eve, but the revelry in the Borghese 'Garden' (another of the symbolic masques which Hawthorne was so skilful in creating) suggests 'the Golden Age come back again' for an hour, rather than Eden; and though the 'friar's' influence over Miriam recalls demonic 'beasts and reptiles,' his death suggests that Hawthorne's attitude towards the Fall was as unorthodox as his interpretation of Greek myth. Criticism has had great difficulty in dealing with this Roman parable of the Fall, and with the passages of speculation which suggest that it may have been fortunate – a *felix culpa*. The leading reasons are that Hawthorne's theme has regularly been described as 'the fall of man into evil'; and the related assumption that he shares the view of Kenyon and Hilda who 'decisively reject the notion of the Fortunate Fall.'[8] The mythology which we have been reconstructing, however, suggests that Hawthorne is little interested in the origin of evil; he does not believe in the real existence of Satan, and he is not interested in metaphysical speculations

8 Hyatt Waggoner, *Hawthorne: A Critical Study*, p. 198.

on the question. Evil is a *donnée*. But he is deeply concerned that women are traditionally held responsible for the Fall; and in the tales of Pandora, Proserpina, and Beatrice Rappaccini he is at pains to show that women are innocent, or at least no more culpable than men. In *Blithedale* he reveals Zenobia's past as erring rather than deliberately evil, and he produces a New England-born woman, Priscilla, who remains immaculate. *The Marble Faun* continues this study in Europe, the source of America's culture, by exploring three things: the initiation of a European 'faun' into the world of experience; the role of the Roman Catholic Church in institutionalizing or ritualizing the facts of human imperfection and goodness; and the symbolic initiation of Kenyon and Hilda, two immaculate Americans who are humanized by the European spectacle and return safely to New England.

Our recognition of Zenobia's status as Eve or the 'primal woman' Pandora, helps us to understand Miriam's identity. Miriam is an artist who is mysteriously connected with aristocrats or people high in the church. She paints such subjects as Judith and Holofernes – virtuous women triumphing over lustful men; and she resembles the pathetic Beatrice Cenci, who took a terrible revenge on her incestuous father. A threatening cousin whom Miriam had refused to marry haunts her studio and stalks her in the catacombs under the city of God. He now wears a friar's habit, and has practiced 'severe and self-inflicted penance' for unspecified sins. Miriam, in short, is another full-length portrait of Hawthorne's Dark Lady, haunted by the Black Man of the Judaeo-Christian tradition. Appropriately, her

160

origins are English, Jewish, and Italian – the races whose religions (Protestant, Judaic, and Roman Catholic) have treated woman as the devil's accomplice. But she asserts her innocence, and Kenyon believes her: ' "No; you were innocent," replied the sculptor. "I shudder at the fatality that seems to haunt your footsteps, and throws a shadow of crime about your path, you being guiltless." ' (VI, 486)

Unlike Zenobia, however, Miriam finds a champion, Donatello – a fanciful anachronism from the unfallen 'state of nature,' elaborately described by Hawthorne as 'Monte Beni.' For such a 'natural man' there is no such thing as evil in a theological sense; his instinct to protect and preserve a loved one is natural. Thus when Miriam's persecutor appears in the garden, Donatello's response is simply to attempt to destroy him. But this is not the Golden Age; it is the Christian era, and the Faun finds himself ineluctably caught in a web of guilt and suffering. 'All nature shrinks from me, and shudders at me!' he cries. 'I live in the middle of a curse, that hems me round with a circle of fire!'[9]

Moreover – and this brings us to the question of the Roman church – Donatello has not really destroyed the Black Man. The corpse, garbed as a Capucin, confronts the guilty couple in a church they visit, and they learn that he will not be permanently buried; his bones will eventually be exhumed and placed on indefinite public display. That is, in the Christian church, western society has created an institution in which the devil will always be alive, so to

9 (VI, 288) The chapter titled 'Myths' in which this passage occurs finds Hawthorne at his mythological best, as compared with the less satisfactory chapter on Fauntleroy in *Seven Gables*.

161

speak – always a reality. But his dark power will be countered by a benign father, a figure whose temporal emblem in this romance is the statue of Pope Julius the Third in Perugia. The church recognizes man's imperfection and knows that he must suffer for it, but – unlike the Puritan faith – promises him an opportunity to work out his own salvation. The Roman's God is not a God of wrath who condemns the unregenerate to eternal flames.

Much has been written about Hawthorne's ambivalent attitude towards the church of Rome. Certainly in their colder moods both Kenyon and Hawthorne see it as a worldly and corrupt institution.[10] But Hawthorne suggests in *The Scarlet Letter* that the Madonna-like mother who attended Hester's trial might have sympathized with the adultress; Coverdale says to Zenobia: ' "I have always envied the Catholics their faith in that sweet, sacred Virgin Mother, who stands between them and the Deity, intercepting somewhat of his awful splendor, but permitting his love to stream upon the worshipper more intelligibly to human comprehension through the medium of a woman's tenderness" ' (C, III, 121–22). Hilda, longing for confession, wonders whether 'the faith in which I was born and bred be perfect, if it leave a weak girl like me to wander, desolate, with this great trouble crushing me down?' (VI, 404) She admires Catholicism for 'the exuberance with which it adapts itself to all the demands of human infirmity.'

The essential fact, however, is that Hawthorne sees Roman Catholicism as a *European* pattern, the product of centuries of human weakness and need. Hilda can find

10 See Rudolph Von Abele's extravagant comments in *The Death of the Artist* (The Hague, 1955), pp. 94–96.

solace and safety in this communion, but she cannot join it. In Perugia, the majestic statue of Pope Julius bends down upon Miriam and Donatello, 'this guilty and repentant pair [,] its visage of grand benignity ... Miriam, Donatello, and the sculptor, all three imagined that they beheld the bronze pontiff endowed with spiritual life. A blessing was felt descending upon them from his outstretched hand; he approved by look and gesture the pledge of a deep union that had passed under his auspices.' (VI, 371) The European Adam and Eve, then, will suffer and find solace within the patterns developed by European religion and culture: Donatello will go to prison, and Miriam will know the anguish of sorrow and loss; but, finally, their crime expiated, they may be reunited.

Miriam clearly sees her own and her lover's suffering as a necessary and valuable spiritual experience, and so does Hawthorne. As he presents the Fall in the story of Pandora, the state of innocence is finally a state of boredom; the garden was in a literal sense a paradise of children, for the innocent state is unreflective; it consists of 'too sunny realities,' and of prohibitions which the innocents must obey but not necessarily understand. But for Hawthorne the state of self-awareness or vision is the goal of human experience. Thus Miriam seriously entertains the idea of the Fortunate Fall:

'Was the crime – in which he and I were wedded – was it a blessing, in that strange disguise? Was it a means of education, bringing a simple and imperfect nature to a point of feeling and intelligence which it could have reached under no other discipline? ... Was that very sin, – into which Adam precipitated himself and all his race, – was it the destined means by which, over a long pathway of toil and sorrow, we are to attain a higher, brighter, and profounder happiness, than our lost birthright gave? Will not this idea account for the permitted existence of sin, as no other theory can?' (VI, 491)

This is the lesson which European experience seems to teach; this is the way of the Old World.

But where do the pristine representatives of the New World, Kenyon and Hilda, fit into this vision of human imperfection? Unlike the 'natural man' and his 'primal woman,' they have not shared in the original sin committed on the Tarpeian Rock, yet they are stained by it, in common with their European friends, and they are forced irrevocably to recognize the existence of evil and to come to terms with it. Here again Hawthorne invokes the mythical pattern of *Seven Gables* and *Blithedale*. The sin of Kenyon and Hilda, the progeny of America (where the letter of the moral law, even in the 1850s, is more important than its merciful intention), is their lack of sympathy. They resemble Holgrave and Phoebe of *Seven Gables*, but Kenyon lives in a cold 'world of marble,' and Hilda, with her 'dove-like' purity and ivory-tower virginity, is completely out of touch with the warm realities which make Phoebe a domestic angel. As Northrop Frye has suggested, the cloud of doves which surrounds Hilda links her, in the most innocent possible way, to Venus,[11] but her 'tower' suggests that she lives only in the pure realm of air, cut off from the squalid realities of the city below. She looks at painted imitations of life and copies them. Late in the action Miriam tells Kenyon directly of his and Hilda's moral failure: ' "I thought of revealing [my secret] ... to you ... on one occasion, especially, – it

11 See Northrop Frye, *Anatomy of Criticism*, p. 137.

164

III: The Marble Faun

was after you had shown me your Cleopatra; it seemed to leap out of my heart, and got as far as my very lips. But finding you cold to accept my confidence, I thrust it back again. Had I obeyed my first impulse, all would have turned out differently." ' (VI, 489) What Kenyon and Hilda must learn, then, is to sympathize, not judge; and evil is their teacher.

The beginnings of this humanizing process in Kenyon and Hilda occur in the long central sections of the romance. Kenyon accompanies the fallen Donatello to his native home, Monte Beni, and observes at first hand the progress of his modern Adam. As Donatello learns to climb the 'dismal stairway' of Monte Beni's tower to a level of knowledge at which the promptings of natural instinct are subordinated to a moral vision, Kenyon is touched by his suffering and grief. Abandoning the cold marble which had been his favourite sculptural medium, he strives to model from clay an expressive image of Donatello. At length, after a secret meeting with Miriam, he agrees to work actively towards a reunion of the unfortunate sinners, and sets out with Donatello on a journey to Perugia. Symbolically, they travel through rugged country along tortuously winding roads witnessing scenes of poverty, selfishness, and ignorance which further enrich the understanding of both pilgrims. Kenyon, we realize, is like the triumphant Perseus; he would like to 'dwell forever' in the cold realm of marble and moonlight, remote from the affairs of earth. But his experience with Donatello and Miriam kindles in him a nascent willingness to identify himself with the real world.

Meanwhile, Hilda, splashed by the dark waves into which her European friends have plunged, can no longer return to her ideal world of art. She confesses her trouble to a priest at St. Peter's, and is comforted; but she does not belong in the Old World communion which serves Miriam and Donatello, and she is innocent of their sin. Nevertheless, she must somehow come to terms with the evil that has been revealed to her.

Kenyon and Hilda, then, are both ready to discover the full implications of what it means to be human, but exactly *how* does this discovery occur? Readers from Henry James on have been baffled by the mysterious events of the last six chapters, in which the American lovers temporarily lose each other and then achieve a permanent reunion. Here the mythological quest tales are again of help.

In a visit to Kenyon's studio Hilda becomes aware of the transformation of Donatello from innocence to manhood when she sees Kenyon's bust of the faun. She is similarly struck by the statue of Cleopatra (Pandora, Eve), a symbol of the warm though erring humanity of Miriam. This new awareness leads Hilda to abandon her tower and disappear into the real world, carrying with her a packet of papers entrusted to her by Miriam. In this positive act of friendship, she acknowledges her connection with her fallen friends. The virgin's lamp, emblem of the super-human ideal of virtue which Hilda has worshipped, is extinguished, and the doves, which similarly suggest a goddess rather than a human being, fly away. Like Proserpina, Hilda has descended into the underworld of darkness. When she delivers Miriam's secret packet she is forcibly detained by the persons who receive it. She was ' "in such kindly custody of pious maidens," ' she explains, ' "and watched over by such a dear old priest, that – had it not been for one or two

166

disturbing recollections, and also because I am a daughter of the Puritans – I could willingly have dwelt there forever." ' (VI, 526) This is magnificently ironic. The Roman church introduces Puritanical Hilda to the awareness of her full nature – of adult responsibility in a fallen world. Like Proserpina, she grows up; she will return, as Miriam says, 'perhaps tenderer than she was' (VI, 485). When she does finally emerge from her labyrinthine experience, she is ready to join the human carnival, for she is a woman.

Kenyon, seeing Hilda's lamp go out, realizes at last the full irresponsibility of his withdrawal from warm, human contact. The knowledge that he may have lost Hilda awakens his emotions fully: he leaves his marble world behind and seeks his loved one in the marketplace of erring humanity. Distracted by doubt and fear, he obeys a mysterious summons and goes to an ancient burial ground on the Campagna. He is accompanied by a frolicsome buffalo-calf which, 'Kenyon half fancied, was serving him as a guide, like the heifer that led Cadmus to the site of his destined city' (VI, 477). Descending into an excavated tomb to await his rendezvous, he discovers the fragments of a superb Venus in whose glorious nudity, says Hawthorne, 'we recognize womanhood ... without prejudice to its divinity' (VI, 480). This image of woman – earthy, pagan, and desirable, yet still divine – is the opposite of Kenyon's earlier view of Hilda as cold, spiritual, and unattainable. The outcome of this discovery, to which Miriam and Donatello have directed him, is that Kenyon is prepared to accept the *living* charms of Hilda. Miriam tells him where he must go if he wishes to rediscover his sweetheart.

At this point it becomes clear that Miriam and Donatello

167

are not merely passive forces in the education of Kenyon and Hilda. If the American innocents are to 'discover' themselves and each other, they must recognize that their fallen European friends are yet capable of love and concern for the happiness of others. Thus Kenyon cannot find his Hilda unless he trusts Miriam and Donatello; in return for this acceptance and trust, they reveal to him, through the image of the ancient Venus, the secret of physical love, and make it possible for him to find his transformed Hilda.

Then, at the end of the tale, Hawthorne gives us the most brilliant and frivolous of all of his allegorical masquerades – the wild Roman Carnival in celebration of the arrival of spring. Kenyon and Hilda's miasmic winter is over. They are about to find their real springtime. As Kenyon wanders through the crowd (Hawthorne is careful to suggest both its kaleidoscopic colour of life, and its labyrinthine confusion) he is approached by a 'gigantic female figure' whose comic amorous advances he repels: 'The rejected Titaness made a gesture of despair and rage; then suddenly drawing a huge pistol, she took aim right at the obdurate sculptor's breast, and pulled the trigger. The shot took effect, for the abominable plaything went off by a spring, like a boy's popgun, covering Kenyon with a cloud of limedust.' (VI, 504) In 'cowboy' terms, the old Kenyon is dead – a lime-whitened ghost, or a figure of marble. As he clings for support to a lamp post at the place at which Miriam had told him to wait, Hilda emerges on a balcony and throws a dewy rosebud which strikes his lips. The two are reunited, and Hawthorne – despite the pressures which forced him to add an explanatory Conclusion – refuses to reveal the meaning of his masque.

168

III: The Marble Faun

Like *Blithedale, The Marble Faun* is not a very happy or optimistic book. But if Hawthorne appears less assured about Kenyon and Hilda than he was about Holgrave and Phoebe, it is clear that he will not have his American heroes and heroines suffer the European fate. The New World lovers have been initiated into human imperfection through their contact with Miriam and Donatello; and their sympathies have been awakened – they have learned not to judge with Puritanical rigour. Moreover, they have not 'fallen' as Miriam and Donatello did; their initiation has been symbolic; they are as immaculate as Priscilla. Like Priscilla, who inherited Zenobia's jewelled flower, Hilda receives from Miriam a precious bracelet containing seven gems, symbol of the sad mystery she has learned to understand. Kenyon avows that his bride has 'softened out of the chillness of her virgin pride' (VI, 420); she will 'be enshrined and worshipped as a household saint, in the light of her husband's fireside' (VI, 521). But though Hilda 'had a hopeful soul, and saw sunlight on the mountain-tops' even for Miriam, one feels a genuine strain in the tone and treatment of the concluding chapters. The triumphant rebirth or 'return' of Kenyon and Hilda resembles the ending of one of the idealized quest myths rather than the close of a sombre tale of experience. Was Hawthorne, like Aylmer, hoping for the impossible? If the richness with which he rendered character is any indication of where his conviction lay, then one would surely conclude that he felt Miriam's story to be closer to the reality of experience. The longer Hawthorne lived, it would seem, the more difficult it became for him to visualize a convincingly happy ending to his American myth.

169

Hawthorne as Myth-Maker

The Marble Faun, nevertheless, marks a thematic progression from the statements of *Seven Gables, Blithedale,* and the mythological tales. It is another realization of Hawthorne's multi-dimensional theme, another face of his poetic *œuvre.* From the analysis of this, and the other 'contemporary' romances considered above, we must now turn to a study of *The Scarlet Letter,* the first major formulation of Hawthorne's myth, and to *Dr. Grimshawe's Secret,* its Kafka-esque twilight.

THE SCARLET LETTER

The point has perhaps been made that Hawthorne's mythological tales, 'these old baby stories,' are closer to the heart of his artistic vision than criticism has generally allowed. The iron men, Dark Ladies, mercurial heroes, and frail princesses of his idealized mythology have their sad relatives in the worlds of American and European experience. What, we must now ask, is their significance for Hawthorne's masterpiece, *The Scarlet Letter?* And what is their relation to those abortive romances with which Hawthorne struggled in the melancholy after-light of his career?

So much has been written about *The Scarlet Letter* that there can now be no question of dealing in detail with what criticism has said. The chief difficulty with many readings is that they fail to get beyond the explicit moral and psychological issues of the tale to see it as expressive action. A second difficulty is that critics do not always keep in mind that Hawthorne is studying the fate of the self in *Puritan America;* that the book is his analysis and critique of the colonial society which evolved, finally, into the stifling narrowness of 'The Custom House.' In one important sense the critics who focus on ideas and moral concepts are right: viewed as a moralized tale, the book does read as a definition of the Christian pattern of sin, its consequences and its expiation. But there are several problems which such analyses fail to resolve. First, if the book is simply a moral tale, then Pearl appears as an improbable and even fantastic creation whose final flight to Europe seems irrelevant. Second, Hawthorne's handling of the central symbol, the *A*, appears fanciful and over-elaborate. Third, the role of the Puritan community and its leaders receives little attention. Fourth, the last chapter appears weak – a polite tying up of ends, and a provokingly ambivalent commentary on the tale's meanings. And finally, the introductory sketch, 'The Custom House,' seems to have no more than a tenuous connection with the romance itself.

Seen in relation to the mythology of the tales and romances discussed above, however, *The Scarlet Letter* would appear to be less about sin than an account of the plight of the Dark Lady and the mercurial hero, menaced by a tyrannical old man of reason in a community which reveres law above all else, sees human nature as depraved, and fears passion and imagination equally. It would also appear to be a quest for the meaning of *A* or Pearl – a meaning which the action of the tale gradually unfolds. These themes are congruent with the themes of the later romances and myths; and the imagery of this tale, which carries much of the burden of meaning, is similarly the imagery of the later work. Without for a moment rejecting the discursive moral aspects of the story, we may observe its shape as myth by reviewing the action chronologically, keeping the images in

171

clear focus, and allowing the protagonists of Hawthorne's later tales to assert their kinship to Hester, Dimmesdale, and the others.

The chronological action of *The Scarlet Letter* begins in Europe. Hester, a beautiful and innocent English maiden, marries a decaying scholar, Chillingworth. Their union, apparently, is a failure, for Hester later reflects that Chillingworth's foulest offence was that 'in the time when her heart knew no better, he had persuaded her to fancy herself happy by his side.' Hers was a 'marble image of happiness' which had been 'imposed upon her as the warm reality' (C, I, 177). Thus at the root of the action we have the Dark Lady-Black Man situation which Hawthorne was later to develop in Zenobia and Westervelt, in Miriam and her model, and Proserpina and Pluto. But Chillingworth, in contrast with his later incarnations, is neither a quack nor a demon-priest; he is, in Europe at least, a kindly enough man, and a great scientific scholar.

Unhappily, reason has so dominated Chillingworth's career that it has cut him off from feeling, from the delights of the heart and the flesh which he sees imaged in Hester. When he first meets Hester in New England he is able to admit that it was the obsession with knowledge that made him an impotent husband: ' "I, – a man of thought, – the book-worm of great libraries, – a man already in decay, having given my best years to feed the hungry dream of knowledge, – what had I to do with youth and beauty like thine own! Misshapen from my birth-hour, how could I delude myself with the idea that intellectual gifts might veil physical deformity in a young girl's fantasy!" ' (C, I, 74) As a 'type' of reason, he is disproportioned from the begin-

172

ning; and when he learns that he cannot rule the lush beauty, passion, and domestic creativity typified by Hester, he becomes vengeful. In a second interview with Hester he describes his relation with Dimmesdale: 'A mortal man, with once a human heart, has become a fiend for his especial torment' (C, I, 172). And Hester expresses her pity for 'the hatred that has transformed a wise and just man to a fiend!'

Hawthorne does not explain why Chillingworth decides to emigrate to America, but it is clear that the Puritan reliance on law and reason are agreeable to his temper, and that the community needs his talents. His tragedy is that, when he fails to establish a true bond with Hester, he (like the Puritans) condemns her passion as demonic, and vows to destroy the person or 'type' that was capable of winning her. As his interest turns from healing to vengeance, he becomes wizened and begrimed by the smoke of his furnace. At length he tells Hester that he recalls his old faith; that their situation is 'a kind of typical illusion' which he is powerless to change. He has become the darkest, most deterministic Puritan of them all.

The third figure of this 'typical illusion' is Arthur Dimmesdale, a brilliant young scholar whose fame has re-echoed at Oxford. His name, Arthur, suggests a great hero (students of Kenneth Burke might pun the name into Arthur-Author, or Art for short) whose role in the community is purely spiritual; he will unendingly battle the powers of blackness as defined by scriptural and civil law. But Arthur is irresistibly attracted to Hester. Where he is pale and ethereal, she is rich and voluptuous; where he is intellectual and imaginative, she is earthy and material – skilled in

173

domestic arts. In secret this couple conceive a child – a Pearl – who unites in herself their two natures.

Arthur resembles the moonlight-mirror types of Hawthorne's mythological tales; in Chillingworth's words, 'the Creator never made another being so sensitive as this' (C, I, 171). But, for all his mercurial ability, Dimmesdale is neither a demi-god nor champion; far from the virile questing Bellerophon, he wanders in the dim dale of a world which his faith assures him is depraved, bearing the burden of a nature which he believes to be evil. As a type of spirit or imagination, his place in Puritan society is the pulpit, and he feels a piercing guilt over the part of his nature which draws him to the things of this world.

At the beginning of the romance, then, we have not a bipolar conflict between Head and Heart, but a situation in which a fecund, richly creative Dark Lady is 'wedded' to two men, neither of whom, in Puritan New England, will admit his connection with her. The minister lacks the courage to admit that his nature has a passionate side; the scientist reviles the lady and swears her to secrecy so that he can pursue an inhuman revenge. And the righteous community brands the lady with a scarlet letter that has 'the effect of a spell, taking her out of the ordinary relations with humanity, and enclosing her in a sphere by herself' (C, I, 54).

As Gordon Roper and John Gerber have argued,[12] the

12 Gordon H. Roper, ed., 'Introduction,' to *The Scarlet Letter and Selected Prose Works* (New York, 1949); John Gerber, 'Form and Content in *The Scarlet Letter*,' *New England Quarterly*, xvɪɪ (March 1944), 25–55.

subsequent course of the story proceeds in a kind of chain reaction in which one character or type dominates, expends its energy, and ignites the fuse that sets a new force in motion. At first the Calvinist community dominates in punishing Hester; then Chillingworth, recognizing Dimmesdale as his victim, begins to torture him; next Hester acts to free her lover from his suffering; and finally the delicate hero, Dimmesdale, takes control, makes his confession, and with a kiss sets Pearl free of the spell that enthralled her. This, in a sentence, is the story of the Puritan-American quest. We must consider each phase of it in detail, for Hawthorne's rendering is so rich that no incident or image is superfluous.

The first force, the Puritan community, provides the theatre for the drama; its ethos is a major target of Hawthorne's criticism. With its stern and drearily unimaginative denial of so much that is rich and warm in human nature, this community would become, in the nineteenth century, the stuffy 'custom' house of Hawthorne's introductory sketch. It believes above all in empirical fact and in law; when feeling or passion, sensual or artistic, go beyond orthodox limits, they are consistently related to the dark – to the Black Man. The sea-captain who witnesses the Puritan holiday at the end of *The Scarlet Letter* calls the rulers 'those sour old Puritans.' Hawthorne's own reflection on their magistrates is: 'They were, doubtless, good men, just, and sage. But, out of the whole human family, it would not have been easy to select the same number of wise and virtuous persons, who should be *less capable* of sitting in judgment on an erring woman's heart, and disentangling

175

its mesh of good and evil, than the sages of rigid aspect towards whom Hester Prynne now turned her face.' (italics mine, C, I, 64)

The fathers of this community (like the twin fathers, Minos-Aegeus, of the Theseus story) are the ageing soldier, Governor Bellingham, and the benign Rev. Mr. Wilson (who, in turn, is related to 'the holy Apostle Eliot' and that 'half-mythological personage,' the Rev. Mr. Blackstone).[13] The chatelaine of the community is Mistress Hibbins, a 'sour-tempered' hag who is 'wedded' in sterile spinsterhood to her domineering brother, the Governor.

In his account of Hester's visit to the Governor's Hall, Hawthorne brings into close dramatic relation all of the forces at work in the Puritan community. The 'chances of popular election' have caused the arch-English Governor 'to descend a step or two from the highest rank' (C, I, 108). Nevertheless, he is still powerful and respected, although his head, separated from his body by a Jacobean ruff, reminds Hawthorne of 'that of John the Baptist on a charger.' Q. D. Leavis has pointed out the relevance of this image to the Puritan separation of mind and body. Governor Bellingham's brilliantly polished armour, the iron facade of the Puritans, is prominently displayed in his hall, where it reflects, greatly magnified, Hester's scarlet letter, the symbol which rouses the iron man's rage.

The composite impression that we get of the Governor's mansion combines gold, sun, iron, splendour, and power –

13 The birth of America was, for Hawthorne, associated with the myth of Europa and Cadmus: 'The Dragon's Teeth.' The Rev. Mr. Blackstone, he records, was 'the first settler of the peninsula; that half-mythological personage who rides through our early annals, seated on the back of a bull' (C, I, 107).

176

the images of the tyrant. Governor Bellingham, as his garden reveals, has not reproduced in New England the culture of the Old Country. The most prominent products of his tillage are cabbages and pumpkins, 'lumps of vegetable gold.' The few rose bushes and apple trees, the flower of English culture, have descended from the Rev. Mr. Blackstone's importation.

The forces which flank the Governor are: the Rev. Mr. Wilson, the saintly but aged gentleman who hopes that 'pears and peaches might yet be naturalized in the New England climate'; Roger Chillingworth, whose empirical 'medical' knowledge has been welcomed by the Puritans, though they fear that he may be in league with the Devil; and Arthur Dimmesdale, the ethereal young minister whose duties in the town, fighting the powers of night, have apparently made him frail and ill. The figures who complete this caste are Mistress Hibbins and Hester. Mistress Hibbins, though the colony's first lady, does not appear in the sunshine, but remains in a shuttered upstairs room. Her daylight role is so empty that she has long since turned vengeful and entered the devil's service. Hester, her New England sister, still appears in public, though condemned to wear the ignominious *A*. But the New England scene has wrought a great change upon her: she dresses in drab gray; her luxuriant hair is concealed; and when she meets the sunny Governor, 'the shadow of the curtain' falls on her and partially conceals her (C, I, 109). New England womanhood, that is, unless it descends to the brutal, 'manlike' callousness of the Boston goodwives, is forced out of the sunshine. Hester, in her New England life, has become like Minerva – a goddess of needle and loom, an intellectual

177

who voyages boldly in the dusky region of mind. She has lost what are, for Hawthorne, the warmest qualities of womanhood (C, I, ch. 13).

The occasion of Hester's visit to Governor Bellingham is the report that Pearl is to be taken away from her – a proposal which Hawthorne places in perspective by suggesting that the Puritan government often meddles in affairs over which it should have no real jurisdiction – affairs as trivial as a quarrel over a pig. On this occasion – the community's second attempt to punish Hester – the erring mother is saved by Wilson and Dimmesdale who, unlike Governor Bellingham, feel great sympathy for the child who personifies the scarlet *A*.

Chillingworth, the second activating force of the story, cares nothing for Pearl's fate. On hearing Dimmesdale's plea for Pearl and Hester, he recognizes his victim, and proceeds with the greatest subtlety to play upon the minister's sense of sin and guilt. He has indeed chosen 'to withdraw his name from the roll of mankind' (C, I, 118). But Hawthorne makes it clear that Chillingworth's power to tyrannize over Dimmesdale results from the Puritan fear of imagination and instinct – the night side of experience. Puritan society cannot recognize these powers as essentially human rather than Satanic. Chillingworth candidly explains Dimmesdale's weakness to Hester: ' "With the superstition common to his brotherhood, he fancied himself given over to a fiend, to be tortured with frightful dreams, and desperate thoughts, the sting of remorse, and despair of pardon; as a foretaste of what awaits him beyond the grave. But it was the constant shadow of my presence! – the closest pro-

pinquity of the man whom he had most vilely wronged!" '
(C, I, 171–72)

In literal terms there is no question that Dimmesdale has
'vilely wronged' the scientist by expressing his love for
Hester. But in 'typical' terms he has wronged himself by
denying the true nature of his powers. Similarly, Chillingworth has wronged Hester by concealing his relation to
her – by failing to be a benign 'father.' Small wonder that
Dimmesdale and Hester – the types of passionate, imaginative men and women – suffer in Calvinist society!

Hawthorne's rejection of the Calvinist view of human
nature, however, does not lead him to espouse the cause of
man's 'natural goodness,' the Transcendental view. For him
there is an ideal, perfect realm, and an imperfect, human
realm. Human nature is inevitably imperfect. But the fatal
error of the Puritans is their failure to recognize all of man's
gifts – to achieve an integration of all of man's forces. The
Puritan life is a half-life, and its outcome is likely to be
tragic.

Hester, the third activating force in this 'typical' drama,
follows a long, tortuous, and erroneous path before she is
able to act decisively, and even then she takes the wrong
course. Isolated by the brand she must wear, she discovers
at the Governor's Hall, and later in the forest, that even the
sunshine now flees from her. She does not share the sin-
centred view of man's nature that obsesses her husband and
lover, and indeed the whole Puritan community; and
'through seven long years' she rejects the view that her act
of love was depraved: 'She was patient – a martyr, indeed –
but she forbore to pray for her enemies; lest, in spite of her

179

forgiving aspirations, the words of the blessing should stubbornly twist themselves into a curse' (C, I, 85). Robbed of her glamour and denied her fecundity, she assumes a 'marble coldness'; 'her life had turned, in a great measure, from passion and feeling, to thought' (C, I, 164), and she speculates with a boldness that 'our forefathers ... would have held to be a deadlier crime than that stigmatized by the scarlet letter.' Mistress Hibbins, recognizing Hester's alienation from the community of iron men, tempts her to hold rendezvous with the Black Man, but she is saved by her responsibility to her 'Pearl.'

The line which her thinking takes is Transcendental, and leads her to assert that her transgression with Dimmesdale 'had a consecration of its own.' But Hawthorne does not agree. He describes her speculations as wanderings in a 'dismal labyrinth' of thought, a moral wilderness. If the Puritan obsession with evil is extreme, Hester goes too far in the opposite direction and begins to think of human nature as 'naturally good.' Her wanderings had taught her 'much amiss'; the scarlet *A* had indeed 'not done its office.'

Hester finds her power to act when Dimmesdale – equally isolated and helpless – mounts the scaffold like a somnambulist in the dead of night to make a desperate and ineffectual admission of his guilt. Hester and Pearl, who have been 'watching at a death-bed,' join him, and as he takes the hands of his wife and child he feels 'a tumultuous rush of new life ... pouring like a torrent into his heart, and hurrying through all his veins, as if the mother and child were communicating their vital warmth to his half-torpid system. The three formed an electric chain.' (C, I, 153) Like Theseus, clutching the thread of sympathy that joined him

180

III: The Scarlet Letter

to Ariadne, Dimmesdale experiences a resurgence of power, but he is still unable to act, for he still fails to understand that Reason is the force that tortures him with guilt. When the leering Chillingworth is revealed across the square, he asks: 'Who is that man, Hester? ... I hate him.' (C, I, 156) Still a Puritan, Dimmesdale cannot challenge the tyranny of the force that is held in such honour in New England. He evades Pearl's charge, 'Thou wast not bold! – thou wast not true!' with the assurance that he will appear publicly with her and Hester 'at the great judgment day.' He is then led away by his familiar fiend, who still triumphs. Ironically, the sexton later finds Dimmesdale's glove on the scaffold and warns him: ' "Since Satan saw fit to steal it, your reverence must needs handle him without gloves, henceforward" ' (C, I, 158).

In this 'black' confessional Dimmesdale has found the secret of his eventual triumph – the identity of his persecutor, and the human bond which will give him the power to act. But Hester has found immediate power to act on her 'speculations.' She informs Chillingworth that she will no longer keep the secret that he is 'wedded' to the scarlet woman. And she meets Dimmesdale in the natural setting of the forest to persuade him that they should escape from the cruel austerities of New England. For a brief time Dimmesdale enjoys this 'natural' setting. He recognizes that Chillingworth's cold and logical investigation of the human heart is an unpardonable sin. Reunited with his lover and their child, he exclaims that this relation – with Hester restored to her original beauty – is indeed 'the better life!' (C, I, 202) And in Pearl he recognizes 'the oneness of their being ... at once the material union, and the spiritual

181

idea, in whom they met, and were to dwell immortally together' (C, I, 207).

But as the minister walks home from the forest his mind wanders in a 'maze' of blasphemous and lustful images – as dangerous as the maze of thought in which Hester had wandered. He realizes that Hester's thrilling plan of escape to a state of nature where there are no formal restraints will be no real escape but rather a second betrayal of himself: 'Tempted by a dream of happiness, he had [momentarily] yielded himself, with deliberate choice, as he had never done before, to what he knew was deadly sin.' The only solution to his problem, then, is to make a 'deliberate choice' which is his own, not Hester's: he must publicly assert his true nature – the nature of the human condition. At this point Dimmesdale finds both his heroism and his humanity. Like Hamlet at the conclusion of Shakespeare's tragedy, he becomes the tragic witness of man's imperfection – 'The readiness is all.' Having gained this insight he is able to write a new election sermon. Thus his last night speeds away 'as if it were a winged steed, and he [like Bellerophon] careering on it' (C, I, 225). And on the next morning he makes his grand confession – proclaims his true self. Tragic 'recognition' has occurred; heroic death ensues. Like Hamlet, Dimmesdale dies for truth.

To say, however, that in his expiring moment Dimmesdale renounces the Puritan faith, would be a distortion of Hawthorne's statement. Dimmesdale is a Puritan to the end. His triumph is his recognition that the dark experience which his brethren regard as demonic is an integral part of man's full nature; as a Puritan he thinks of it as 'the worst,' but he knows that it must be acknowledged, for by repressing it man makes it a source of unending torture. Thus his act of self-recognition and self-assertion – the public reunion with Hester – releases Pearl from the 'spell' which had made her seem a demon child. For Hester and Dimmesdale, the types of passion and imagination in Puritan society, there can be no conventional happy ending. But Pearl, through their fortitude, becomes a complete woman instead of a Puritan half-woman – the first representative of a new breed, the first *complete* American.

Given this understanding of Dimmesdale's drama, we may now interpret fully the meaning of that meteor-like *A* in the sky – the portent which many of Hawthorne's critics have thought merely fanciful. When Dimmesdale is reunited upon the scaffold with his lover and child, the 'great vault' of the sky

brightened, like the dome of an immense lamp. It showed the familiar scene of the street, with the distinctness of mid-day, but also with the awfulness that is always imparted to familiar objects by an unaccustomed light ... [Every detail became sharply visible] but with a singularity of aspect that seemed to give another moral interpretation to the things of this world than they had ever borne before ... They [the family] stood in the noon of that strange and solemn splendor, as if it were the light that is to reveal all secrets, and the daybreak that shall unite all who belong to one another. (C, I, 154)

This clear moment, that is, is the moment of vision: it reveals the deep truth of nature that 'all who belong to one another' should be united. But Dimmesdale, still shackled like the 'others of his superstitious brotherhood,' can understand this clear light only as a portent of doom. Having 'extended his egotism over the whole expanse of nature,' he

183

misses the meaning of the revelation; 'the disease in his own eye and heart' lead him to see a vast letter A, the universal witness that he (and this whole night realm of experience) is depraved (C, I, 155). The beauty of the vision is quenched in his obsessive awareness of sin. Only after the final forest scene will he grasp the real meaning of the A, and find the power to proclaim it.

This brings us finally to the centre of the romance – to Pearl and to the meaning of the scarlet A, Hawthorne's richest symbol. Hawthorne discovered the A in the Custom House, that deadening institution whose rigid commitment to routine, mechanical measurement, and rules, threatened the complete annihilation of his imagination. As a man 'who felt it to be the best definition of happiness to live through-out the whole range of his faculties and sensibilities' (C, I, 40), Hawthorne regarded the A as a bright point of hope – a release from the latterday Puritan 'custom' house of his age, and a promise of imaginative fulfilment.

From the outset the A is an ambivalent symbol. Its 'scarlet woman' meaning for the Puritans is clear, but by the last line of the story when we see it as an heraldic A *Gules* on Hester's and Dimmesdale's common tombstone, it has assumed a meaning that is beyond the philosophy of any Puritan. All of the meanings with which Hawthorne invests it are relevant; and all are united organically in Pearl, the 'living embodiment' of the A. The scarlet letter, finally, becomes Hawthorne's emblem of the human heart – of its imperfection, and its labyrinthine mixture of good and evil. The letter is blood red (*gules*) rather than scarlet, for it betokens 'our common nature.'

From the Puritan point of view, the A stands specifically

III: The Scarlet Letter

for adultery and, in general terms, for sin – for the fallen aspects of man's nature which must be brutally suppressed: sexual knowledge, sensory indulgence, and the broad area of fancy and intuition which Puritanism labelled 'witchcraft.' Man has only the law of Scripture and reason to guide him, and even reason may deceive him in his study of God's providence. The *A* is thus further associated with the sin of Adam, with hell, infernal fire, Satan, demons, fairies, and so on. The magistrates' intention in branding Hester with this lurid mark is to make her a living warning to others who are tempted to give in to unlawful impulses. Its corrective function will be to reduce Hester's rich femininity to the drab, un-sexed coarseness of the community goodwives (C, I, 50); to make her colourless, submissive, and unthinking – denying her nature on earth to gain life eternal.

But the effect of the scarlet brand on Hester is not at all what her male judges expected. She clings stubbornly to the belief that her sin 'had a consecration of its own,' and the whole seven years of her torment fail to convince her that her natural impulse is depraved. Puritanical men are the people who fear her gifts. She tells Pearl that 'Once in my life I met the Black Man! ... This scarlet letter is his mark!' (C, I, 185) Hawthorne underlines in various ways Hester's failure either to accept the Puritan meaning of the *A* or to arrive at an adequate personal understanding of it. At one moment she speaks of being 'disciplined to truth' by the *A*, and at the next she confesses that she is lost in a 'dismal maze' of thought (C, I, 166). Her bitterness over Chillingworth's attempt to kindle 'a household fire' (C, I, 74) in his heart by marrying her leads Hawthorne to remark: 'But

185

Hester ought long ago to have done with this injustice ... Had seven long years, under the torture of the scarlet letter, inflicted so much of misery, and wrought out no repentance?' (C, I, 177) She does feel a throb of pain whenever another sinner's eyes fall on her badge, as though other people understand her guilt, and themselves wear the *A* secretly. And she does understand that a green *A*, which Pearl makes out of seaweed, 'has no purport'; the *A* is an emblem that speaks of mankind and his moral dilemmas, not of Nature. But a genuine understanding and acceptance of the *A* will come only after Dimmesdale's heroic revelation and death. Then, having witnessed in Europe the fulfilment of Pearl's womanhood, Hester will return to New England and do what she can to prove that the *A* is not a demonic badge: 'Here had been her sin; here, her sorrow, and here was yet to be her penitence. She had returned, therefore, and resumed – of her own free will ... the symbol of which we have related so dark a tale.' (C, I, 263)

Hester's understanding of her scarlet emblem comes slowly and painfully, but Hawthorne's treatment of the *A* leads the reader fairly quickly to question its Puritan meaning and consider other possibilities. The sympathy which the Madonna-like young mother of the first scaffold scene feels for Hester suggests that the emotions of motherhood are perhaps closer to the truth of human nature than the stern legality of 'the righteous Colony of the Massachusetts, where iniquity is dragged out into the sunshine!' (C, I, 54) If Governor Bellingham's hollow steel armour reflects only glaring sun, an enormously exaggerated *A*, and Pearl's impish smile, the simple Puritan 'folk,' guided more by human feeling than doctrine and law, sometimes think of

III: The Scarlet Letter

Hester's *A* as meaning able or angel. The *A*, it is rumoured, looks like 'a nun's cross'; it repels the devilish arrows of the Indians (C, I, 163); as embroidered by Hester, it is a work of art; it is a portent in the sky which the 'disease' in the minister's 'own heart and eye' (the Puritan ethos) makes him see as a cosmic revelation of his depravity, but which Hawthorne sees as a sign of 'the daybreak that shall unite all who belong to one another' (C, I, 154). The point to be made here is that Hawthorne, however 'tasteless' his critics find his symbolism, is not merely fanciful. Every *A*-image that he uses adds a new shade of meaning to the symbol. The *A* becomes the centre towards which all extremes tend. And it is a living centre, for Pearl represents it in the flesh.

The traditional meaning of 'pearl' as the soul or self is surely Hawthorne's meaning. We have already noted that Dimmesdale sees the child as the 'material union, and the spiritual idea' of himself and Hester. But Hawthorne's elaboration of Pearl, *A*, and crimson images serves the serious purpose of deepening and expanding the meaning of his symbol. To the Puritans Pearl is an imp, a demonic child, or a witch; she is outside the law; unrestrained, apparently, by any of the strictures which shape little Puritans. Hester, in her defiance of the Puritan interpretation, deliberately dresses Pearl in scarlet fashions, as if to underline the absurdity of regarding as evil an infant who 'was worthy to have been brought forth in Eden; worthy to have been left there, to be the plaything of the angels, after the world's first parents were driven out' (C, I, 90). This costume, however, reminds the Rev. Mr. Wilson of 'one of those naughty elfs or fairies' who, in pre-Reformation England, were benignly regarded. In Old England, that is, such magical qualities were valued rather than feared; people believed in *good* fairies.

The scarlet or crimson colour also links Pearl to roses, the traditional symbol of beauty and love. She claims to have been plucked from the native rosebush which blooms bravely at the prison door; and she imperiously demands to have the sunshine reflected from the Governor's house, and the English roses in his garden. But the Governor's light and flowers are not hers; the young American, as Hester expresses it, must 'gather ... [her] own sunshine' (C, I, 103). In Boston, the flower which overshadows the wild rose is 'the black flower of civilized society, a prison.' Pearl combines in herself the attributes of the sturdy native rose and its cultivated English sister; she does not recognize the 'black flower.'

This rose imagery helps us to understand why Pearl must go to Europe at the end of the romance. She cannot thrive in the black-flowering garden of New England where English roses flourish but feebly and native roses are unregarded. When Pearl pelts the scarlet *A* with roses, Hester feels only pain, but the child understands intuitively that it is her mother's true badge. She seems to know, too, that this is the mark on her father's breast; and, however inappropriate in terms of realistic fiction, she embraces the full legacy of the *A* by kissing it (C, I, 212).

Through love, the force which binds her father and mother, Pearl has learned an intuitive acceptance of the *A*. But her integration of the gifts of Hester and Dimmesdale has no place in Puritan America. She must therefore find her fulfilment in Europe as the first representative of a new

188

breed – the figure who presages James's immaculate heroines, 'the heiress of all the ages.' Pearl, moreover, looks forward to Phoebe Pyncheon and Priscilla. One might safely say that she is the first genuine Miss America.

Thus, though the Puritan phase of the American quest ended darkly, the picture was not overwhelmingly black. 'In the spiritual world,' the 'mutual victims,' Chillingworth and Dimmesdale, may find their hatred transmuted into 'golden love.' And even in America the full self – the forces of reason, feeling, and imagination or spirit – may yet be recognized. If Hester's foresight can be trusted, 'at some brighter period, when the world should have grown ripe for it, in Heaven's own time, a new truth would be revealed, in order to establish the whole relation between man and woman on a surer ground of mutual happiness' (C, I, 263). America, that is, will accept fully the bright, creative powers of its womanhood, and the imaginative gifts of its men. Pearl has even inherited Roger Chillingworth's wealth, the greatest thing that the Puritans created – so great, indeed, that the witch-child, had she wished, 'might have mingled her wild blood with the lineage of the devoutest Puritan among them all.'

The story of Hester's and Dimmesdale's struggle through 'seven long years' to learn the meaning of *A* is Hawthorne's central theme. In the mythological tales the hero and the Dark Lady surmounted their difficulties happily enough, but in the world of experience they seldom triumph. Man is fallen; his characteristic atmosphere is that dusky area in which warm hearthlight and clear moonlight mingle; or, in nature, the 'cool brown light' of sun and shadow. This is the realm of the integrated self. The statement of *The*

189

Hawthorne as Myth-Maker

Scarlet Letter is basically what Hawthorne has said elsewhere. The 'seven long years' of Hester's torture are like the seven generations, or Seven Gables, of the Pyncheon-Maule conflict, and the seven years of Hollingsworth's quest to establish an institution for criminal reform. In the same way, the embroidered scarlet *A* is a 'talisman' or token of 'our common nature'; it is the talisman which later appears in *Blithedale* as Zenobia's exotic flower (handed on to Priscilla) and in *The Marble Faun* as the seven stones in the bracelet which Miriam presents as a wedding gift to Hilda. But Hawthorne will not have his New World inherit the guilt of the Christian tradition. Pearl is surely the luminous prophecy of the coming of Phoebe Pyncheon and Holgrave – a prophecy upon whose fulfilment we have, in Blithedale's Priscilla and Coverdale, Hawthorne's later, less sanguine comments, and in Hilda and Kenyon, his qualified hope.

The Last Quests

The transition from *The Scarlet Letter* to *Dr. Grimshawe's Secret* is a leap off a cliff: from the pinnacle of Hawthorne's artistic achievement we plummet to the ruins of a mind and an art. But the ruins, far from being the meaningless trivia which a superficial inspection of them would suggest, reveal the agony of the prematurely aged Hawthorne attempting to get at the *truth* of his 'last phase,' the chaotic world of the sixties. In the fifties he had seen Europe and felt its beauty and tragedy; and he had now come back to his brave new world of America – the hero of his historical myth – to find it on the brink of a deadly civil war. The agony of this tragic homecoming – the piercing awareness that he was an

190

III: The Last Quests

orphan of two worlds – is the sombre ground upon which his last romances trumpet out their sound and fury. In the isolated tower-cell of The Wayside, over whose trapdoor he placed his chair, Hawthorne struggled valiantly to synthesize once more the shattered elements of his vision and produce the romance that would be his crowning achievement. *Dr. Grimshawe's Secret* (which Hawthorne commanded his heirs never to publish) is the chief testament of these years; it is Hawthorne's crown of thorns.

Any study of the last romances must defer gratefully to Edward H. Davidson's biographical researches and to his definition of the texts.[14] What Mr. Davidson says about Hawthorne's failure in the 'last phase' is both wise and restrained. First, and most obviously, Hawthorne was a sick man. This is one fact which critics of the psychological school have not as yet explained away. Second, driven by the need for money, and by the feeling that he must re-establish his reputation, he forced himself to write a great deal – to write, perhaps, before he was ready. Third (and this 'takes us to the fringes of Hawthorne's curious mind'), the America to which he returned was not the circumscribed theatre that he had left: 'The tight world of New England society, together with its moral themes, was gone and he discovered that his artistic world was in ruins.' He was, in a word, 'baffled by the times in which he lived.'[15]

These are sensible, solidly-rooted explanations of what happened to Hawthorne – the best that can be said, perhaps,

14 *Hawthorne's Last Phase* (New Haven, 1949); ed., *Hawthorne's 'Dr. Grimshawe's Secret'* (Cambridge, Mass., 1954). Page numbers inserted in the text will refer to Davidson's edition of *Dr. Grimshawe*.
15 *Hawthorne's Last Phase*, pp. 150–53.

191

in explanation of his failure to complete any works of fiction after 1860. Since, apart from his characteristically controlled private letters, there is not a shred of documentary evidence to suggest that he suffered any severe emotional or psychological disturbance in these years, the kind of criticism which applies the images of his art (the chest of 'golden curls,' the 'iron box,' and so on) to the exegesis of his sexual-artistic neuroses is at best a fanciful exercise in etiology. Mr. Davidson avoids this trap, but he appends a further explanation of Hawthorne's failure which should not pass unchallenged. His fourth point is this: 'Perhaps ... he completely lost [the] interest in right and wrong which had moved him so profoundly in the decade before ... The old problems still remained but the mind had lost the keen edge to be profoundly interested in them or work them out in well-motivated human character.'

With the last part of this statement we cannot quarrel. In terms of realistic roundness, not one of the protagonists of the last romances lives. But had Hawthorne completely lost interest in right and wrong? Were the problems of the last romances, in other words, merely literary malingering – meaningless games with which, day in and day out, Hawthorne vexed himself in his tower study? Certainly all of the interpolated soul-searchings in *Dr. Grimshawe*, and the decisions to 'Try back again ... Stubbornly, stubbornly,' argue against this assumption. Hawthorne was very clearly struggling with the greatest problem of his artistic career. The only basis on which he had lost interest in the moral problems of right and wrong was on the superficial level of statement – of pointing a moral. And it is not surprising that, precipitated into the chaos of pre-civil-war America,

192

he should abandon the sanctimonious and ineffectual practice of 'pointing morals.'

This objection to Mr. Davidson's explanation must be the occasion for a new definition of Hawthorne's imaginative method – a definition towards which the entire argument of this book has been leading, and which is now made possible by the evidence that the editor has so scrupulously produced in *Hawthorne's 'Dr. Grimshawe's Secret.'*

In the foregoing pages, two important aspects of Hawthorne's mind and art have been stated or implied: first, he was not a systematic thinker nor in any sense a disciplined scholar; second, he was a highly self-conscious artist. How, then, if not by systematic thought, does he achieve in his art that coherence and shape which we have noted in the major romances? In *Hawthorne's Last Phase*, Mr. Davidson has answered this question admirably: the genesis of Hawthorne's tales, as the *Notebooks* so fully demonstrate, was an image or situation which struck him as being not merely picturesque but susceptible of moral interpretation. From this basic image and its moral meaning (Hawthorne's secular adaptation of the Puritan type or 'Providence') he then proceeded to elaborate an action and a set of dramatis personae. Mechanical as this process seems, it sometimes produced the transcendent suggestiveness of 'Young Goodman Brown' or 'My Kinsman, Major Molyneux.' About the 'iron rod' of the moral image, Hawthorne was sometimes able to construct a psychological web which enabled his readers to perceive for a moment the deepest impulses of human action.

The secret of his artistic method is less a mechanical working out of a moral idea than the synthetic act of

193

creation which Coleridge recognized as the highest imaginative act. As Mr. Davidson expresses it: 'Hawthorne depended upon the mystical operations of his imagination to fuse moral and image and then to evolve the whole panoply of romance.'[16] In these terms, the prime standard of judgment which Hawthorne applied to his own works was whether they 'felt right,' whether he had 'got it.' They had to be true above all to his imaginative vision, to his personal myth. It is this imaginative coherence that is at the base of Hawthorne's artistic method; it is this that allows him to say: 'Do not stick at any strangeness, or preternaturality; it can be softened down to any extent, however wild in its first conception.'[17] If only he can work out an expressive action that 'feels right' imaginatively, then any absurdities (witness the so-called Gothic elements of *Seven Gables* and *Blithedale*) can be made palatable to the reader.

Hawthorne's failure in *Dr. Grimshawe's Secret*, therefore, is anything but a loss of interest in moral problems; it is a failure to achieve that imaginative coherence, that 'right feel' which made him aware of the mechanical obviousness of 'The Great Stone Face,' and made him recognize the Greek myths as stories which were so perfect that they 'seem never to have been made.'[18]

In effect, *Dr. Grimshawe's Secret* is the last step in Hawthorne's development away from the early short-story form, a step which, after four years of struggle, he failed to complete. The problems which he set himself in the early

16 *Ibid.*, p. 153.
17 Davidson, ed., *Dr. Grimshawe*, p. 151.
18 See Julian Hawthorne, *Hawthorne and His Wife*, I, p. 287, on 'The Great Stone Face.'

III: The Last Quests

tales were small in compass; like Poe, he strove with brilliant success to create a single effect or to realize a single idea. The romances took him beyond this compass to the considerably more complex definition of a society (or self) with all of its opposing forces, but the short-story technique still applied. In *The Scarlet Letter* and *Seven Gables* he was able to find a central symbol which – once intuited and worked out imaginatively – became the rock upon which the entire action was founded. In *Blithedale* and *The Marble Faun* he took a further step: although the central symbols of Blithedale and the faun were important, the characters of these romances assumed an autonomy of their own; they were no longer aspects of an *A* or a seven-gabled house but opposed forces in search of an equilibrium of their own. This accounts in part for the original, discontinuous technique of *Blithedale*. In *Dr. Grimshawe* Hawthorne wanted to look into the future – to sum up his English experience by working out the true relation of America to its parent country. This was a new and difficult problem, an effort – with no maps to rely on – to see a happy ending to both the American quest and the quest of his mercurial hero; to bring his 'life of allegory' to a triumphant conclusion. This subject presented complexities that he had never before encountered, and in the end his art wrecked itself in trying to bring in a true verdict.

The America to which Hawthorne returned was far from being the land of 'heroes prov'd / In liberating strife, / Who more than self their country lov'd / And mercy more than life.'[19] Up to this point his American myth – the myth in which man discovers his true nature and learns to make the

19 See 'America the Beautiful,' stanza three.

best use of his natural imperfections – had progressed very favourably. In the early tales and *The Scarlet Letter* he had understood the meaning of Puritanism, had recorded its failures, and sent its liberated spirit, Pearl, off to Europe to await a 'brighter time.' In *Seven Gables* he had seen, after seven generations, the triumph of the American consciousness, in the marriage of Phoebe and Holgrave. In *Blithedale* he had seen that Zenobia (Hester, Eve) still had no place in the community and that love of the absolutist-reformer had estranged America's developing womanhood (Priscilla) from the imaginative man who understood her (Coverdale). Things mended in *The Marble Faun* when Hilda and Kenyon, initiated without sin into the mysteries of human nature, returned with their wisdom to New England. But even for them the new day had not arrived. There was no more than 'light on the mountain tops.'

What Hilda, Kenyon, and Hawthorne found on their return to the glorious democracy was a New England which had now turned bitterly on its former leader, Franklin Pierce, and was self-righteously intent upon subjugating the South, that part of the Union which was not most sympathetic to England. In these terms, Hawthorne's dream of a glowing young son of America who returns to England, establishes his claim to a title equal to any in the realm (and perhaps declines it for the greater privilege of remaining an American) – this dream becomes a nightmare. The comparison, on the realistic level, between English and American manners becomes odious, and the young American claimant's noble speech of rejection becomes a galling irony: ' "You will laugh at me, my friend; but I cannot help feeling that I, a simple citizen of a republic, yet with none

III: The Last Quests

above me, except those whom I help to place there – and who are my servants, not my superiors – must *stoop* to take these honors. I leave a set of institutions which are the noblest that wit and civilization of man has yet conceived, to enlist myself in one that is based on a far lower conception of man, and which therefore lowers everyone who shares in it." ' (141)

What, Hawthorne must have wondered bitterly, was now the relation between England and America? What had become of that young democrat of 'A Select Party' whom Hawthorne had imagined as follows:

Yet he was a young man in poor attire, with no insignia of rank or acknowledged eminence, nor anything to distinguish him among the crowd except a high, white forehead, beneath which a pair of deepset eyes were glowing with warm light. It was such a light as never illuminates the earth save when a great heart burns as the household fire of a grand intellect. And who was he? – who but the Master Genius for whom our country is looking anxiously into the mist of Time, as destined to fulfil the great mission of creating an American literature, hewing it, as it were, out of the unwrought granite of our intellectual quarries? From him ... we are to receive our first great original work, which shall do all that remains to be achieved for our glory among the nations ... Nor does it matter much to him, in his triumph over all the ages, though a generation or two of his own times shall do themselves the wrong to disregard him (II, 79–80).

Could America hope, with genuine confidence, for such a hero? What narrative action could objectify the relation between the America of the 1860s and the 'Old Home' which Hawthorne had discovered, as consul and tourist, to be in many ways his spiritual home?

It will not be possible within the length of this study to

197

follow Hawthorne's tortured attempts in the 70,000 words of the first draft of *Dr. Grimshawe's Secret* to give shape to this, the greatest problem of his career. There is page upon page of introspection in which he 'tries back again' to discover the meaning, the controlling principle or symbol of his story. We may, however, examine the 'forces' or *dramatis personae* of the tale, and witness the various transformations which Hawthorne makes in them as he struggles to find the 'feel,' the imaginative coherence of his action. From the outset it is clear that the artificial, set-piece dialogues and passages of reflection in which English and American manners are contrasted are not the centre of Hawthorne's interest; there is at once a bitterness and a perfunctoriness about them which mark Hawthorne's real animus against English snobbery and his ultimate disdain for mere *mœurs*. Nor are his descriptions of English scenery – the things which travelbook tourists of the picturesque might like best – of more importance. Setting does not speak as eloquently as it did in the scaffold and forest scenes of *The Scarlet Letter*.

The principal characters and the action itself are at all times, as the passages of introspection reveal, Hawthorne's prime concern. Study A begins with an American, 'a person of high rank, who has reached eminence early' (20), who comes to England to investigate his 'interesting' connection with his ancestral family. There he meets an 'unflinchingly' English young lady who turns out to be one of his relatives – one of the many, in all stations of life, who inhabit the neighbourhood. He also meets 'an American Defalcator' who has lived in solitude in this district, and a nobleman

198

III: The Last Quests

(possessed of a secret vice) who is also a relative. Un-expectedly, the American discovers that it is in his power to overturn 'whatever seems fixed. The nobleman's title and estate, for instance ... It must be shown, I think, throughout, that there is an essential difference between English and American character, and that the former must assimilate itself to the latter if there is to be any union.' (20–21)

In Study B we learn that the American, a lawyer, shall 'feel himself the master of this nobleman's fate ... The great gist of the story ought to be the natural hatred of man – and the particular hatred of Americans – to an Aristocracy; ... At last, I think, the American must have it in his power to put an end to the nobility of the man; and shall do so, not without reluctance and pain.' (22)

Study B1 suggests that the American is the 'rightful heir' to the English estate, but 'the gist of the story shall be not to install him in possession of the property' (23). Study c wonders what the secret vice – or 'impending calamity' (hereditary) – of the English family will be. Study D opens the story in Salem with a kindly but eccentric old doctor (Dr. Grimshawe) who has charge of the young American (an almshouse foundling) and a sweet young girl who will later reappear as the 'English' girl whom the young fortune-hunter meets. Fifteen years later the old doctor dies. The young American, now a politician, goes to England to seek out his ancestry. He is robbed 'and left for dead' near his family's ancestral seat, but is rescued by an 'old pensioner' (the American defalcator, brother to Dr. Grimshawe) and taken to a charitable home which the old family has en-dowed. The old pensioner it appears, had once been a

199

financial baron. Study E concludes that the American's 'generosity, and a feeling of shame, must prevail with him not to claim his rights' (26).

As this evidence reveals, Hawthorne began with the intention of writing a romantic fairy tale – an adolescent 'conquering-hero' dream – in which a young American returned to his old home to depose the wicked uncle, inherit the wealth of England, and claim the hand of his distant cousin, the beautiful English maiden. On the level of realism, the tale would afford many opportunities for the contrast and comparison of English and American manners as recorded in Hawthorne's notebooks. But even at the outset this plot was complicated by two factors: Dr. Grimshawe, the benevolent old foster-father, had died, but the American defalcator remained to save the hero from death; and the nobleman was to be overthrown for a crime which Hawthorne could not specify. *Who* was the defalcator, and *what* was the nobleman's crime?

As Hawthorne delved deeper and deeper into these questions, his problems grew more and more complex. On the surface the action bears a close relation to the Theseus myth. The benign old doctor (Aegeus) sends his unacknowledged 'son' to England to find out his ancestry, to destroy the black monster (Minos – the nobleman) who has wreaked so much harm on America, and to marry the 'English' daughter (Ariadne).[20] In terms of the romantic American dream this is very easy. The young American, now grown to manhood and political prominence, can easily assert the superiority of his way of life over the sinful old

20 Hawthorne's imagery repeatedly suggests that the ancestral home is a dusky and mysterious labyrinth.

III: The Last Quests

English family. But would this childish wish-fulfilment narrative really be a 'true' account of British-American relations?

The real reason for the American 'hero's' needs to assert his claim to English roots, it soon appears, is that England is really his spiritual home. He is not quite the symbol of a superior breed that Hawthorne's story-line implies. As Etherege (the hero) tells the old Pensioner:

'The current of my life runs darkly on, & I would be glad of any light on its future, or even its present course ... I have tried to keep down this yearning [for roots], to stifle it, annihilate it, with making a position for myself, with being my own past; but I cannot overcome this horror of being a creature floating in the air, attached to nothing; ever this feeling that there is no reality in the life and fortunes, good or bad, of a being so unconnected. There is not even a grave, not a heap of dry bones, not a pinch of dust, with which I can claim connection, unless I find it here.' (144–45)

The English garden is 'the sweetest and coziest seclusion he had ever known' (100). His dream of attaining it is, perhaps, a 'fool's Paradise,' but after the 'turbulent life' of his American career, he wants this security. America is always changing: 'Posterity! An American can have none' (83, 97).

The American's 'return' to England, then, is not the conquering hero's progress which Hawthorne had first imagined. England, with its permanence, its resemblance to a 'cultivated Eden' and its age-old tradition of beauty and art, is not wholly evil. Perhaps it is more good than bad. And America, for all its glorious democratic vistas, is turbulent, rough, changeable, rootless. The proof that Hawthorne was profoundly disturbed by this discrepancy between what he would like to believe and what his experience

201

of England made him feel is amply recorded in Mr. Davidson's edition of *Dr. Grimshawe's Secret*. On the one hand Hawthorne clung stubbornly to his American myth, the belief that the new institutions of America would produce a new breed of men and women, a breed whose crowning glory would be a Master Genius. This belief was the basis of his entire artistic career and he could not give it up unless he were willing to admit that the belief of a lifetime – and the heart of an *œuvre* – was an illusion. On the other hand, though he could bristle angrily at the smugness, self-complacency, and insularity of the English, his hero could not 'stifle' or 'annihilate' his yearning for the wisdom and security and beauty that England displayed on every hand.

If, therefore, he was to have his cake and eat it too – to give his American a legitimate claim to the riches and titles of England, without sacrificing his 'superiority' – he would have to conceive an action of greater subtlety than the conquering-hero quest. This he attempted to accomplish by suggesting that, at the end of Charles the First's reign, the English family of his story had unjustly expelled a younger son. This younger son, who was not, as the English family claimed, the king's executioner (a father-killer), had emigrated to Virginia, and the family, losing track of the emigrant's posterity, had passed into the hands of a collateral British line who held the inheritance through two centuries, though it rightly belonged to the American branch of the family. Thus, after two hundred years, the American heir would return to England bearing proofs of his ancestry; he would decline to accept the title, which would then devolve upon the old pensioner (the American defalcator), now disciplined to saintliness after his career of fraud. The young American would marry his English 'cousin' (the little girl brought up in America by Dr. Grimshawe, and now identified as the daughter of the old pensioner). In this case the inheritance would go not to the aggressive young politician but to the old man whose shady career in 'the world' and in America had led him to retire to England and claim his right, by virtue of relationship, to the charity of the old family.

As Hawthorne works and reworks these materials, his *dramatis personae* change radically. The benevolent Dr. Grimshawe, lost in his cobwebby dreams of regenerating the world through the medicinal properties of spiders, becomes a wizard, a Dr. Rappaccini, whose symbol is a malevolent African spider. Like this monster, sitting at the centre of its web – the web of time – he plans to destroy the English family, root and branch, by involving them in a plot which will function inexorably, even after the Doctor's death. The best motive that Hawthorne discovers for the Doctor's diabolism is that a member of the English family seduced his sister and caused her death – a crime which the Doctor will never forgive.

In line with this plan, the young American now becomes a dupe of the Doctor, an imposter whom the Doctor plans to impose upon the English family. Meanwhile, the seventeenth-century emigrant is described as almost 'saintly'; and the old Pensioner, now the emigrant's 'rightful heir,' becomes a similarly uncomplaining saint who will come, 'in spite of himself,' into the inheritance which he knows about but is too gentle to claim. The usurping nobleman's 'vice' will be his knowledge of an imprisoned ancestor, a man driven into perpetual hiding by Dr. Grimshawe. This prisoner will be discovered by the young American dupe and will die of shock at the mention of Grimshawe's name. The young American's supposed fortune will be a coffin 'filled with golden curls,' the only remains of the sweetheart of the first emigrant. Meanwhile the deserving old Pensioner will come into his English estate.

Hawthorne could get no further than this with his chaotic plot. The further he pursued his action, the more complex and fantastic it became, and although he had discovered arresting symbols (the Bloody Footstep to represent the English family's crime, the coffin of curls to represent the young American's delusion, and the African spider to symbolize Dr. Grimshawe's malevolence) he could not pin down their meaning. What was the crime of England against the American branch of the family? Who was the old Pensioner? Why was Dr. Grimshawe so diabolical? In attempting to establish the crucial reason for the young American's quest, Hawthorne mixed himself up completely in a chronological tangle. The crime against the first emigrant was very difficult to define or symbolize. This, therefore, was reinforced by the family's later crime against Dr. Grimshawe's sister. But Dr. Grimshawe had no real relation to the English family; and neither the two-hundred-year-old crime against the emigrant nor the Doctor's loss of his 'sister' served as adequate justification for the diabolical web in which he deliberately enmeshed the English family. There was no 'dark necessity' here comparable to the necessitarianism of the Puritan ethos in *The Scarlet Letter*.

Hawthorne abandoned *Dr. Grimshawe* without solving its problems. He had failed in the most difficult task that he had ever undertaken. And the fundamental reason for his failure was that, for the first time in his career, his sanguine views about the career of America clashed in mortal conflict with a mythical narrative that irresistibly denied the American hero's triumph. There was no solution to this impasse; it meant the 'death of the artist.'

But the sheer power of the imaginative, myth-making centre of Hawthorne's mind would not die without a titanic struggle. Whatever the strength of his rational opinions, they could not prevail against the deeper knowledge of the imagination; hence the almost autonomous transformations of the characters in *Dr. Grimshawe*. As Hawthorne 'tries back' again and again, the young American, who dreams of having a past and a family, becomes a brash, over-confident young fool who seeks to establish an illusory claim to English rank. But this illusion is not entirely the young man's fault. The old Doctor encourages him to believe in his superiority over the English; and as this motif develops, Hawthorne's prose echoes the sun-gold-lust-power imagery which characterizes Jaffrey Pyncheon and 'blinds' nineteenth-century New England. In the same way, the ineffectual old Pensioner – a man who suffers from too much conscience rather than, like Dr. Grimshawe, from none at all – finally becomes the rightful heir to English culture. His approach to England, after a stormy career in the prize-ring of high finance, is to assert meekly his claim of kinship; to accept the 'charity' of his relatives and, finally, to be acknowledged as heir 'in spite of himself.' Hawthorne could not 'make out' rationally what such transformations meant; or if he could, he would not accept their import. He could not give up his dream; he could not bring himself to a daylight avowal of his terrifying sense of America's true nature in the eighteen sixties.

Septimius Felton, the aftermath of this imaginative agony, is a logical outcome of it. Lacking a reliable edition of its text, we shall not attempt here to analyze the work in detail. One thing, however, can be stated with certainty. If Hawthorne's art – and his vision of America – had not produced the crowning achievement for which he hoped, then the achievement would have to wait for a later age. It was perfectly natural, therefore, that Hawthorne should turn, perhaps quite unconsciously, from the shattering defeat of his hopes and dreams recorded in *Dr. Grimshawe* to the subject of 'earthly immortality.' This is precisely the subject of the final season of his career. Although 'he had aged so much that he could hardly grasp a pen,'[21] he determinedly set out to create a hero who would live beyond the chaos of the sixties and achieve a selfhood which would prove his real independence of the old king-father (England), and assert his equality or his superiority over him. The idea was not new to Hawthorne; he had broached it as early as 'Dr. Heidegger's Experiment'; but it was not a major theme of his fiction, and he turned to it now with desperation and misgiving. The 'undying man' of The Wayside, of whom Thoreau had told him, would be his hero. (As with Etherege, we again sense self-portraiture in this 'owner' of The Wayside.) This hero, Septimius Felton, would live beyond the troubled era of war – Hawthorne chose the Revolutionary war as a symbolic period – and would

21 Davidson, *Hawthorne's Last Phase*, p. 151.

eventually claim his inheritance from the English family of the Bloody Footstep. As Hawthorne expressed the idea in Study G of his story: 'Septimius thinks that he shall live to see the glory and the final event of the American Republic, which his contemporaries, perishing people, are fighting to establish.'[22] This glory, of course, cannot be achieved now, in a time of war, but it will come nevertheless. The urgency of this idea for Hawthorne is expressed in a marginal note at the top of the first page of Study D: 'Express strongly the idea that the shortness &c of life shows that human action is a humbug.' And in the first paragraph of this study: 'Septimius muses much on life and death, and is dissatisfied with death, on noble grounds, because it so breaks off and brings to naught all human effort; so as [to] make a man a laughing stock of whoever created him.'[23]

On the whole, *Septimius Felton* approaches closer to success than does *Dr. Grimshawe*. Hawthorne has retreated from the immediate need to see the vindication of his American hero and is content to see his problem work itself out in the timeless drama of imagination. But even with this imaginative distancing, the action does not achieve that coherence which was Hawthorne's prime requirement of his fiction. The discrepancy between his faith in his American dream and his intuitive fear that it would not be fulfilled produces another, a final, impasse.

As the tale develops, we see that the English protagonists are now the villains. Dr. Grimshawe has become the crudely-named Dr. Portsoaken whose mysterious daughter, Sibyl Dacy (Hester, Pandora), finally gives her life to keep

22 *Ibid.*, p. 88.
23 *Ibid.*, pp. 82–83. The square-bracketed parenthesis is Davidson's.

Septimius from drinking the fatal elixir which her father has concocted. With Sibyl's death, the Doctor also dies, mysteriously, and his talisman-spider proves to be the empty shell of a dessicated insect. Septimius then, it is rumoured, goes off to England and asserts his claim to the ancient title to which he is the 'rightful heir.'

As pure fantasy, this is a much more acceptable story than *Dr. Grimshawe*. Its only difficulty, as Hawthorne must have realized, is that it really is pure fantasy. It is an escape from the dilemma of *Dr. Grimshawe*, for Sibyl Dacy, Dr. Portsoaken, and Septimius are, as symbols, historically meaningless in comparison with their earlier incarnations – Hester, Chillingworth, and Dimmesdale. England was not, for Hawthorne, the demon that we see in Dr. Portsoaken, and England's creative force would not, as Sibyl Dacy did, commit suicide so that the American hero might march off in triumph to claim his inheritance or assert his superiority. Oddly enough, there is an almost prophetic element in Hawthorne's choice of a wartime situation as the occasion of a realignment of American and British relations. Hawthorne's intuition fell just short of seeing that in the next cycle of the myth America, though estranged and reluctant, would finally come to the aid of its ageing, war-afflicted parent, and inherit quite naturally the title of leader in the western community.

It would be much too harsh a judgment to say that in these works Hawthorne betrayed his artistic vision. He knew that *Dr. Grimshawe, Septimius Felton*, and *The Dolliver Romance* – the last flicker of his creative energy – were failures. And he had the good sense to know that they should not be published. He was, in a sense, completely true to his vision. Always his own best critic, he recognized the heartbreak of failure. His family, we must suppose, were no more than accessories in this betrayal, for they had no idea of the meaning of the artistic problems with which their father attempted to deal in his last phase. These fragmentary romances, therefore, in no sense diminish our conception of Hawthorne's greatness. For his readers they are a piercing and pathetic record of the dying struggles of a genius. At the same time they give us – more than anything else that he wrote – an insight into his artistic methods and a glimpse of his overwhelming concern for the future of the America which he loved so well. Edward H. Davidson has expiated the sin of exploring these forbidden fragments by helping us to know Hawthorne better, through an analysis of his methods. The present analysis has attempted to perform a similar service by reconstructing his myth of America.

PART IV

Hawthorne's Character Types: The Personae
of His Myth

LITERATURE, PHILOSOPHY, RELIGION, AND THE SOCIAL sciences try to make 'human sense' of experience by revealing or creating patterns which suggest an order or meaning that permeates reality; hence such varied formulations, ancient and modern, as Buddhism, Platonism, Christianity, Freudianism, Miltonic cosmography, and Yeatsian historical theory. Man may regard such structures as unalterable, divine revelations, or treat them as imaginative patterns which help him to learn, in the words of Conrad's Dr. Stein, 'How to be.' Self-conscious man has always needed such patterns; and twentieth-century man no doubt lives by his myths as faithfully as his Greek or Puritan ancestors did, and perhaps as credulously.

In literary study, where criticism has become newly aware of the myth-making or mythopoeic aspect of the subject, there has been a good deal of analysis that is justly described as 'Symbol Simon' interpretation: Freudian critics, for example, argue that Hawthorne and a host of other writers cannot stay away from landscapes which are disguised images of male and female genitalia; and as Douglas Bush has remarked, religion-oriented symbolist critics are likely to see every garden as the Garden of Eden and every tree as The One True Cross.

All too frequently such criticism fails to recognize that a serious artist's patterning of character, action, and imagery

213

is likely to be unique, whatever his debts to tradition; Milton's world is not Blake's or Conrad's or Faulkner's. Therefore, one of criticism's prime tasks is to define as fully as possible the nature of an artist's particular vision. If the artist's propensities are 'towards Fairy Land' (VII, 150), as Hawthorne avowed that his were, then the critic must try to discover what his particular fairyland was like. Who are the people who live in it? What are their powers? And what are their typical conflicts?

The analysis of Hawthorne's character types which this essay presents is schematic, indeed diagrammatic, but it attempts to be faithful to Hawthorne rather than to Freud, Frazier, or Christian apologists; and it is offered not as a doctrinaire interpretation of Hawthorne's mythology but as a set of signposts which may bring us closer to the heart of his 'cryptic preoccupation.' Like any schema, it cannot compass the resonance and richness of the work itself; it will not even attempt to account for every character whom Hawthorne created. But it may reveal in a new way the currents of energy that shaped his deepest vision.

As we have seen above, the images and symbols that Hawthorne attaches to the *personae* of his mythological tales are closely related to images which define character in his tales of experience. In broad outline, all of these images suggest that Hawthorne thought of two kinds of people; far from exemplifying the Head and Heart division so popular with criticism, his world contained one large and complex group associated with the daylight realm of sunshine, animal energy, and empirical things; and a second, equally complex group associated with the night realm of moonlight, imaginative energy, and spiritual reality. This basic

IV: Hawthorne's Character Types

division is Hawthorne's personal expression of what F. O. Matthiessen and W. Stacy Johnson have seen in theological terms as his fundamental dualism – a division between 'this world' and the ideal or heavenly world.[1] But Hawthorne does not define these realms in religious terms; instead, his imagery relates them to 'empirical' truth (see part I, p. 15, note 12, on the special use of this term), and imaginative or spiritual truth. In the empirical realm we are faced with the hard, unyielding particulars of sensory experience and concrete objects. The images which characterize this world are sun, gold, lust, power, 'Oriental' female beauty, and scientific exactness. But these images are complemented by benign images of sunniness (as of disposition), golden hair, motherliness, and parental warmth – in short, the domestic warmth of the hearth. In the moonlit realm of night, we are in the clear territory of spirit or imagination, uncluttered by the particulars of objects and self-aggrandizement. The images which characterize this realm are moon, water, mirrors (Mercury), magic, coldness, artistic detachment, and sometimes wizardry or monstrousness (Medusa).

Hawthorne's art, however, does not oscillate between these polarities; nor are they simple oppositions. As we shall see below, each of the two realms contains a group of active characters and a group of passive characters; and within each sub-group, active or passive, there is a generous spectrum of personalities, male and female, who typify various aspects of empirical and imaginative experience. These people may move towards the extreme limits of their particular realm as does the demonic Roger Chillingworth

1 Johnson, *Hibbert Journal*, L (1951), 40; Matthiessen, *American Renaissance*, pp. 337–51.

on the one hand, and the artist-wizard of 'The Prophetic Pictures' on the other. But there is a third realm which lies somewhere between the extremes. This is the mysterious centre of Hawthorne's art; it is the essential area in which fact and insight, the empirical and the imaginative, intersect – the mixed realm of human nature in which man's (or society's) opposing qualities may achieve a balance or synthesis.

In its benign aspect, this central human realm of action is characterized by sun and shade, ideally imaged in the atmosphere of Monte Beni; or by Phoebe Pyncheon's domestic sunniness; or by the 'cool brown light' of the forest. In 'The Custom House' it is a combination of warm hearthlight and clear moonlight reflected in a mirror – a blend of the two worlds which is the ideal atmosphere for artistic creation (C, I, 35–36). In the figure of Pearl, the living embodiment of the A, we see the union of imagination and the warm gifts of the heart and hearth. The presiding values of this area are sympathy, generosity, and love. In its malign aspects, the human realm presents a darkling scene of ugliness, indifference, passion, and selfishness. Finally, to use Hawthorne's central symbol, this shadowy area is the human Heart, that 'foul cavern' and ideal garden which is the vessel of 'our common nature.'

Stated in abstract terms, Hawthorne's basic myth is a quest to recognize the powers of both the sunlit and moonlit realms of experience, and to use both creatively in the mixed, human realm. Ideally, the cool vision of the night realm 'marries' the benign warmth of the empirical world; only then does an individual or a society find its full self, its vision and power – its Heart. This fundamental action

216

IV: Hawthorne's Character Types

or conflict – as in the mythological formulations of Blake and W. B. Yeats – gives shape and coherence to Hawthorne's art. It enables him, moreover, to speak equally (and sometimes simultaneously) of the self, the society, and the artist – of *mythos, ethos,* and *dianoia.* Before turning to the individuals who flesh out this pattern of active and passive, empirical and imaginative types, I shall present it as a diagram that suggests graphically the major oppositions in Hawthorne's 'life of allegory.' The commentary that follows will consider the problems of the sixteen contrasted character types (and four others not shown in the diagram). Why are some condemned to isolation and suffering? Who can 'marry' or find his place in the central human realm?

In his Introduction to *The American Notebooks by Nathaniel Hawthorne* (1932), Mr. Randall Stewart included a valuable analysis of Hawthorne's character types. In returning to that subsequently neglected subject, I am inevitably indebted to his work; the analysis which follows, however, expands the field by including the *personae* of the Greek mythological tales, and alters the emphasis of the original by considering the various characters as types of one or another force in Hawthorne's personal mythology. Thus some of the small groups considered by Mr. Stewart are here united under one heading; for example, among the 'tyrant father' figures, kings, military men, judges, and reformers are grouped together since all are linked by similar motives, similar talents, similar imagery, and similar hostility to imaginative young heroes. I should add that the titles which I have chosen for each group are not merely capricious: they describe the nature of the characters so grouped; but because my classification departs radically

217

from earlier groupings I have felt it necessary to avoid titles such as Head and Heart, with their implications of simple bi-polar opposition.

The broad pattern of character contrasts – active and passive, empirical and imaginative – has been discussed above. A few general comments on figure I should be made before we turn to individual character groups. First, there are more male than female types in Hawthorne's imaginative world. Among the eight 'active' types in the diagram only two are female – the Dark Ladies and the so-called 'female monsters' (a type which I shall suggest is largely illusory). Among the eight 'passive' types, four are female. In the empirical realm there are large groups of aggressive fathers and scientists, and a large group of benign but ineffectual fathers; but Hawthorne's principal heroes belong in the imaginative realm; there are very few young heroes in the empirical or 'sun' realm of Hawthorne's vision. Second, there are no tyrant fathers in the imaginative realm, and no tyrant mothers in the empirical realm. Imaginative fathers such as Matthew Maule, who have been denied their function in the daylight world, are likely to become wizards who plague iron materialists; and mothers like Hester, who have been denied their natural intuitions, may enter the night realm; but such parents do everything possible in support of their sons and daughters.

Third, four figures who are best described as 'prime movers' have been omitted from the diagram: Jupiter, Phoebus-Apollo, Fauntleroy, and Old Moodie. Hawthorne, as we know, believed firmly in an ideal or divine order, and a state of perfection beyond life, but he did not accept

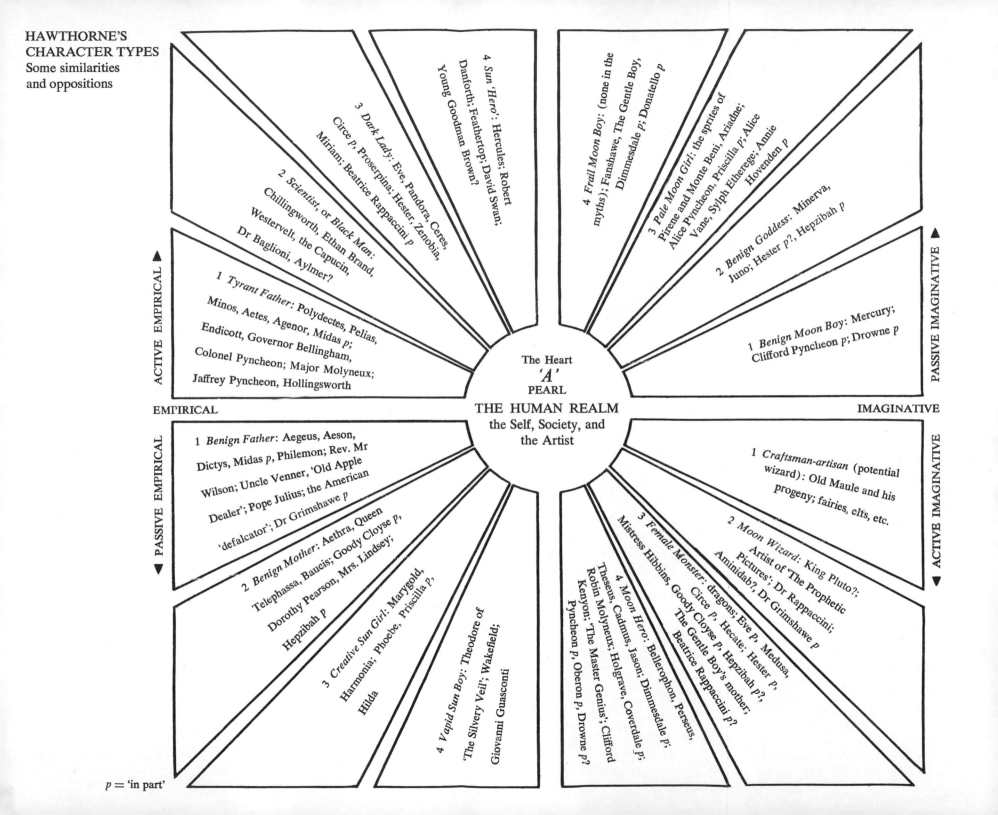

HAWTHORNE'S
CHARACTER TYPES
Some similarities
and oppositions

The Heart
'A'
PEARL
THE HUMAN REALM
the Self, Society, and
the Artist

ACTIVE EMPIRICAL

PASSIVE EMPIRICAL

EMPIRICAL

PASSIVE IMAGINATIVE

ACTIVE IMAGINATIVE

IMAGINATIVE

4 *Sun 'Hero'*: Hercules; Robert
Danforth; Feathertop; David Swan;
Young Goodman Brown?

3 *Dark Lady*: Eve, Pandora, Ceres,
Circe *p*, Proserpina; Hester, Zenobia,
Miriam; Beatrice Rappaccini *p*

2 *Scientist, or Black Man*:
Chillingworth, Ethan Brand,
Westervelt, the Capucin,
Dr Baglioni, Aylmer?

1 *Tyrant Father*: Polydectes, Pelias,
Minos, Aetes, Agenor, Midas *p*;
Endicott, Governor Bellingham,
Colonel Pyncheon; Major Molyneux;
Jaffrey Pyncheon, Hollingsworth

4 *Frail Moon Boy*: (none in the
myths); Fanshawe, The Gentle Boy,
Dimmesdale *p*; Donatello *p*

3 *Pale Moon Girl*: the sprites of
Pirene and Monte Beni, Ariadne;
Alice Pyncheon, Priscilla *p*; Alice
Vane, Sylph Etherege; Annie
Hovenden *p*

2 *Benign Goddess*: Minerva,
Juno; Hester *p*?, Hepzibah *p*

1 *Benign Moon Boy*: Mercury;
Clifford Pyncheon *p*; Drowne *p*

1 *Benign Father*: Aegeus, Aeson,
Dictys, Midas *p*, Philemon; Rev. Mr
Wilson; Uncle Venner, 'Old Apple
Dealer'; Pope Julius; the American
'defalcator'; Dr Grimshawe *p*

2 *Benign Mother*: Aethra, Queen
Telephassa, Baucis; Goody Cloyse *p*,
Dorothy Pearson, Mrs. Lindsey;
Hepzibah *p*

3 *Creative Sun Girl*: Marygold,
Harmonia; Phoebe, Priscilla *p*,
Hilda

4 *Vapid Sun Boy*: Theodore of
'The Silvery Veil'; Wakefield;
Giovanni Guasconti

1 *Craftsman-artisan* (potential
wizard): Old Maule and his
progeny; fairies, elfs, etc.

2 *Moon Wizard*: King Pluto?;
Artist of 'The Prophetic
Pictures'; Dr Rappaccini;
Aminidab?, Dr Grimshawe *p*

3 *Female Monster*: dragons; Eve *p*, Medusa,
Circe *p*, Hecate; Hester *p*,
Mistress Hibbins, Goody Cloyse *p*, Hepzibah *p*?,
The Gentle Boy's mother;
Beatrice Rappaccini *p*?

4 *Moon Hero*: Bellerophon, Perseus,
Theseus, Cadmus, Jason; Dimmesdale *p*;
Robin Molyneux; Holgrave, Coverdale *p*;
Kenyon; 'The Master Genius'; Clifford
Pyncheon, Oberon *p*, Drowne *p*?

p = 'in part'

IV: Hawthorne's Character Types

Puritan views of the creation and Fall, or their emphasis on the guilt of Eve. Indeed he was little concerned with the Miltonic need to 'justify the ways of God to men'; his great concern was man himself, and man's need to affirm the spiritual side of his nature. But when in *Blithedale* he was faced with explaining the origins of the sensuous Zenobia and the ethereal Priscilla, he created a two-sided spectral figure, Fauntleroy-Moodie. Fauntleroy is a vain and dazzling spirit who neglects his Eve-like daughter; Old Moodie, his New England double, is a humbled and ineffectual deity who asks that the colonists cherish his immaculate second 'daughter.' Fauntleroy, in short, is the prime mover in the materialistic sun realm; his passive counterpart in the sun realm is the foppish Phoebus-Apollo, seen only once in the tale of Proserpina – a figure who has no interest in human sorrow or suffering. Old Moodie, with his vain hopes that Priscilla will be made Zenobia's equal in Blithedale, belongs in the passive night realm; and his active counterpart is Jupiter, the all-powerful though unnamed deity who sires Perseus, spirits away the pristine child Europa, and rewards the sympathy of Baucis and Philemon with immortality.

These figures or forces, though not of central interest to Hawthorne, suggest very clearly the nature of his conception of divine power. Jupiter, with his gifted servants Mercury and Minerva, and his benign wife Juno, is the imaginative hero's champion; and Moodie, though under a cloud, champions the spiritual maiden. Fauntleroy, the materialistic spirit, loses his 'noble' wife and allows his exotic daughter to get into trouble; Apollo, his passive but glittering counterpart, is an epicene cipher; and Hercules (Helios), their

219

demigod champion is principally a muscle-man. In the sun realm, Ceres and Juno, though not supreme forces, appear to be the deities most sympathetic to human needs.

These general comments bring us to the particular groups presented in the diagram. Some of the figures appear to be allied to more than one group, and to recognize such ambivalence I have placed a *p* after their names to indicate that they may belong 'in part' in the opposite quarter of the diagram. Thus Priscilla begins as a Pale Moon Girl, but the sunny Blithedale period of her experience suggests that she might be a Creative Sun Girl. And since the diagram is an hypothesis, I have sometimes added a question mark following a character's name to indicate that I find my attribution open to question.

The Empirical Realm: Active Types

The leading type here is a tyrant father figure (1). In the mythological tales he appears as a grasping old monarch – Polydectes, Pelias, Minos, Aeetes, or Agenor. He is the 'man of iron' who resists any change in the status quo, who ruthlessly destroys or suppresses the talent of his aspiring sons and relatives. He cannot allow them to share in his power, and is condemned as a result to a magnificent, isolated eminence. Like Polydectes, he is lustful; like Pelias, cruel; like Midas, greedy; and like Aeetes, who so carefully guards his Golden Fleece, jealous. He is also, as Hawthorne suggests in the Midas story, 'blind'; the glare of sun-gold closes his eyes to human values.

Related to these mythological types are a variety of menacing father figures who appear in the tales and romances.

IV: Hawthorne's Character Types

Those 'sour old Puritans' – Endicott, Governor Bellingham, and old Colonel Pyncheon – are grimly inflexible figures whose blind regard for law, doctrine, and conformity drives the imagination into witchcraft and wizardry. In a later age their sternness becomes the 'sultry' sunshine and the 'hot, fellness of purpose' of Jaffrey Pyncheon. In *Blithedale*, it takes a new turn in the blind, reforming zeal of Hollingsworth, the ex-blacksmith who thinks of human nature as criminal. But this type – which we know in modern dress as E. M. Forster's Wilcox men and Galsworthy's Forsytes – is not wholly to be condemned, for they are in possession of man's physical power – his aggressive competence to get things done, his creative energy in the realm of things. The danger is that this figure will exaggerate his useful qualities until they become a curse. The man who lives only for sun – for law, logic, and hard fact – may perish of heat and glare; he becomes isolated, cut off from the sun and shade of the human realm.

When the power or creative energy of this figure is intellectual, Hawthorne portrays him not as a ruler but as a scientist (2). This man's mastery of the empirical world can bring infinite benefit to mankind, but an exclusive pursuit of knowledge can cut him off from humanity entirely. If, moreover, he turns his skill to the cold analysis of the human heart, he commits the unpardonable sin; he has, like Chillingworth and Ethan Brand, 'violated in cold blood, the sanctity of a human heart' (C, I, 195). When the scientist works against rather than for mankind he becomes a demon. In the New England context he is the Black Man who makes the imperfection of his fellows a crime with which he endlessly tortures them, and who

221

regards woman as a sinful temptress. Chillingworth and Westervelt are Hawthorne's New England scientist-demons, and Dr. Baglioni is a European variant. Miriam's model, the Capucin, though not a scientist, belongs with Chillingworth and Westervelt as a Black Man, Roman Catholic style.

A curious variation of the scientist figure is Aylmer, 'a type of the spiritual element' whose physical nature is typified in his simian 'underworker,' Aminidab. In attempting to remove the single blemish in his wife's otherwise perfect beauty, the over-intellectual scientist destroys her. Aminidab, whose Old Testament name suggests the leader of a priestly family, knows that Aylmer has sought the impossible, and laughs his 'hoarse, chuckling laugh.' 'Thus ever,' Hawthorne comments, 'does the gross fatality of earth exult in its invariable triumph over the immortal essence which, in this dim sphere of half-development, demands the completeness of a higher state' (II, 69). Aylmer's intentions were noble, but he lacked the vision to recognize that in the human realm perfection is unattainable.[2]

The female counterpart of these forceful sun men is a richly endowed, glamorous brunette (3) who appears in the mythological tales, and in many passing allusions, as Eve, Pandora, Proserpina, or a nymph. Like the father figures and scientists, the Dark Lady is very much of this world. Though she appears in New England as Hester and

2 This tale, published in 1834, is not typical of Hawthorne's later formulations of the obsessed scientist. Though Hawthorne calls Aminidab's talents 'earthly,' the 'underworker's' awareness of Aylmer's delusion suggests that, like Matthew Maule, he is wiser than his master – that he is intuitively in touch with human nature, and that Aylmer's scientific spirit is the more dangerous force.

IV: Hawthorne's Character Types

Zenobia, she is not native born; she belongs to another land, as do the other incarnations of the type, Miriam and Beatrice Rappaccini. She is a fecund creature, gifted with an extraordinary range of talents – sewing, painting, gardening, nursing; and in her bolder (and perhaps misguided) moments she is a thinker. Hawthorne clearly admires this primal woman and takes elaborate pains to say that she is guiltless, or at least no more guilty than men; she simply follows the laws of her nature. Thus both Pandora's and Proserpina's only weakness is that they give in to natural impulses; Coverdale and Kenyon both insist that their Dark Ladies are not blameworthy; even Dimmesdale ends by claiming his Hester, though as a good Puritan he demands that her strength be 'guided by the will which God hath granted me!' (C, I, 253) Still more clearly, Hawthorne's angelic 'Beatrice' Rappaccini is only what her father made her; in her last breath she asks the sunny Giovanni: 'Was there not, from the first, more poison in thy nature than in mine?' (II, 147)

But if the Dark Lady of tradition is blameless, Hawthorne nevertheless has great difficulty in finding a role for her in America, for she is a very strong personality. If her creative energies were given full scope in society, she might serve as a benign creative force. But men keep denying her, and when her daylight creativity is denied she may enter the dusky realm into which Hester was forced by her Puritan judges; and here she can appear to be a witch, a destructive force which haunts men's dreams. In mythology she is Gorgon Medusa, Medea, or Circe (though we must remember that Hawthorne cleared Circe of blame; the men she transformed *wanted* to behave like beasts). In Christian

223

terms, the Dark Lady is Eve, cursed by the Puritans but admired by Hawthorne.

Yet even though innocent, the Dark Lady is not the mate Hawthorne wants for his nineteenth-century heroes. Such men as Holgrave and Coverdale want a sunny, spiritual, golden-haired creature who will understand the rare nature of their love and accept their mercurial vision. They need a woman who will 'marry' them to the sunny realities of the empirical realm. The obsessively sexual Dark Lady really belongs to the European tradition. The American hero's bride will be free of the Christian and Puritan taint – an immaculate Phoebe or Priscilla who, like Cadmus's Harmonia, will be at once a 'daughter of the sky' and a fecund 'domestic saint.'

A fourth figure who belongs with the active trio of sun people described above is the young sun-hero (4), a type whom Hawthorne neither understands fully nor particularly likes. In the mythological tales he is Hercules, a hearty but somewhat thoughtless blunderer. Hawthorne does not treat Hercules satirically, but the muscle-man's adventures clearly do not absorb the author as Perseus' and Bellerophon's do; the result is two of the most formless of the mythological tales, with a variety of pasted-on morals. In the New England tales, the young sun-hero appears to triumph only once: this figure is Robert Danforth, the hearty young blacksmith in 'The Artist of the Beautiful.' Danforth, however, belongs to the Puritan period, and though he wins the girl whom Owen Warland desired, and produces a lusty child, it is clear that the artist reaps a spiritual reward – perhaps the best he can hope for in Puritan society. In two other tales, a young 'sun hero' appears in even less promising guise. 'Feathertop' is a scarecrow, the creation of a 'witch,' Mother Rigby (all the names in this tale are allegorical). Mother Rigby, an embittered Puritan woman who has long since recognized the daylight shams of her community, endows her scarecrow with all the external splendour of a public figure, in which guise he courts the daughter of a gullible merchant, Mr. Gookin. But Feathertop, who is a spirit from the night realm, sees in a mirror that his finery is only that of a scarecrow, and in rage and despair dashes out the pipe which gives him spiritual being. Mother Rigby, equally alienated from the empirical realm, reflects sardonically: ' "My poor, dear, pretty Feathertop! There are thousands upon thousands of coxcombs and charlatans in the world, made up of just such a jumble of wornout, forgotten, and good-for-nothing trash as he was! Yet they live in fair repute, and never see themselves for what they are." ' (II, 278)

David Swan, another naive hero, sleeps stolidly by a flowing spring while possibilities of wealth, love, and violent death pass by without awakening him. Hawthorne's concern in this allegory is the unconsciousness of youth; his final question is whether there may be a 'superintending Providence' which operates with 'regularity enough in mortal life to render foresight even partially available?' (I, 218) David Swan awakens, unscathed, in time to stop the stagecoach for Boston where he will become an apprentice to his merchant uncle. Perhaps Providence or instinct will indeed watch over him, for his name suggests a great king and a soaring white bird; but there is no sign that he has seen the reflections in the prophetic mirror of the spring. David Swan is perhaps typical of youth; Hawthorne cannot assure us that he will discover any vision beyond the marketplace.

The Empirical Realm: Passive Types

The second quartet of empirical character types is passive or benign. As we have seen in the mythological tales, the tyrannical father is frequently linked with an ineffectual but pleasant old man, a benign father (1) who relinquishes his authority and supports the younger generation. Tired old Aegeus, Theseus' father, is such a man; he is full of love for his son but totally incompetent to better the young man's fortunes or to triumph over Minos.[3] The young man must champion his father and his country. In the Jason myth, the benign father, Aeson, is such an unimportant character that Hawthorne omits him entirely from his version of the tale; and Dictys, King Polydectes' brother in the Perseus story, remains unnamed. It is clear, however, that Hawthorne felt sympathy for these losers in life's power struggle. 'The Old Apple Dealer,' a basic study of this type, is a sympathetic figure; and Uncle Venner, the 'patchwork philosopher' of *Seven Gables*, knows that the avuncular role is to advise the young rather than command. The great virtue of such sunny characters is their power of sympathy and affection. In the European setting, Pope Julius of *The Marble Faun* is hearteningly benign, but relatively powerless – a monument to an earlier age. Very often, however, these disinherited fathers are restored to honour by their questing sons; and

3 James Joyce anagramatically transforms Minos into the false father, 'Simon' Dedalus, in *A Portrait of the Artist As a Young Man*.

226

the American defalcator of *Dr. Grimshawe* is honoured in spite of himself. The meek, in some degree, do inherit the earth, though they may not receive a palace from Jupiter as Baucis and Philemon do.

The counterpart of the benign father is a female figure whom we may call the benign mother (2). So rare is this type in Hawthorne's fiction that one is tempted to account for her obscurity in biographical terms: was she the kind of woman whom Hawthorne was likely to have known in his own family? In the mythological tales she appears as Aethra, Theseus' 'widowed' mother to whom he finally returns; as Queen Telephassa, the loyal companion of Cadmus' quest; and as Philemon's spouse, Baucis. In the New England context, dominated by the callous goodwives of Boston, and the younger Hesters and Priscillas, she appears as Mrs. Lindsey of 'The Snow Image,' a woman who 'all through her life ... had kept her heart full of child-like simplicity and faith' (III, 406); and in a more sombre context she is the quietistic Dorothy Pearson, foster-mother of the Gentle Boy.

Third, and of the highest importance for Hawthorne's vision, this benign and sunny group contains the ideal native-born American woman (3) whose prototype is Phoebe (sun goddess) Pyncheon. Phoebe has a number of counterparts in Hawthorne's fiction: her mythological relations are the sunny Marygold of 'The Golden Touch' and the charming Harmonia, Cadmus' bride; she is a practical, domestic angel, a household divinity. She is seen again in ultra-refined terms as Kenyon's Hilda; and there is a brief period during the Blithedale experiment when it appears that Priscilla may blossom into the kind of sunny good health and gaiety which Coverdale finds 'bewitching.' The ideal woman (and we recall Hawthorne's many reflections on the refining and etherealizing influence of New England upon the coarse 'beef and ale' constitution inherited from England) – the ideal woman is a sunny, intelligent creature, firmly in touch with reality, who constitutes for her husband that link with the warm, human realm which every imaginative quester needs. She is a domestic goddess, and in her American incarnation she is immaculate – free of the Black Man's mark.

Finally, the passive group of sun figures produces an ineffectual male who might be best described as a vapid sun boy (4), the sun-hero *manqué*. He is inclined to be dull, or perhaps merely thoughtless; whatever the reason, he tends to be the victim of circumstance rather than its master, and he is sadly lacking in the powers of vision which characterize Hawthorne's heroes. Chief among these, perhaps, is Giovanni Guasconti of 'Rappaccini's Daughter.' Though blessed with youth and vitality, Giovanni becomes the dupe of Dr. Baglioni. At the critical moment when he should have believed in the unspotted purity of Beatrice, Giovanni heeds Baglioni's traditional, rule-book ideas, and destroys his innocent Dark Lady. Similarly Theodore, the doubting young materialist in Zenobia's legend, 'The Silvery Veil,' fears that the Veiled Lady may be Gorgon, and in refusing to kiss her before seeing her features loses forever the immaculate spirit he might have won. Wakefield, too, belongs to this class. Late in life he decides, for no clearly defined reason, to enter the dusky, anonymous realm of night; but his aimless effort brings him only old age and waste. He has observed life from the outside, as an artist might, but to no point; and meanwhile he has missed the real life which he might have enjoyed.[4]

These are Hawthorne's sun people, the types of human nature (or society) that express the power of the empirical realm of objects and the senses. They are indispensable forces in the kind of life which it is man's fate to live. In opposition to these two groups – and sometimes in sympathy with them – are two groups of moon-mirror types who in Hawthorne's mythology are even more important in the dynamics of the self and the society.

The Imaginative Realm: Active Types

The second major group of Hawthorne's character types are allied to the night realm of experience – to moonlight, mirrors, fountains, and air. These are the people to whom imagination, intuition, and spirit are important. Transcending the hard particulars of the empirical realm, they are concerned with form and meaning as opposed to measurement and law. There can be no question that Hawthorne allied himself to this world of Oberon and Mercury; this alliance, indeed, gives his mythology its unique personal character.

In the night realm there is no counterpart of the tyrant father figure, for no spiritual father would behave as Colonel Pyncheon does. As suggested above, Jupiter is the omnipotent mythological father or god. In the New England

4 An obscure but valuable article on 'Wakefield' is Andrew Schiller's 'The Moment and the Endless Voyage,' *Diameter*, I (March, 1951), 7–12. Wakefield's boredom anticipates the monotony of contemporary life, but his solution – to opt out and become an observer – is inadequate. In this tale Hawthorne is close to the thought of Existentialism.

setting, the imaginative father is necessarily less than a god; he is the gifted artisan (1) Matthew Maule, condemned as a witch by Colonel Pyncheon. Dispossessed of his 'garden ground,' Matthew becomes more terrible than the sternest Puritan – a wizard who has power over the minds of ordinary people and over their dreams. His heirs build the labyrinthine seven-gabled house for their oppressors, but Matthew's curse kills the Colonel; the deed to the fabulous Eastern land is lost; the fresh-flowing Maule's Well turns brackish; and old Matthew becomes a bitter spectre who plagues the Pyncheons through seven generations. Finally the whole Maule line disappears from the daylight realm to reappear triumphantly and humanely in its last representative, Holgrave.

It is extremely important to recognize that Matthew Maule and his progeny are not devils, but sorcerers or wizards. Devils, for Hawthorne, are persons who, like Chillingworth, use their knowledge perversely to make man ashamed of the night side of his nature. Wizards are moon people whose creative power appears evil to rationalists; and, if their magic is denied, they may use it vengefully. In Puritan terms they are associated indiscriminately with demons or witches; but as the Rev. Mr. Wilson and Arthur Dimmesdale correctly recognize, the 'demon child' Pearl is really like 'one of those fairies or elfs' that they had known in England. Related to this figure are nymphs and water-sprites such as the legendary Pirene of 'The Chimaera' or the creature who dwelt in the fountain at Monte Beni. Hawthorne's intention in this imagery, it would seem, is to suggest that his moon people are 'nature spirits'; their magic seems demonic only when they are repressed, or when their real gifts are misunderstood, as they are by the Puritans.

More dangerous than the disinherited 'father' who becomes a wizard, is an isolated 'moon wizard' type (2), the counterpart of the scientist. This character, either an artist or organic chemist, lives only for the values of his own realm. His ordeal, instead of flame, is likely to be frost. There is no mythological representative of this figure, though the powerful King Pluto of 'The Pomegranate Seeds' seeks to warm the 'cold chamber' of his heart with a little human love.[5] In New England, Holgrave is tempted to become a moon-wizard, but instead catches Phoebe in 'love's web of sorcery.' The 'foreign' artist of 'The Prophetic Pictures,' and Dr. Rappaccini, however, dwell so completely in the visionary realm that they become inhuman. The one emotion which the painter, 'insulated from the mass of human kind,' is unable to comprehend is love; thus he will never know why Elinor has remained with Walter Ludlow despite his prophecy of a disaster in their marriage. Dr. Rappaccini, Hawthorne's supreme intellectual wizard, attemps to reverse the traditional account of mankind's fall from innocence. Failing to accept that the broken fountain and ancient walls of his 'garden' are at best an ironic Eden, he attempts to arm his innocent and vulnerable daughter against such golden materialists as Giovanni, the vain and

5 Pluto, 'king of the mines,' reminds us of Chillingworth, but he is not a vengeful figure. Perhaps the most that can be said, since Hawthorne gives us so little to go on, is that he is a 'dark' alter-ego of Jupiter: Jupiter's servants launch the imaginative hero into a daylight role. Pluto craves the sunlit vitality of Proserpina to bring warmth to the 'tiresome magnificence' of his wealth.

231

rather stupid young sun hero who is encouraged to see his angelic Beatrice as poisonous. The basic struggle in this tale is between Dr. Pietro (stone) Baglioni who lives in the 'barren city' outside the garden, and follows the ancient rules of tradition, and the organic chemist, Dr. Rappaccini, whom Baglioni describes as a 'vile empiric.'[6] Dr. Rappaccini, however, believing that woman is 'exposed to all evil and capable of none,' infuses Beatrice's system with the 'poison' of a plant that reminds us of Zenobia's exotic flower and the jewel-like shrub that Proserpina plucks. Baglioni, the traditionalist, can only see such homeopathic medicine as demonic, and counsels Giovanni to resist *la femme empoisonneuse*. The two 'physicians,' clearly, are mortally opposed; and both are sufficiently megalomaniac that, like Chillingworth, they think less of healing than of vindicating their own positions. Baglioni, in terms of Hawthorne's mythology, is a demon, a conventional practitioner who believes that woman is the devil's instrument. Rappaccini is a wizard, a powerful 'organic' scientist intent on endowing his immaculate daughter with a power that will protect her from lovers who think of her as 'guilty' or (in the language of the tale) 'poisonous.' But both doctors have lost touch with the human realm; both use the young people whom they dominate as puppets. The result is tragedy: Giovanni, like the vacuous Theodore in the tale of the Veiled Lady, loses his beloved; and the pure Beatrice, rather than accept his vision of her nature as poisonous,

6 Hawthorne's scientific terms are outmoded in 1968, but his distinction is clear; the golden Baglioni follows ancient laws rather than making empirical observations and experiments which will reveal the organic facts of human nature. Baglioni belongs to the tradition-bound past, whether European or Puritan.

drinks Dr. Baglioni's lethal draught. This tale is not the most clearly designed of Hawthorne's myths, but it is perhaps the most significant of his shorter works. In the opposed medical 'fathers' we see the extremes of the empirical and imaginative worlds; in Giovanni we see the failure of imagination in the sun hero; and in Beatrice we see the tragedy of the immaculate Dark Lady whose father has misguidedly attempted to arm her against crass men. Woman's true fulfilment may be realized in Europe in the 'marriage' of Miriam and Donatello; her American fulfilment will come only in the marriages of Phoebe and Hilda.

The third active personality of the imaginative realm is a 'female monster' (3) who menaces men – whether iron materialists or young imaginative heroes. Freudian critics would have it that she represents the maternal sex taboo which the young hero must overcome; she is the 'terrible mother,' a dragon that guards the golden fleece or the three golden apples; or she is the dragon whose teeth Cadmus must extract and plant in order to become a city-builder. Admittedly, such creatures suggest male sexual fears, but criticism has failed to emphasize that Hawthorne sees such fears as largely illusory, for in his view woman is guiltless. In the idealized myth the imaginative heroes invariably triumph over the dream-like 'monsters' of the night.

It would seem, however, that the female nature, denied its legitimate power in the daylight world, may cross over into the night realm where its power appears menacing, castrating (Hawthorne's word would probably be 'unmanning'). Circe, disillusioned by men's vanity and sensuality, encourages them to become beasts; Medea promises to rejuvenate old men by boiling them in her cauldron; and

Beatrice Rappaccini, as Dr. Baglioni sees her, is lethal. This so-called 'monstrous' woman is peculiarly the plague of sun men, particularly Puritans. Mistress Hibbins, though less extreme than the enchantress-wife of King Aegeus, is a witch who indulges in midnight orgies while her bachelor brother, Governor Bellingham, sleeps. Goody Cloyse, the companion of Goodman Brown's night journey, is similarly linked with Satan; Hester, reviled by society, is thought to be a witch, but is saved from that fate by her motherhood; and the Quaker mother of 'The Gentle Boy' has renounced her benign mother's role because of Puritan persecution.

But these are Puritan ways of describing disaffected women. In a later age, Coverdale laughingly describes the same figure, Zenobia, as a witch, or more accurately as a 'Sprite laughing at me from the bottom of a deep well' (C, III, 48), an image that Hawthorne had used a year earlier to describe the depths of the helpful Medea's eyes.[7] In her morning attire, Hepzibah of *Seven Gables* resembles the Gorgon, but her whole attention is devoted to her mercurial brother Clifford; and in their flight from the house they are described as owls, the bird that Hawthorne knew was sacred to Minerva. Nevertheless there can be no question that Hawthorne found his Dark Ladies formidable; indeed, as Miriam's fate suggests, he may finally have thought of them as a part of the European Judaeo-Christian past rather than of the American present. But he would not think of them as Gorgons: Theodore's lack of faith in the 'angel' of the 'Silvery Veil' legend is Hawthorne's clear answer to the 'dark' conception of womanhood. The people who believe

7 Poe, describing the mysteries of Ligeia's eyes, referred to Democritus who wrote that *truth* lies at the bottom of a well.

in female monsters are materialists who, like Westervelt, are 'incapable ... of so much as one spiritual idea.'

Fourth among the active moon people is the imaginative young hero (4), Hawthorne's central character. The mythological prototypes of this figure are Bellerophon and Perseus. In late Puritan times he appears as Owen Warland, the 'artist of the beautiful,' rejected by the Puritan watchmaker and blacksmith, but nevertheless achieving a spiritual triumph of his own in the creation of a golden butterfly (psyche), wrought out during long night labours. The butterfly cannot survive in the empirical realm, even though it is made of the Puritan's most prized element, but Owen has found his authority nevertheless, though not his place in the community. In the nineteenth century the prototype of this figure is a man of fantasy, the Master Genius of 'A Select Party'; it is he who must hew out 'the unwrought granite of our intellectual quarries' – must reveal to society the value and the dangers of its achievements. The true story of the American moon hero is less sanguine. Dimmesdale, in the last day of his life, achieves a full knowledge and acceptance of his gifts. Holgrave, after seven generations of family struggle, marries a benign type of the empirical realm. Coverdale feels himself a supernumerary in his society, though he records its drama faithfully, if ironically. And Kenyon, the 'humanized' man of marble, may perhaps be welcomed in New England. In Hawthorne's terms, this young hero *must* find his place in the empirical realm, for if he carries his 'cryptic preoccupation' to extremes he is in danger of the same isolation and inhumanity that the scientist suffers. He cannot become a demon, since he does not use his insight vengefully, or as a weapon of

235

power; but he may become a wizard and commit the Unpardonable Sin of probing coldly into the secrets of the human heart. This hero's acceptance or 'marriage' into the community does not, as Frederick Crews and others have argued, mean 'the death of art'; what he seeks is balance or integration of 'the full range of his faculties and sensibilities'; in such a situation his vision will prevail.

The Imaginative Realm: Passive Types

In parallel to the passive and benign people of the sunlit realm are a group of unaggressive, spiritual moon people. The first of these, the night realm's counterpart of the benign father, is a delightful son or brother whom we see in the mythological tales as a 'benign moon boy,' Mercury (1). This imaginative personality, possessed of infinite wit and sensitivity, is a lover of life who is interested in everybody's affairs but is never more than a messenger or intermediary. In other terminology he resembles the Coleridgian 'fancy': he is a charming, epicene person who aids the hero but is always auxiliary to his creative energy. In the New England myth of experience Quicksilver has no counterpart, for there is no youthful male figure willing to support the imaginative hero, or capable of helping him to achieve recognition in the community. Instead, the hero himself takes on mercurial qualities. Holgrave's art as Daguerreotypist is an up-to-date version of the mercury-mirror imagery associated with the artist; Oberon belongs in the silvery night realm; Coverdale possesses a mercurial ubiquity; and Kenyon, until humanized, lives in a cold, marble realm of imagination. Clifford Pyncheon, the almost hermaphroditic dreamer-idealist whose

236

bright talents have been crushed beyond recovery by thirty years of imprisonment, is similarly mercurial, but must be regarded as an historical portrait of the failed American hero. The story of the woodcarver Drowne suggests primarily the power of love to inspire a minor artist-artisan to high achievement. Indeed, Hawthorne's artist heroes need love more than anything else to lead them from their haunted chambers into the human realm.

The sister of the Mercury figure is a benign goddess (2), the night realm's counterpart of the benign mother. In the mythological tales she is Minerva, goddess of wisdom and household crafts. Minerva, like Mercury, is celibate, the invisible benefactress who helps Perseus and Jason but who, like Quicksilver, does not perform great deeds herself. In Hawthorne's New England fiction we see her briefly in chapter XIII of *The Scarlet Letter*: Hester, who is neither a witch nor a sprite, is pictured here as a figure of 'marble coldness,' wandering with desperation and daring in a dark labyrinth of mind. But, for the Puritan Dimmesdale – and for Hawthorne perhaps – this is not the proper realm for women. The liberal Coverdale wishes that Zenobia could have fulfilled her intellectual talents, but despite his sympathy he clearly values his own insights above hers.

A second version of the New England Minerva is seen in Hepzibah Pyncheon, the ugly old spinster who finds herself responsible for the House of the Seven Gables and in her extremity opens a cent shop. For her, the role of household manager is a blatant piece of miscasting. In her dominant, daylight role she wanders about like an owl. Her relief comes with the advent of Phoebe and Holgrave and the return of Clifford –, the people whom she might properly aid and protect. For Hepzibah it is too late to become an imaginative heroine like Alice Pyncheon (she has never been allowed to play Alice's harpsichord); but she does find an indoor role as benign mother to Clifford and her protégés Phoebe and Holgrave.

Third among the passive moon people is a female type who becomes one of the leading characters of Hawthorne's fiction. She is the pale moon girl (3) whom we see in the mythological tales as Ariadne. This type is delicate, ethereal, and pure, a woman who has escaped the Black Man's mark. As Hawthorne's version of the Theseus story makes clear, she prefers to remain with her domineering old father rather than enter into a sexual union with the young hero. Cadmus' Harmonia, however, descends into the daylight world and becomes a mother. Hawthorne portrays this figure in New England as the easily swayed Alice Pyncheon, Alice Vane, Sylph Etherege, and so on, but he defines her nature most clearly and fully in Priscilla of *Blithedale*. This young lady is sensitive, imaginative, and other-worldly, a true daughter of Old Moodie's New England phase. She lacks, unfortunately, a free will of her own, and is therefore a promising victim of the Black Man, of mesmerists, or such empirical zealots as Hollingsworth. The imaginative Coverdale expresses his appreciation of this sweetly spiritual type but, since she is almost completely ethereal on her arrival at Blithedale, she cannot give him the contact with empirical reality that he so badly needs. He has high hopes of her in the ideal colony, where she so thrives and blooms that he sees her as a May Queen. She might almost be another Phoebe Pyncheon. But Coverdale's hopes are crushed when she succumbs to the powerful blacksmith-reformer Hollingsworth – the nineteenth-century Puritan spirit. In New England the proper partner of the artist is dominated, rather, by narrow, fact-bound men.

Finally, among the passive moon people we have a frail moon boy (4), the imaginative counterpart of the vapid sun boy. Since he is a figure of vision, however, he is anything but vapid; he is, in effect, the moon-hero *manqué*; he is a delicate scholar or dreamer rather than a leader. Needless to say, he has no place in Hawthorne's ideal myth, for the mythological heroes always achieve their quests, but in the narrative of experience he is a prominent figure. We meet him first as Fanshawe, the delicate scholar who momentarily asserts his superiority, but whose inclination leads him to the library and thence the tomb. In another incarnation he is the Gentle Boy who could not survive the grossness of Puritan society. The young minister, Arthur Dimmesdale, who 'trod in the shadowy by-paths, and thus kept himself simple and childlike,' is a figure of this type until, through the energy of the electric 'chain of humanity' in the midnight scaffold scene, he finds his power and becomes a hero in death. It would not be an exaggeration, indeed, to say that the typical imaginative man of the Puritan community is a frail moon boy, for in that society he cannot be a leader. Rather incongruously, the final example of this figure is Donatello of *The Marble Faun*. Superficially, he appears to be a figure of sun and gold, but the sunshine of Monte Beni is not the blazing light that blinds materialistic tyrants; it is the joyous light of the state of nature. Monte Beni produces not real gold but the 'bottled sunshine' of a delicious wine; and its owners, we recall, are related to fountains and pools – the mercurial moon-mirror cluster of images. Donatello, moreover, does

239

not lead but is led; however, he may emerge from his dark ordeal in a Roman prison as a genuine imaginative hero, though Hawthorne does not explore that possibility. Hawthorne's ultimate concern is the fate of 'new' (or New World) men and women. As A. N. Kaul has expressed it: 'He shared something of the land-of-promise hope together with a great deal of doubt whether any lands of promise are to be ... discovered anywhere – unless it be in the altered hearts of men.'[8]

In Jungian terms, the sixteen character types described above form a mandala – a circular figure at whose centre lies the Self. D. H. Lawrence, in a less-comprehensive discussion in his essay on Hawthorne, describes the pattern as follows: 'We are divided in ourselves, against ourselves. And that is the meaning of the cross symbol.'[9] But Hawthorne's cross-purposes are much more complex than Lawrence's opposition of 'mind knowledge' and 'blood knowledge.' James sensed the ambivalence of Hawthorne's insight, as Melville had, and as Faulkner was to do in the twentieth century. All of them knew that there is no accounting for 'marriages'; and they knew equally that there must somehow be a productive marriage of spirit and fact if man is to fulfil his humanity.

The key personality in Hawthorne's emblematic treatment of marriage is Pearl, the character who inherits the physical gifts of her mother, the spiritual gifts of her father, and the practical wealth of her 'legal' father, Chillingworth. In Puritan America this synthesis of forces is unwelcome,

8 A. N. Kaul, *The American Vision*, p. 154.
9 D. H. Lawrence, *Studies in Classic American Literature* (New York, 1953), p. 94.

though Pearl's money would persuade the community to overlook or tolerate the unconventional union which produced her. But Pearl cannot be a complete woman in America. Her mother, however, finally returns to Boston in the hope that 'when the world should have grown ripe for it,' a new ground of 'mutual understanding' would be established in the relations of man and woman. This new ground, as revealed in the broad pattern of Hawthorne's character types, is governed by two principles. First, active or aggressive types can best marry passive personalities. Second, imaginative people are best complemented by practical people of the sunlit realm, and vice versa.

In these terms we might construct a second diagram suggesting which forces in Hawthorne's symbolic world should, or should not, marry, but it will be enough, perhaps, to consider some of the alliances and misalliances which struck him most forcibly. Given the dual attraction of active for passive, and sun for moon, it is clear that the aggressive, empirical male typically chooses a passive moon girl, a 'gentle parasite' in Coverdale's phrase, whose role will be to serve her master without question. The active moon hero will prefer a domestic, happy, sun girl to whom he will give great latitude of action. The vigorous Dark Lady needs a passive, imaginative moon boy whom she can protect and mother. There are no imaginative father figures who seek to marry, except for the mythological King Pluto who seeks a sunny companion to brighten and warm his cold heart.

Hawthorne's personal bias on the question of marriage is obvious: in the new world that he envisions, imaginative heroes should be rewarded with angelic blonde wives who are at once immaculate and sexually enticing. There will be no

241

sin in such unions, but simply a fulfilment of the whole range of man's (and woman's) faculties and sensibilities. This is the New World ideal.

It is not difficult, then, to see why Zenobia's attachment to the Puritanical Hollingsworth would prove disastrous; their temperaments were by nature so similar that marriage might have proved an unending struggle for dominance. Zenobia speculates, following her rejection by Hollingsworth, that she might have found fulfilment with Coverdale: ' "It is an endless pity," said she, "that I had not bethought myself of winning your heart, Mr. Coverdale, instead of Hollingsworth's. I think I should have succeeded, and many women would have deemed you the worthier conquest of the two." ' (C, III, 226–27) But this second choice might not have been much happier, for Coverdale is potentially an active type and Zenobia's career with him might well have been stormy, despite his avowal that he would give woman even more freedom than she would ask. Of the trio of Dark Ladies, Miriam makes the most successful choice. Temperamentally the gentle, intuitive Donatello is the perfect foil for Miriam's rich strength; she is vibrantly in touch with the material world, and will use her power and protective love to ameliorate her husband's painful initiation into experience.

Throughout most of *The Scarlet Letter* Hester is the active figure who boldly faces the community, while Dimmesdale passively suffers in his guilt-haunted world of shadow. In the end, Hester's strength – the 'electric chain' of sympathy and love – enables him to become an active figure who takes their destiny into his own hands. Appropriately, after her lover's confession and death, Hester too becomes a new personality; freed of the necessity to fight for her child

242

and her lover, she becomes a benign and comforting figure – a passive sun type. And when at length she dies, she is reunited with her lover under the symbol A. The final 'victory' of the tale thus suggests a reversal of the roles of Hester and Dimmesdale; the 'surer ground of mutual happiness' may involve benign Dark Ladies and un-Puritanical heroes who make their vision prevail. But the American environment has an etherealizing effect on women; by the nineteenth century they will be prettier, more feminine, gentler, and capable of sharing their lives as equals with imaginative men.

This question of marriage – of the union of the empirical and imaginative worlds in a human frame – is Hawthorne's presiding concern, his 'cryptic preoccupation'; and it applies to the opposed forces of the self, the relations of men and women, and the conflicting forces within society. For readers who wondered whether Donatello's ears really were pointed, or whether Young Goodman Brown had merely had a bad dream, Hawthorne was a good Gothic entertainer – a man who wrote 'for his own age.' His triumph is that he created a fabric of such richness that readers in other ages find him deeply rewarding; as he said of Shakespeare, 'There is no exhausting the various interpretations of his symbols.' His achievement, indeed, is now seen to be as brilliant as any that American literature has produced. He brought to his imaginative analysis of the human condition and of American society a sensitivity and a stubborn independence that none of his contemporaries but Melville could fully appreciate or match. However much the winds of Puritan piety and the waves of New England circumstance buffetted him, he did not for a moment abandon that cool and resolute point of view which enabled him to penetrate to the bottom of man's

243

heart and to the heart of America. His vision, consistently followed through almost forty years, is so richly comprehensive that it transcends the particulars of his age and achieves the universality that distinguishes major art from topical portraiture. It is not a new vision; it is as old as the myths which Hawthorne recreated for his age and place; but it has – as he rendered it in his early tales, in the tragedy of *The Scarlet Letter*, and in the ironic tragi-comedy of *Blithedale* – the freshness of revelation. This is the kind of *œuvre*, perhaps, which Hawthorne foresaw as the creation of his Master Genius. But Hawthorne's characteristic modesty would have kept him from claiming that achievement as his own.

Index

Index

246

Index

247

Index

248

Index

Index

Index

Index

Index

253

Index

Index

255

Index